THE NEW SILK ROAD

China Meets Europe in the Baltic Sea Region

A Business Perspective

Foreword by Pascal Lamy

THE NEW
SILK ROAD

China Meets Europe
in the Baltic Sea Region

A Business Perspective

Editor

Jean-Paul Larçon

HEC Paris, France

W **World Scientific**

NEW JERSEY · LONDON · SINGAPORE · BEIJING · SHANGHAI · HONG KONG · TAIPEI · CHENNAI · TOKYO

Published by

World Scientific Publishing Co. Pte. Ltd.

5 Toh Tuck Link, Singapore 596224

USA office: 27 Warren Street, Suite 401-402, Hackensack, NJ 07601

UK office: 57 Shelton Street, Covent Garden, London WC2H 9HE

Library of Congress Cataloging-in-Publication Data

Names: Larçon, Jean-Paul, author.

Title: The new silk road : China meets Europe in the Baltic Sea Region /
  Jean-Paul Larçon, HEC Paris, France.

Description: New Jersey : World Scientific, [2017] | Includes bibliographical references.

Identifiers: LCCN 2017009360 | ISBN 9789813221802 (hard cover)

Subjects: LCSH: China--Commercial policy. | China--Foreign economic relations. |
    China--Commerce--Europe. | Europe--Commerce--China. |
    China--Commerce--Baltic Sea Region. | Baltic Sea Region--Commerce--China.

Classification: LCC HF1604 .L36 2017 | DDC 382.09510479--dc23

LC record available at https://lccn.loc.gov/2017009360

British Library Cataloguing-in-Publication Data

A catalogue record for this book is available from the British Library.

Desk Editor: Tay Yu Shan

Typeset by Stallion Press
Email: enquiries@stallionpress.com

Printed in Singapore

To my daughter Anne-Sophie

Foreword

Pascal Lamy

Honorary President of Notre Europe — Jacques
Delors Institute and former WTO director-general

Trade and investment are at the core of the China-Europe relationship and China's "New Silk Road" initiative adds a new dimension to the interaction between the two partners.

China's accession to the World Trade Organization (WTO) in 2001 has been a milestone in China's reform and opening-up policy, and a step forward in the transformation of its economy. It required a lot of efforts from China on the domestic front, and led to a rapid increase of China-Europe trade, of the flow of foreign direct investment entering into China, and later to a major increase in Chinese outward foreign investment.

International trade is also at the center of China's "Belt and Road" initiative which aims at enhancing trade openness: removing investment and trade barriers, lowering non-tariff barriers, promoting mutual assistance in law enforcement, enhancing customs cooperation and developing cross-border e-commerce.

China's initiative, announced in 2013, has two unique characteristics:

1. Huge investments in transport infrastructure and logistics hubs along both the "Maritime Silk Road" and the Eurasian Land Bridge connecting China to Europe through Central Asia

2. New financial instruments and development banks to finance these investments such as the Asian Infrastructure Investment Bank (AIIB) created in 2014

China's announcement of the "One Belt One Road" (OBOR) initiative has been followed by discussions between China and countries potentially interested by the project, as well as with new investments in transport infrastructure in Asia, Africa, Central Asia and Europe.

In Europe, China is developing its initiative mainly through bilateral cooperation agreements at the country level, with special attention to the countries of Central and Eastern Europe. China's first few remarkable investments in Europe in the framework of the OBOR initiative have been in the Greek port of Piraeus and in the railway connection between Greece, Serbia and Hungary.

China's "New Silk Road" initiative will contribute to a reduction of the duration and cost of transportation between China and Europe, and will stimulate the development of a modern transport infrastructure based on mega container ships, large automated container terminals, better connectivity between large European seaports and their hinterland, and rapid railway connections connecting seaports, large metropolis and final consumer markets.

Among European countries, Germany should benefit directly from the increase of China-Europe trade at the level of its logistics hubs, such as Hamburg and Duisburg, as well as for logistics companies such as DB Schenker, the transportation and logistics subsidiary of Deutsche Bahn. But more generally the development of trade should serve the interests of German firms operating in China and Chinese firms investing in Germany. It should also contribute to the development of China-Germany advanced technology cooperation.

The reduction in distance-related costs will also have a major influence on the localization of economic activities and the reorganization of the global value chain (GVC) along the trade routes between China and Europe. From that point of view, China's initiative is a new opportunity for landlocked countries along the way such as Belarus and Central Asian countries.

The EU Baltic Sea Region is connected to China by both the maritime routes and the new Eurasian Land Bridge, which creates new opportunities of cooperation for the Northern provinces of Poland and Germany, and for the Nordic and Baltic countries. Companies operating in the region, which have strong experience in international trade and a management culture oriented towards innovation, are developing joint projects with Chinese firms in sectors such as renewable energy, ICT, marine engineering and environmental technology.

China's "New Silk Road" forward-looking initiative represents an opportunity for European companies and regions, and a source of progress and innovation for both partners.

Preface

HEC Paris and Tsinghua University School of Economics and Management (Tsinghua SEM) are among leading contributors to China-Europe cooperation in the field of management education and research, promoting faculty development and faculty exchange, students' international mobility, cooperation in executive education and joint research projects. The collaboration between the two schools started in 2001 with the objective of producing knowledge on economics and managerial topics relevant to the Chinese-European cooperation.

China's "go global" policy, initiated by the Chinese government in 1999, has led to a rapid increase of China's outward foreign investment, and to significant initiatives of Chinese companies in foreign markets. Since 2001, the date of China's entry into the WTO, Chinese foreign investment has resulted in an exponential curve and the internationalization process of Chinese firms became one of the priority research topics of the two partner schools.

In 2006, HEC Paris and Tsinghua SEM decided to develop a research project on "Chinese Multinationals" with the support of the National Natural Science Foundation of China (NNSF). It mobilized researchers from the HEC Paris strategy department, Tsinghua SEM business strategy and policy department, the Enterprise Research Institute of the Development Research Center (DRC) of the State Council, and the

Institute of World Economics and Politics of the Chinese Academy of Social Sciences (CASS).

The results of this research on "Chinese Multinationals" was published in 2008 by World Scientific, providing a comprehensive overview of the international strategies of Chinese firms in terms of marketing and branding, management of technology, organization, M&As, international joint ventures and human resource management. The strategies of several well-known companies such as Baosteel, Beijing Jeep, CNOOC, CNPC, Haier, Hisense, Huawei, Lenovo, TCL, Tsingtao Brewery or Wahaha were described in detail.

During his visit to Kazakhstan in 2013, Chinese President Xi Jinping suggested that China and Central Asia could join hands to build a "Silk Road Economic Belt" to boost economic cooperation. It was the first official announcement of China's "Belt and Road" (B&R) initiative. This announcement was quickly followed by the creation of new financial institutions, the signature of new international agreements, and the emergence of new Sino-foreign projects in Central Asia, Southeast Asia, Africa and Europe.

As Europe and China are leading world trade and investment partners, we decided to study the impact of China's B&R initiative on China-Europe economic cooperation, and to focus on one of the regions of Europe where the two wings of the "New Silk Road" are converging: the Baltic Sea Region (BSR).

The BSR is accessible from China through sea ports ranging along the coast of the North Sea and the Baltic Sea, and through the land-road crossing Central Asia and Russia towards the Baltic Sea and Central European countries. Thus, the B&R initiative creates new strategic opportunities for Chinese and European enterprises operating along the way, as well as new challenges for government agencies and regional authorities in charge of foreign trade, infrastructure development and the country's attractiveness.

This is why we are delighted to share our findings with the corporate leaders, entrepreneurs, management scholars and representatives of the public sector working on this unique project connecting people, organizations and cultures across Eurasia.

Jean-Paul Larçon

Acknowledgment

This book is dedicated to the founding fathers of the cooperation between HEC Paris and of Tsinghua University School of Economics and Management (Tsinghua SEM):

- Zhao Chunjun, Dean Emeritus of Tsinghua SEM
- Bernard Ramanantsoa, Honorary Director General of HEC Paris

The editor and the authors are particularly indebted to personalities who supported the "China's 'Belt and Road' initiative and the Baltic Sea Region" project from the beginning:

- H. E. Wei Ruixing, Ambassador Extraordinary and Plenipotentiary of the People's Republic of China to the Republic of Lithuania
- Alfonsas Daniūnas, Rector of Vilnius Gediminas Technical University
- Rita Bendaravičienė, Dean of the Faculty of Economics and Management, Vytautas Magnus University
- Vytas Gruodis, Co-founder of Baltic Management Institute
- Véronique Malleret, Academic Dean of Baltic Management Institute
- Gabriella Mazzini, Head of International Development, E.M.E.A. — Russia, HEC Paris
- Jaunius Pusvaškis, Director General of Baltic Management Institute

- Pierre Semal, Vice-Dean International Affairs, Louvain School of Management
- Rolandas Valiunas, Chairman of Baltic Management Institute

The authors also want to name the research centers and think tanks which contributed greatly to the production and dissemination of knowledge related to the economic dimension of China's "Belt and Road" initiative: BOFIT, Helsinki (Finland); Bruegel, Brussels (Belgium); CAREC Institute, Urumqi (China); CEPII, Paris (France); HKTDC, Hong Kong (China); Clingendael, The Hague (Netherlands); IES, Chinese Academy of Social Sciences, Beijing (China); Ifri, Paris (France); and MERICS, Berlin (Germany).

Authors and Contributors

BARRÉ Geneviève, HEC Paris, France

Geneviève Barré is a graduate of Paris-Sorbonne University in Chinese language and history and holds a Ph.D. in management from Conservatoire National des Arts et Métiers (CNAM, Paris). Specialized in Asia's industrial, research and education policies, she contributed to projects of economic cooperation between Europe and China-India for 30 years, working with the EU, the OECD and the World Bank. She joined HEC Paris in 2001 and contributed to the HEC-Tsinghua research on "Chinese Multinationals". She published *Quand les entreprises chinoises se mondialisent: Haier, Huawei et TCL* (CNRS Editions, 2016).

BRUNSTAD Rolf Jens, NHH Norwegian School of Economics, Norway

Rolf Jens Brunstad has been a full professor at NHH since 1999. Since the fall of the Berlin wall, Brunstad has been active in establishing modern business education in Russia, as well as in Central and Eastern Europe. He is currently chair of the Academic Council of Baltic Management Institute and of the Council of Founders of Warsaw University of Technology Business School. His main research areas include labor economics, industrial organization, agricultural economics and applied welfare economics in the transport sector.

DAPKUS Mindaugas, Vytautas Magnus University, Lithuania

Mindaugas Dapkus is an associate professor in the Department of Economics at Vytautas Magnus University (VMU) since 2003. He is responsible for the Masters program in International Economics at VMU. His research interest focuses on areas of macroeconomics related to economic growth and development, macroeconomic policy and economic behavior at the national and international level. One of his recent research is oriented towards the estimation of overheating in the economy during the business cycles.

DUSSAUGE Pierre, HEC Paris, France

Pierre Dussauge is a professor of Strategic Management at HEC Paris. He was a visiting professor of Corporate Strategy at the Ross Business School of the University of Michigan in Ann Arbor from 1991 to 2003 and at other leading international institutions such as Insead, ISB (Hyderabad), and Tsinghua SEM (Beijing). He is the author or coauthor of several books in the field of strategic management and strategic alliances, notably *Cooperative Strategy* (J. Wiley & Sons, 1999).

KALENDIENĖ Jonė, Vytautas Magnus University, Lithuania

Jonė Kalendienė is an associate professor in the Department of Economics at VMU. She has been working in the same department since 2006. She is a visiting professor at ISM university of Management and Economics for seven years. During 2007 to 2008 she was serving as an economist in the macroeconomic analysis and forecasting division in the Department of Economics at Lietuvos bankas (Central Bank of Lithuania). She has published several papers about the competitiveness of exports of different European countries nationally and internationally.

LARÇON Jean-Paul, HEC Paris, France

Jean-Paul Larçon is emeritus professor of International Strategy at HEC Paris. He was a visiting professor at CEIBS (Shanghai), Fundação Getulio Vargas (EAESP), São Paulo (Brazil), Saint Petersburg University Graduate School of Management (Russia), and Tsinghua University School of Economics and Management (China). He is the author or coauthor of several books and articles in the field of entrepreneurship in economies in transition and strategy in emerging markets. His current research focuses on emerging market multinationals.

LI Donghong, Tsinghua University, China

Li Donghong serves as vice chair and associate professor of the Department of Innovation, Entrepreneurship and Strategy of Tsinghua School of Economics and Management. He is the associate dean of the Institute for Global Industry 4.5 Center of Tsinghua University. He graduated from Renmin University of China, School of Business Administration, with a Ph.D. in business administration in 1999. Now he teaches courses like Strategic Management, Enterprise Management Foundation, Strategic Alliances, Diversification Strategy, etc.

LIU Zuokui, Chinese Academy of Social Sciences (CASS), China

Dr. Liu Zuokui is a senior research fellow, director of the Department of Central and Eastern European Studies, Institute of European Studies, CASS. He is also the director of the Secretariat Office of the "16+1 Think Tanks Network" of the CASS. Liu Zuokui has a rich international experience, including France, Germany, Latvia and Central Europe, as well as Japan. His major research interest is Central and Eastern Europe, China-EU relations and EU Integration Studies, China-Turkey relations, and Balkan studies. He published in 2014 "The Role of Central and Eastern Europe in the Building of the Silk Road Economic Belt", *China International Studies*.

PANIBRATOV Andrei, Saint Petersburg State University, Russia

Andrei Panibratov is professor of Strategic and International Management at the Graduate School of Management, and the head of the Center for the Study of Emerging Market and Russian Multinational Enterprises, both at Saint Petersburg State University, Russia. His research interests and lecturing area focus on internationalization of emerging market firms, outward FDI from emerging economies, and Russian multinationals. His publications include *International Strategy of Emerging Market Firms: Absorbing Global Knowledge and Building Competitive Advantage*

(Routledge, 2017) and *Russian Multinationals: From Regional Supremacy to Global Lead* (Routledge, 2012).

POMFRET Richard, University of Adelaide, Australia

Richard Pomfret has been professor of Economics at the University of Adelaide since 1992. Before coming to Adelaide, he was professor of Economics at the Johns Hopkins University School of Advanced International Studies in Washington DC, Bologna (Italy) and Nanjing (China). He previously worked at Concordia University in Montréal and the Institut für Weltwirtschaft at the University of Kiel in Germany. His most recent books are *The Age of Equality: The twentieth century in economic perspective* (Harvard University Press, 2011) and *Trade Facilitation*, coauthored with Patricia Sourdin, (Edward Elgar, 2012).

PUKELIENĖ Violeta, Vytautas Magnus University, Lithuania

Violeta Pukelienė is professor of Economics from 2008 and head of the Economics department of VMU. She has experience in integration economics and social economics from 1998. She is Jean Monnet chair in Integration Economics and has written a textbook *Economic integration: theory, EU policy and processes* (Kaunas: Vytautas Magnus University, 2008). She was a visiting professor at ISM university of Management and Economics, University of Latvia for more than ten years. She is the author or coauthor of several books and articles in the field of migration, welfare economics and tax.

ŠAKALYS Algirdas, Vilnius Gediminas Technical University, Lithuania

Algirdas Šakalys holds an engineering degree and a doctorate in transport technology from Vilnius Gediminas Technical University. He served as an advisor to the prime minister and as a vice minister for transport and communication in the government of Lithuania. He has 24 years of experience in transport policy, green transport, freight transport and logistics, and management of international transport corridors. Since 2007, he is the head of the Competence Centre for Intermodal

Transport and Logistics at Vilnius Gediminas Technical University, and, since 2010, the president of the international East-West Transport Corridor Association (EWTCA) uniting 37 logistics and transport partners from 13 Asian and European countries. In 2016 he was appointed as coordinator of the European Union Strategy for the Baltic Sea Region in the transport area.

SHI Jianxun, Tongji University, China

Professor Shi Jianxun is doctor of economics, the professor of Finance at the School of Economics and Management, Tongji University. He is the director of the Institute of Economics and Finance at Tongji University. He is the chief expert of China National Social Science Fund Decision Consulting Think Tank. He is the special correspondent of *The People's Daily* overseas edition. He also serves as a pluralistic professor at Southeast University. His research interest involves international finance, the international monetary system and Renminbi internationalization. He has published on economic and management more than 200 papers in newspapers and magazines, as well as 18 books, such as *Understanding the China and the World Economy in the Post-crisis era* (China Machine Press, 2014).

TANG Lingling, Tsinghua University, China

Tang Lingling is a postdoctoral researcher of the "Belt and Road" and international capacity cooperation at Tsinghua University SEM. She graduated from Soochow Unversity of China, Dongwu Business School, with a Ph.D. in business administration in 2014. She has published several papers in international and Chinese academic journals. Now she serves as a research director of the Institute for Global Industry 4.5 of Tsinghua University.

ZHAO Yixuan, Nanjing University, China

Dr. Zhao Yixuan is an assistant researcher in the Department of Human Resource Management, School of Business, Nanjing University, China. She has been conducting research on millennial employee management, employee well-being and leadership. She has published several papers in international and Chinese academic journals.

ZHAO Shuming, Nanjing University, China

Dr. Zhao Shuming is chair professor and honorary dean of the School of Business, Nanjing University, China. He serves as president of the International Association of Chinese Management Research (IACMR, Third Term), president of Jiangsu Provincial Association of Human Resource Management, vice-chairman for the Steering Committee for National Business Degree Programs of the Ministry of Education of China, vice president of Chinese Society of Management Modernization. His research area is human resource management, multinational business management, and entrepreneurship. He has chaired several research projects for the National Natural Science Foundation of China and has published more than 10 books and over 300 academic papers and articles.

The authors are grateful to Dr. Wang Panpan for his contribution to the research on the financing of the "Belt and Road" initiative. Wang Panpan has a Ph.D. in economics and finance from the School of Economics and Management, Tongji University. His research interests focus on monetary economics and international finance.

The book has benefited from the copy editing services of Bryan Bradley of Textus Aptus Communications.

About the Editor

LARÇON Jean-Paul, HEC Paris, France

Jean-Paul Larçon, former director of HEC Paris Grande Ecole, is a professor of International Strategic Management. Larçon has been working with Chinese companies and institutions since 1984. He has been teaching and researching in economies in transition of Central and Eastern Europe, Russia and Central Asia since 1989. He published *Entrepreneurship and Economic Transition in Central Europe*, (Kluwer Academic Publishers, 1998). From 2007 to 2008, he led the research project on "Chinese Multinationals" developed by HEC Paris and Tsinghua University School of Economics and Management. He was the editor of *Chinese Multinationals* (World Scientific, 2008).

He is a member of the academic advisory board of Louvain School of Management (Belgium), NHH Norwegian School of Economics (Norway), and Shanghai Tech School of Entrepreneurship (China). He is the co-chair of Baltic Management Institute (BMI) and a senior researcher at the Institute for Global Industry 4.5 of Tsinghua University.

List of Cases, Figures, Maps, and Tables

Tables

Acronyms

ADB	Asian Development Bank
AIIB	Asian Infrastructure Investment Bank
APEC	Asia-Pacific Economic Cooperation
ASEAN	Association of Southeast Asian Nations
B&R	Belt and Road
BCP	Border Crossing Post
BOT	Build-Operate-Transfer
BRICS	Brazil, Russia, India, China and South Africa
BSR	Baltic Sea Region
CAREC	Central Asia Regional Economic Cooperation
CBSS	Council of the Baltic Sea States
CDB	China Development Bank
CEEC	Central and Eastern Europe Countries
CIS	Commonwealth of Independent States
EBRD	European Bank for Reconstruction and Development
EEA	European Economic Area
EEU	Eurasian Economic Union
EFTA	European Free Trade Association
EU	European Union
Eurostat	The Statistical Office of the European Union
Exim Bank	Export-Import Bank of China
FDI	Foreign Direct Investment

FTA	Free Trade Agreement
GDP	Gross Domestic Product
GSP	Generalised Scheme of Preferences
GVC	Global Value Chain
IIF	Institute of International Finance
IMF	International Monetary Fund
KRU	Kazakhstan, Russia and Ukraine
LNG	Liquefied Natural Gas
M&A	Mergers and Acquisitions
MNE	Multinational Enterprise
MSR	Maritime Silk Road
NATO	North Atlantic Treaty Organization
NDB	New Development Bank
OBOR	One Belt One Road
OSJD	Organization for Cooperation between Railways
OTIF	Intergovernmental Organization for International Carriage by Rail
PPP	Public-Private Partnership
PRC	People's Republic of China
RMB	Renminbi
SASAC	State-owned Assets Supervision and Administration Commission of the State Council
SCO	Shanghai Cooperation Organization
SOE	State-owned Enterprise
SREB	Silk Road Economic Belt
SRF	Silk Road Fund
TEU	Twenty Foot Equivalent Unit
UN	United Nations
UNCTAD	United Nations Conference on Trade and Development
UNMCSR	UN Maritime and Continental Silk Road Cities Alliance
WB	World Bank
WTO	World Trade Organization

Introduction

China-Europe economic cooperation and the "New Silk Road"

The objective of China's "Belt and Road" initiative is to develop simultaneously the maritime and the inland trade roads linking China, Europe and Africa: the "21st Century Maritime Silk Road" and the inland "Silk Road Economic Belt". This project is likely to influence significantly China-Europe trade: reducing the cost and the duration of transportation, increasing trade in volume, promoting Chinese investment in Europe, developing new trade routes and logistics hubs, and creating new opportunities for economic development along the way.

The "Maritime Silk Road" is key for China-Europe trade. Most of the goods currently exchanged between China and Europe are transported by very large container ships reaching Europe through the Mediterranean Sea via the Suez Canal. China is a key trading partner for the largest European container ports such as Rotterdam, Hamburg and Antwerp, and a key factor of economic development of their hinterland. The acquisition in 2016 of the port of Piraeus by Chinese company Cosco gives Greece a clear advantage in China-Europe trade with Southern Europe, Central and Eastern Europe and North Africa.

China is also investing in large infrastructure projects along the inland railroad, the "Silk Road Economic Belt", connecting West China (Xinjiang province and western metropolises such as Chengdu or Chongqing) to Central Asia, Russia and Belarus, and reaching Baltic Sea countries: the Baltic States, Northern Poland and Germany, as well as Nordic countries.

This book focuses on the economic and managerial dimensions of the "Belt and Road" initiative: Chinese economic objectives, the impact on trade and investment in Northern Europe, the characteristic of international projects currently operated along the way, the influence on the economies of Central Asia, the strategies of Chinese and foreign companies and the challenges they meet in terms of financing and human resources.

Organization of the book

- Chapter 1 identifies the key dimensions of China-Europe economic cooperation in the Baltic Sea Region.
- Chapter 2 describes China's vision of the "Belt and Road" initiative, the objectives, policies and institutions from a business perspective.
- Chapter 3 focuses on the economy of the countries of the Baltic Sea Region and the strategy of the firms of the BSR in a relationship with China.
- Chapter 4 analyses the trends in terms of trade and investment between China and the Nordic-Baltic countries.
- Chapter 5 is dedicated to international transportation and logistics: the alternative for connecting Europe to China through the Eurasian Land Bridge.
- Chapter 6 addresses the impact of China's "Silk Road Economic Belt" initiative on Central Asia from the point of view of global value chains.
- Chapter 7 studies the new institutions and financial instruments developed by China to finance the large infrastructure projects along the "Belt and Road".
- Chapter 8 focuses on human resource policies needed to nurture and manage talents along the "Belt and Road".

Finally, two *Special Contributions* provide an insightful look at the role of collaboration agreements between Chinese firms and their foreign partners along the "Belt and Road":

- the case of Russian Multinationals and their Chinese partners, and
- the diversity of alliances and joint ventures along the "New Silk Road".

The book includes 17 short case studies focusing on Sino-foreign projects currently developed along the "Belt and Road": investments in infrastructure, new logistics hubs, collaborative agreements and joint ventures, new financing scheme, operation management and human resource dilemma.

It also includes 15 maps of the "Maritime Silk Road", the "Silk Road Economic Belt", the Baltic Sea Region, and Central Asia to help understand China's vision and strategic moves.

Contents

Chapter 1

China Meets Europe by the Baltic Sea

Jean-Paul Larçon and Geneviève Barré

HEC Paris

The "One Belt One Road" concept was introduced for the first time by Chinese President Xi Jinping during his visit to Kazakhstan in 2013. This announcement was carefully prepared and very rapidly followed by the first steps of implementation: the negotiation with key foreign partners, and the publication of an action plan on the "principles, framework, cooperation priorities and mechanisms" of the "New Silk Road" strategy (Table 1.1).

1. China's B&R Initiative and Chinese Companies

Renewing the ancient Silk Road trade tradition, the objective of the "One Belt One Road" (OBOR) or "Belt and Road" (B&R) initiative is to promote the development of the maritime and inland trade roads linking China, Europe and Africa simultaneously: the "21st Century Maritime Silk Road" and the inland railroad "Silk Road Economic Belt" (Map 1.1).

The Chinese plan calls for "policy coordination, greater connectivity, unimpeded trade, financial integration and strengthening people-to-people bonds". It focuses on three dimensions: eliminating trade and investment barriers, developing bilateral economic cooperation through

Table 1.1   Chronology of China's "Belt and Road" initiative

The B&R routes run through the continents of Asia, Europe and Africa, connecting the vibrant East Asia economic circle at one end and the developed European economic circle at the other.

The "Silk Road Economic Belt" focuses on bringing together China, Central Asia, Russia and Europe (the Baltic); linking China with the Persian Gulf and the Mediterranean Sea through Central Asia and the Indian Ocean. The "21st Century Maritime Silk Road" is designed to go from China's coast to Europe through the South China Sea and the Indian Ocean in one route, and from China's coast through the South China Sea to the South Pacific in the other. The major events in the development of China's B&R initiative so far are as follows:

September 2013 — The SREB concept was introduced by Chinese President Xi Jinping during his visit to Kazakhstan. In a speech delivered at Nazarbayev University, Xi suggested that China and Central Asia cooperate to build a "Silk Road Economic Belt". It was the first time the Chinese leadership mentioned the strategic vision.

October 2013 — President Xi proposed building a close-knit China-ASEAN community and offered guidance on constructing a "21st Century Maritime Silk Road" to promote maritime cooperation. In his speech at the Indonesian parliament, Xi also proposed establishing the Asian Infrastructure Investment Bank (AIIB) to finance infrastructure construction and promote regional interconnectivity and economic integration.

November 2013 — The Third Plenary Session of the 18th Central Committee of the Communist Party of China called for accelerating infrastructure links among neighboring countries and facilitating the B&R initiative.

December 2013 — Xi urged strategic planning of the B&R initiative to promote connectedness of infrastructure and build a community of common interests at the annual Central Economic Work Conference.

February 2014 — Xi and his Russian counterpart, Vladimir Putin, reached a consensus on construction of the B&R, as well as its connection with Russia's Euro-Asia Railways.

March 2014 — Premier Li Keqiang called for accelerating B&R construction in the government work report. The report also called for balanced development of the Bangladesh-China-India-Myanmar Economic Corridor and the China-Pakistan Economic Corridor.

May 2014 — The first phase of a logistics terminal jointly built by China and Kazakhstan went into operation in the port of Lianyungang in East China's Jiangsu province. The terminal, with a total investment of 606 million yuan (US$98 million), is considered a platform for goods from Central Asian countries to reach overseas markets

October 2014 — 21 Asian countries willing to join the AIIB as founding members signed the memorandum of understanding (MOU) on Establishing AIIB. As agreed, Beijing will be the host city for AIIB's headquarters. The AIIB is expected to be formally established by the end of 2015.

(*Continued*)

Table 1.1   *(Continued)*

November 2014 — President Xi announced that China will contribute US$40 billion to set up the Silk Road Fund. During the Beijing APEC meetings, Xi announced that the fund will be used to provide investment and financing support for infrastructure, resources, industrial cooperation, financial cooperation and other projects in countries along the B&R.

December 2014 — The Central Economic Work Conference sketched out priorities for the coming year, which include the implementation of the B&R initiative. Earlier in the month, Thailand approved a draft MOU between Thailand and China on railway cooperation.

January 2015 — The number of AIIB founding members, many of which are important countries along the Silk Road routes, rose to 26 after New Zealand, Maldives, Saudi Arabia and Tajikistan officially joined.

February 1, 2015 — At a special meeting attended by senior leader Zhang Gaoli, China sketched out priorities for the B&R initiative, highlighting transportation infrastructure, easier investment and trade, financial cooperation and cultural exchange.

March 5, 2015 — Premier Li, in his government work report, again highlighted the initiative, saying China will move more quickly to strengthen infrastructure with its neighbors, simplify customs clearance procedures and build international logistics gateways.

March 8, 2015 — Chinese Foreign Minister Wang Yi dismissed comparisons of the initiative to the US-sponsored Marshall Plan. The initiative is "the product of inclusive cooperation, not a tool of geopolitics, and must not be viewed with an outdated Cold War mentality," Wang said, adding that China's diplomacy in 2015 will focus on making progress on the B&R initiative.

March 28, 2015 — The National Development and Reform Commission, Ministry of Foreign Affairs and Ministry of Commerce jointly released an action plan on the principles, framework, and cooperation priorities and mechanisms in the B&R initiative after President Xi Jinping highlighted the strategy the same day while addressing the opening ceremony of the 2015 annual conference of the Boao Forum for Asia (BFA) in the coastal town of China's southernmost island province of Hainan.

Source: Xinhua (2015, March 28).

joint investment projects, and cooperation in the conventional and renewable energy sector (NDRC, 2015).

The B&R strategy is based substantially on huge investments in overseas infrastructure projects such as roads, railways, seaports, airports, pipelines, logistics hubs, as well as information and communications technology (ICT). The initiative, which is extremely ambitious, serves several major Chinese objectives simultaneously: developing Chinese exports and international investment, promoting Chinese technology

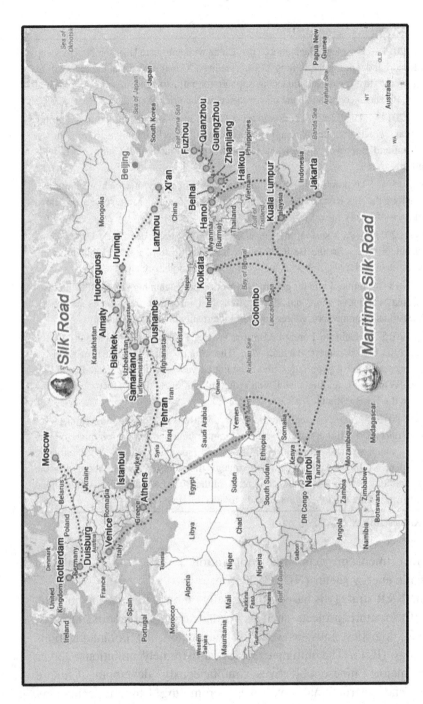

Map 1.1   The "Silk Road Economic Belt" and the "21ˢᵗ Century Maritime Silk Road"

Source: Xinhua (2015).

internationally, contributing to the economic development of West and Central China, increasing China's economic and political influence in Central and Eastern Europe, Central Asia and Africa, and accelerating the internationalization of the renminbi (RMB). The B&R initiative can be viewed as a great leap forward, a "new round of opening to the outside world" (Godement and Kratz, 2015).

The B&R initiative is a major move in terms of both foreign affairs and internationalization of the economy. It is also a major move for Chinese companies which have the opportunity to go a step further in their internationalization process. This process already differed in the past from the one of former US, European and Asian multinationals: Chinese companies did not wait to enter into foreign markets for the accumulation of clear competitive advantages over their foreign competitors. On the contrary, it is their internationalization which helped them to build or acquire the missing strengths or capabilities. Their internationalization process was based on four key factors (Larçon, Ed., 2008):

- The size of the Chinese domestic market, giving national champions a unique competitive advantage in terms of volume;
- The relative cost advantage linked to the cost of manpower;
- The experience of internationalization in the mainland itself through sino-foreign joint ventures, giving Chinese engineers and staff the opportunity to learn from their foreign partners and develop their own managerial best practices and innovation capabilities; and
- The massive support of the Chinese government in terms of Research and Development (R&D) investments, financing large projects and international diplomacy supporting the presence of Chinese firms.

Barré (2016), examining the key success factors of the international strategy of Chinese multinationals such as Haier (home appliance), Huawei (telecom and IT), and TCL (multimedia), identifies a unique combination of factors:

- Accelerated internationalization process and business strategies based on the acquisition of knowledge, the emphasis on new products and advanced technologies, and the investment in human potential; as well as
- Government support for both innovation and investment abroad.

These key factors explain the success of companies that have not only been catching up with their foreign competitors, but also become leaders in their industry. They have done so by developing a successful presence in both emerging economies and developed markets such as the European market, either by acquisition or organic growth.

With the B&R initiative, Chinese multinationals will benefit from even better conditions to develop their exports and investments to Europe. The initiative will also open the door to Europe to a new wave of Chinese national champions specialized in the area of energy, logistics and infrastructure, such as oil and gas, construction, engineering, shipping and railway companies. China's national champions at the forefront of Chinese investments along the B&R will mostly be state-owned giants, such as China National Petroleum Corporation (CNPC) in the oil industry, China Merchants Group and China Ocean Shipping (Cosco) in port management and shipping, or China Railway Rolling Stock Corp (CRRC), the world's largest rail company, created in 2015.

2. China, Europe and the Baltic Sea Region (BSR)

China and Europe trade more than 1 billion Euros a day. The European Union (EU) is China's biggest trading partner and records a significant trade deficit with China. China is the second most important EU trading partner behind the United States, accounting for 14% of total extra-EU trade in goods in 2014, and China is one of the fastest growing markets for European exports.

The EU and China have been negotiating a comprehensive EU-China investment agreement for progressive liberalization of investment and the elimination of restrictions for investors since 2013. The rise of Chinese foreign direct investment (FDI) in the EU sparked a debate about the control that China may be seeking to take over European economies (Nicolas, 2014). Granting China market economy status was still in question in 2016: it would boost Chinese exports to the EU by 3.9% to 5.3% in volume (Bellora and Jean, 2016). The EU Commission proposed, among key objectives for a new EU-China policy, that the EU should: "Drive forward infrastructure, trading, digital and people-to-people connectivity between Europe and China based on an open rules-based platform with benefits for all the countries along the proposed routes" (EU Commission, 2016).

Thus the perceived mutual benefits of the new B&R projects in Europe will have a direct influence on the outcome of these negotiations. In any case, China's B&R initiative, as well as China's foreign investment policy, are likely to accelerate Chinese investments in Europe and especially in Germany (Hanemann and Huotari, 2015).

China's official announcement of the B&R initiative is quite recent, but the first investments in terms of transport infrastructure are already producing very tangible results. Along the "Maritime Silk Road" (MSR), Cosco has invested in terminal infrastructures in Piraeus, the port of Athens, regularly from 2009 to 2015 and finally acquired a 67% stake in the Port of Piraeus for 368.5 million Euros in 2016. These investments contribute to saving between four to ten days of transport if alternative ports of Northern Europe such as Hamburg (Germany), Rotterdam (The Netherlands) and Antwerp (Belgium) are used instead. It creates the opportunity for Greece and Southern Central Europe countries to build their comparative advantage for attracting China-Europe transit flows. It also demonstrates the direct influence of Chinese investments in the framework of the B&R initiative on the trade routes between the EU, China and East Asia (Van der Putten and Meijnders, 2015).

Along the inland railroad, the "Silk Road Economic Belt" (SREB), which ranges from China to Western Europe through Central Asia, Turkey and Russia, is also creating new opportunities and challenges. The Yuxinou Railway, the freight rail route connecting Western China to Germany, stretches 11,000 kilometers (km), running from Chongqing to Duisburg via Kazakhstan, Russia, Belarus and Poland in fourteen days — a much shorter journey than the maritime way. Thanks to international customs cooperation, this rail operates a "one-stop declaration, inspection and release" system all along the route. Kazakhstan railways (KTZ), which is also a Yuxinou shareholder, is investing massively in infrastructure and manufacturing. Alstom, one of the leaders in the market of heavy freight electric locomotives, is manufacturing, with its Kazakh partners in Astana, electric locomotives which will contribute to make the journey even faster: less than ten days.

The Baltic Sea Region

The BSR refers geographically to the nine coastal states bordering the Baltic Sea: three Nordic countries (Denmark, Finland and Sweden), the three Baltic States (Estonia, Latvia and Lithuania), and Germany, Poland and Russia (Map 1.2). Norway does not border the Baltic Sea but it belongs to the broad Baltic Sea historical, cultural, political and economic environment. Norway, which was in a union with Denmark or Sweden or

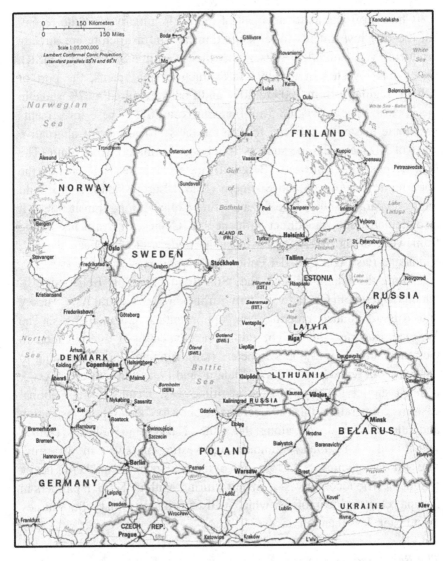

Map 1.2   The Baltic Sea Region

Source: Courtesy of the University of Texas Libraries, the University of Texas at Austin.

both for many centuries, is a part of the Scandinavian Peninsula (Norway and Sweden) which separates the Baltic Sea from the North Sea and the Atlantic Ocean.

In the past, the region had been a theater of intense rivalry between the leading powers of Northern Europe, such as Germany and Russia, but it had also given birth to a unique economic alliance and trade association in European history: the Hanseatic League. The League, founded in the 13th century by port cities of Northern Germany and merchant communities, had dominated trade for some 400 years in Northern Europe. It was a powerful economic network of independent cities and enterprises operating along the trade routes of both the Baltic Sea and the North Sea.

Leading modern metropolis — capital cities, ports and trade centers — of Northern Europe are the successors of the Hanseatic cities: Antwerp and Bruges (Belgium), Tallinn (Estonia), Bremen, Hamburg and Lübeck (Germany), Riga (Latvia), Klaipėda (Lithuania), Bergen (Norway), Gdańsk (Poland), Kaliningrad and Novgorod (Russia), Stockholm (Sweden) and London (UK). Amsterdam (Netherlands) was not a member of the Hanseatic League but was still the central warehouse from which the grain exported from the Baltic was sold to the hinterland and other European countries. The Dutch called the Baltic grain trade the "mother of all trade".

The success of the Hanseatic League was "based on trust, reputation and reciprocal relation, as well as on the art of keeping their transaction costs low" (Schulte Beerbühl, 2012). This lesson is still valid today with the development of global value chains (GVC) along the B&R. The European countries of the Baltic Sea and the North Sea regions have maintained their longstanding trade and cultural ties and are more and more economically integrated.

Eight countries of the BSR are members of the EU and Norway, which is not an EU member state, but is very closely integrated economically and culturally into the EU policy frameworks. The BSR is characterized by a strong industrial tradition, a culture of international cooperation and trade, an institutional environment favorable to business, skilled and educated workforce, good infrastructure and easy access to key European markets. The region has also acquired strong experience and capabilities in the development of viable solutions in various fields such as "climate change adaptation and mitigation, food production, land use, urban-rural interaction, waste management, sustainable consumption and production as well as renewable energy" (Council of the Baltic Sea States, 2014).

The BSR and China's initiative

Germany is China's leading industrial and commercial partner in Continental Europe; Poland is a key economic hub among Central and Eastern Europe countries, and the Nordic-Baltic countries play a major role in cooperation at the level of innovation-driven strategies. The BSR is a leading force in the European high-tech sector. In 2015, four of the BSR countries — Sweden, Denmark, Finland and Germany — were top innovation leaders among EU nations in terms of product or process innovation, marketing or organizational innovation, sales of new-to-market and new-to-firm innovations.

Both wings of the B&R initiative, China's MSR and the SREB play a major role in the Baltic Sea Region:

- China's MSR has major economic importance for the ports of the Baltic Sea: Kiel and Lübeck (Germany), Gdańsk and Gdynia (Poland), Göteborg (Sweden), HaminaKotka and Helsinki (Finland), Aarhus (Denmark), Klaipėda (Lithuania), Riga (Latvia) as well as Saint Petersburg (Russia), which is building a new marine transshipment complex that should be the deepest port in the Baltic Region. To promote trade and economic cooperation with China, these port cities tend to build special collaboration mechanisms with Chinese port cities and regions with similar interests. This was the case for Schleswig-Holstein, the northernmost state of Germany, located between the North Sea and the Baltic Sea, and with China's Zhejiang province (Case 1.1). Thus, the success of China-Europe cooperation along the B&R depends on the quality of contacts at three different levels: the EU level, the national level, and the level of the city and its hinterland.
- The SREB which connects Western China to Moscow and Minsk (Belarus) through Kazakhstan is a great opportunity for Poland, Lithuania and Latvia, which offer good railroad and port facilities closely connected to Moscow, Minsk, as well as to Northwest Russia,

especially Saint Petersburg and Kaliningrad. Here the quality of cooperation depends not only on national and regional interests, but also on broader policy issues such as the quality of cooperation between the EU and the Commonwealth of Independent States (CIS).

Chinese companies, already present in the region, have mainly been attracted by the search for talent and technology. This was the case for Huawei's investments in R&D in the telecom sector in Finland, Sweden and Poland. The acquisition of Volvo cars from Ford Motor in 2010 by Chinese billionaire Li Shufu and its company Zhejiang Geely in a US$1.8 billion deal is an interesting example (Case 1.2). Under Geely's ownership, Volvo has been able to invest in new products and rapidly develop its sales and capacity of production; and in 2015, the company was planning to export cars made in its new Chengdu plant to the US.

Chinese banks are also present, supporting Chinese investments. The Bank of China (BoC) is opening branches in Finland and Poland, while Industrial and Commercial Bank of China (ICBC) is opening a branch in Poland, where China Investment Corporation (CIC), the Chinese sovereign wealth fund, is also expected to invest. Be it infrastructure, trade, investment or financing, Chinese firms are ready for a new phase of expansion in the BSR. Finnish companies are discussing opportunities for development with their Chinese counterparts, through joint projects in the high-tech sectors in third world countries, outside China and Finland, and in emerging markets and mature economies.

In this context, institutions and companies of the BSR are actively promoting their specific competitive advantages and creating new business models and modes of international collaboration with their Chinese, Russian and Central Asia counterparts.

The BSR and the Eurasian Land Bridge

From China to the Baltic Sea through Eurasia, there are two mainland roads: the Northern Route through Siberia crossing Russia from Northern China to Moscow and Saint Petersburg, and the Southern Route from Western China to Kazakhstan, Russia and Eastern Europe.

The BSR is a natural interface with Russia and Belarus, both members of the CIS with Kazakhstan, and one of the most attractive western gates of the Chinese "New Silk Road" from an economic point of view. However, tensions between the EU and Russia linked to the prolonged crisis in Ukraine since November 2013 have hampered the development of trade and investment between Russia and European countries of the Baltic Rim.

Russian position towards the SREB initiative has evolved from skepticism in the early days to a supportive attitude in 2015. On the one hand, Russia wants to develop its economic cooperation with China, and China is interested in Russia's natural resources, especially oil and gas, and its transportation through Kazakhstan and Western China.

Kazakhstan, which is a close partner of the Federation of Russia, sees itself as the economic hub at the core of the "Eurasian transport corridor". Kazakhstan belongs to the Eurasian Economic Union (EEU): Armenia, Belarus, Kazakhstan, the Kyrgyz Republic and the Russian Federation, and its major trading partners include the CIS countries, Italy, China and Russia. China-Kazakhstan cooperation is already well established in the oil business with 20% of Kazakhstan's oil flowing from the Port of Atyrau along the Caspian coast to Alashankou in China's northwest Xinjiang region. The pipeline is a 50-50 joint venture between the China National Petroleum Corporation (CNPC) and KazMunaiGaz. Kazakhstan is also potentially interested in the development of joint infrastructure projects, pipelines, railways, free trade zones and mining activities. In 2012, Kazakhstan's President Nursultan Nazarbayev, announcing the development of the "New Silk Road", said "Kazakhstan must revive its historical role and become the largest business and transit hub of the Central Asian region, a bridge between Europe and Asia".

China is developing a major logistics hub at the China-Kazakhstan frontier. Khorgos free-trade zone, established in 2012 at the China-Kazakhstan border in China's Xinjiang Uyghur Autonomous Region, is a huge international railway, energy and logistics hub. Chinese authorities describe it as "China's mainland port" on the SREB. Finally, the Chinese SREB initiative is "the only international project aimed at the development of the transit potential of Central Asia" (Astana Club Report, 2015). It creates the opportunity for Central Asian countries to participate actively in the GVC and to become a manufacturer of goods and services (Vandenberg and Kikawa, 2015).

The development of trade and investment along the SREB will create the need or opportunity for large companies operating simultaneously in China, Central Asia and Europe to reorganize their activities along the way in terms of value chain, manufacturing hubs, assembling and distribution centers. It will also create opportunities for new actors to develop new products and services, as well as new business models (Vadcar, 2016).

In this context Russia seeks to combine its own long-term strategic interests with the flexible Chinese SREB vision, offering alternative trade routes from Western China through Kazakhstan to Turkey and Western Europe. After a mixed reception by Russian authorities to the Chinese initiative in 2013, President Putin and Xi signed an agreement in 2015 linking the B&R with the EEU, pledging to create a "joint economic space" in Eurasia. However, Simola (2016) notes that, despite the increase in cooperation between the two countries, "the economic dependency is rather a one-sided dependency of Russia from China than a deeper interdependency".

Belarus, traditionally a close economic partner of Russia, is already participating actively in a B&R project with the development of a logistics hub in Minsk, at the junction of the EEU, the EU, and the new SREB.

3. Financing the B&R Infrastructure

According to the BoC, the need for infrastructure investments in Asia could represent a total amount of US$8 trillion in 2010–2020. These funds will come from various sources: new financial institutions initiated by China, Chinese banks and the CIC-China's sovereign wealth fund created in 2007, as well as foreign banks and financial markets. In 2014, China developed three new major financial institutions to support its projects: the Silk Road Fund (a China-led fund of US$40 billion), the Asian Infrastructure Investment Bank (AIIB) and the New Development Bank (NDB).

The AIIB, established in 2014 by the representatives from 22 countries with headquarters in Beijing, will focus on the development of infrastructure and other productive sectors in Asia, including energy and power, transportation and telecommunications, rural infrastructure and agriculture development, water supply and sanitation, environmental protection, urban development and logistics. The president-elect of the AIIB is Jin Liqun, China's former vice finance minister. Britain, France and Germany have been the first European countries to join the AIIB in 2015.

The BRICS NDB, a multilateral development bank, was created in mid-2014 by the governments of Brazil, Russia, India, China and South Africa. Each country will have one vote and no country will have veto power. The bank headquarters are in Shanghai, with an African Regional Center opened in Johannesburg in 2016. It will have a fairly large capital contribution — initially of US$50 billion — from BRICS countries and can grow up to US$100 billion with contributions from other countries.

The internationalization of China's RMB has been described as "the most significant global financial markets development since the formation of the Euro" (Deutsche Bank, 2014). The internationalization of the RMB, initiated in 2002 with the internationalization of China's bond market, made a major step in 2015 with its inclusion as the 5th currency in the Special Drawing Rights (SDR) basket of currency of the International Monetary Fund (IMF). Recently, the IMF announced that the RMB would be included in the basket of currencies that makes up the IMF's SDR. Transactions along the SREB would preferably be established in Russian rubles or in Chinese RMB. The internationalization of the RMB will benefit from the expansion of new RMB-clearing banks, providing direct access to RMB liquidity in China, and contributing to the expansion of offshore RMB.

4. Managing across Cultures, Languages and Nationalities

History has left a uniquely diverse variety of cultures, languages and nationalities along the SREB. The Xinjiang Uyghur Autonomous Region, which has common borders with Mongolia, Kazakhstan, Kyrgyzstan, Tajikistan, Afghanistan, Pakistan and India, is home to a number of ethnic groups including the Uyghur, Han, Kazakhs, Tajiks, Hui, Kyrgyz and Mongols.

In Central Asia, the five largest ethnic groups are the Uzbek, Kazakh, Tajik, Turkmen and Kyrgyz. Except for the Tajik, these peoples speak languages related to Turkish, facilitating the cooperation with modern Turkey, one of the major investors in the region. Islam is the dominant religion and culture amongst these populations, but other minorities live in the region such as the Russians, Ukrainians and Germans who migrated to Central Asia under the Russian or the Soviet Union regimes. Kazakhstan is a typical multiethnic country, with a Kazakh majority of some 63% followed by the Russian (23%) and other ethnic groups (14%): Uzbeks, Ukrainians, Uyghurs, Tatars and Germans.

On the Baltic end of the Silk Road, Estonia and Latvia have particularly large ethnic Russian minorities, with about 24% and 27% of the general population. In Lithuania, only 8% are native Russian speakers. However, Russian is still widely spoken and taught at school in the three Baltic Republics, which facilitates the contacts with neighboring Russian speakers in Belarus, Ukraine, Federation of Russia and Central Asia.

Thus, managing large projects in these areas means taking into account these differences and benefiting from this diversity. Zhang *et al.* (2015) found that people of two seemingly opposite cultures are able to work together in a project-based environment to complement each other and reap mutual benefits for a win-win result. In the framework of the Silk Road projects, Chinese authorities are already developing systematic language courses in all Eurasian languages for Chinese employees and executives. At the company level, top management will have to pay attention to cultural differences and avoid the dominance of one culture among the others. The choice of a common language for business purposes will already be a difficult choice.

References

Astana Club Report (2015). *Geo-Economics of Eurasia*. Astana, Kazakhstan: The Institute of World Economics and Politics (IWEP).

Barré, G. (2016). *Les entreprises chinoises et la mondialisation*. Paris, France: CNRS Editions.

Bellora, C. & Jean, S. (2016). *Granting market economy status to China in the EU: An economic impact assessment*. CEPII Policy Brief 11 September. Paris, France: CEPII.

Council of the Baltic Sea States (2014, June 20). Decision by the Council of the Baltic Sea States on a review of the CBSS long-term priorities. Stockholm, Sweden: CBSS.

Deutsche Bank (2014, March). *At the center of RMB Internationalisation. A brief guide to offshore RMB.* Frankfurt am Main, Germany: Deutsche Bank.

European Union Commission (2016, June 22). Elements for a new EU strategy on China. Joint Communication to the European Parliament and the Council. Brussels, Belgium: EU Commission.

Godement, F. & Kratz, A. (Eds.) (2015). *One Belt, One Road: China's great leap forward.* European Council on Foreign Relations.

Hanemann, T. & Huotari, M. (2015, June). *Chinese companies in Europe and in Germany — Preparing for a New Era of Chinese Capital.* Report. Berlin, Germany: Mercator Institute for China Studies and Rhodium Group.

Larçon, J.-P. (Ed.) (2008). *Chinese Multinationals.* Singapore: World Scientific Publishing.

National Development and Reform Commission (NDRC) (2015). Vision and Actions on Jointly Building Silk Road Economic Belt and 21st-Century Maritime Silk Road. Beijing, People's Republic of China: the National Development and Reform Commission, Ministry of Foreign Affairs, and Ministry of Commerce of the People's Republic of China, with State Council authorization in March 2015.

Nicolas, F. (2014). China's Direct Investment in the European Union: Challenges and Policy Responses. *China Economic Journal,* 7(1, 2), 103–25.

Schulte Beerbühl, M. (2012). *Networks of the Hanseatic League,* in: European History Online (EGO). Mainz, Germany: Leibniz Institute of European History (IEG).

Simola, H. (2016). *Economic relations between Russia and China — Increasing inter-dependency?* BOFIT Policy Brief 6. Helsinki: Bank of Finland Institute for Economies in Transition.

Vadcar, C. (2016). Value creation and global chains: New business models. *ParisTech Review,* June 29.

Van der Putten, F.-P. & Meijnders, M. (2015). *China Europe and the Maritime Silk Road.* Clingendael report. The Hague, Netherlands: Clingendael.

Vandenberg, P. & Kikawa, K. (2015, May). *Global Value Chains along the New Silk Road.* ADBI Policy Brief. Tokyo, Japan: Asian Development Bank Institute (ADBI).

Zhang, Y., Marquis, C., Filippov, S. & Steen, M. van der (2015, February). The Challenges and Enhancing Opportunities of Global Project Management: Evidence from Chinese and Dutch Cross-Cultural Project Management. Harvard Business School Organizational Behavior Unit Working Paper No. 15-063. Available at SSRN: http://ssrn.com/abstract=2562376.

Case 1.1   The cooperation between Schleswig-Holstein and Zhejiang
province

The economy of Schleswig-Holstein

Schleswig-Holstein is the northernmost of Germany's 16 states. Its position
between two seas — the North Sea and the Baltic Sea — is unique in Germany.
Schleswig-Holstein borders Denmark to the north, the North Sea to the west,
the Baltic Sea to the east, and the German states of Lower Saxony, Hamburg,
and Mecklenburg-Western Pomerania to the south. In 2015, its population was
2.841 million, 3.48% of the national total. The capital city is Kiel; other main
cities are Lübeck, Flensburg and Neumünster; the distance between Kiel and
its neighboring city-state of Hamburg is less than 100 km.

Large companies include Dräger (medical and safety technology with
around 13,000 employees worldwide), ThyssenKrupp Marine Systems
(system provider for non-nuclear submarines and high-end naval vessels with
around 3,200 employees in Germany), Jungheinrich Norderstedt (material
handling equipment, warehousing engineering and machine building),
Caterpillar Motors (marine diesel engines), and Autoliv B.V. (the world's
largest automotive safety supplier). The regional high-tech cluster "Life
Science Nord", covering Schleswig-Holstein and Hamburg, is dedicated to
biotechnology, pharmaceuticals and medical technology.

The logistics sector

The ports of Kiel and Lübeck have a significant role in cargo shipping from
Germany to Scandinavia, the Baltic States and Russia. Both cities are offering
train connections to the German "hinterland", industrial areas such as Munich
or Stuttgart, and other destinations such as the Port of Duisburg, the biggest
inland port all over Europe. Schleswig-Holstein connects Scandinavia with
Southern Germany and ongoing to Austria, Benelux, France, Italy and Spain.
New infrastructure projects such as the Baltic Sea highway should easily
connect Schleswig-Holstein with Eastern Europe. A direct maritime connection
already exists between Klaipėda (Lithuania) and Kiel by daily ferryboat.

Cooperation with China

Schleswig-Holstein and the Chinese province of Zhejiang entered into a
partnership since 1986. Both Zhejiang and Schleswig-Holstein are coastal

(*Continued*)

Case 1.1   (*Continued*)

regions, and in 2011, the two regions agreed to step up their economic collaboration in the fields of shipbuilding, maritime technology and renewable energy; there is also a big potential for cooperation in port infrastructure, aquaculture and offshore wind energy. The two regions develop their cooperation at the university level, such as joint programs offered by the University of Kiel and Zhejiang University. Schleswig-Holstein and Hamburg consider China as a key partner and are supporters of China's B&R initiative, including the development of the China-Europe Land Bridge via the Baltic Sea.

Sources: Europa, European Business Network: Hamburg Schleswig-Holstein, Logistik Initiative Schleswig-Holstein.

Case 1.2   Zhejiang Geely's acquisition of Volvo Cars (2010)

"Volvo Cars will be run by Volvo management, and be strategically independent. They are distinct companies. Volvo is a Swedish business with a strong Scandinavian heritage."

Li Shufu, CEO Geely (2010)

Zhejiang Geely background

Zhejiang Geely, a Chinese motorcycle manufacturer founded in 1986, decided to enter the automobile industry in 1997. In 2002, it signed agreements with Daewoo in Korea and Carrozzeria Maggiora in Italy. Geely's headquarters are in Hangzhou, the capital of East China's Zhejiang province. Geely is controlled by Li Shufu, listed by Forbes as one of China's richest men. Mr. Li was born in 1963 in a village of the Zhejiang province, the homeland of many of China's wealthiest entrepreneurs.

   Geely operates via two key legal entities, Zhejiang Geely Holding Group and Geely Automobile Holdings. Zhejiang Geely Holding Group is Geely's ultimate parent company. It is an independent privately-owned firm registered in the People's Republic of China (PRC). Geely Automobile Holdings is listed on the Hong Kong Stock Exchange. In 2011 Geely was among the top ten Chinese automakers.

(*Continued*)

Case 1.2   (*Continued*)

The Chinese auto market

The Chinese car market has seen a remarkable acceleration since China's entry into the World Trade Organization (2011) and it has been a period of increased competition between manufacturers. Foreign car manufacturers have a strong presence in China in partnership with local companies: Volkswagen (Shanghai, Nanjing, Changchun, Chengdu), Toyota (Tianjin, Chengdu, Changchun, Guangzhou), Nissan (Zhengzhou, Wuhan), Hyundai (Beijing), Chevrolet (Shanghai, Yantai, Shenyang), Buick (Shanghai, Yantai, Shenyang), Honda (Wuhan, Guangzhou), and Ford (Nanjing, Chongqing, Shanghai).

From 2001 to 2011, foreign investors have increased their investment in China, building added capacity, introducing new models, developing their dealers' networks and developing their collaboration with their Chinese counterparts. Since 2001, there was also a boom in Chinese export of cars, auto parts and motorcycles. In 2009, China overtook the United States as the world's No. 1 auto market, with 13 million cars sold. The Chinese government is encouraging the emergence of national champions and the consolidation of an industry which is yet too fragmented.

International strategies

Shanghai Automotive (SAIC), a state-owned enterprise and the largest car manufacturer in China, acquired the Korean manufacturer SsangYong in 2004. In 2005 the company acquired from British manufacturer MG Rover the design rights of the Rover 25 and 75 car models. The Rover 25 model is branded as Roewe in China. In 2007 SAIC became the owner of MG's plant in Birmingham (UK) after the acquisition of Nanjing Automobile Group Corp. Among Foreign Multinational Corporations (MNCs), Honda was the first exporter of cars made in China in 2005, with the Jazz model made in Guangdong province for the European market. Components manufacturers, such as Wanxiang — a leading supplier of foreign MNCs in China — have started exporting and investing abroad. Among private car companies, Chery was the leading exporter of Chinese cars in 2005. It started to export to Malaysia and plans to build plants in Venezuela and Pakistan to assemble cars with local partners.

Geely's total overseas sales are over 100,000 vehicles. Its key markets are the CIS, Middle East, Africa, Southeast Asia, and Central and South America.

(*Continued*)

Case 1.2   (*Continued*)

In 2009, overseas assembling plants were established in Ukraine, Russia and Indonesia to produce vehicles in semi-complete or completely knocked down (CKD) kits.

Geely's acquisition of Volvo and projects

In 2010, Geely bought Volvo Cars from Ford; it paid US$1.3 billion in cash and issued a US$200 million note for the acquisition. Li Shufu became Chairman of the Board of Volvo Car Corporation and Hans-Olov Olsson the Vice-Chairman. FDI by Chinese firms is usually motivated by the quest for natural resources, the control of foreign brands and access to distribution networks, or by the transfer of technology and know-how.

While the Swedish public opinion and Volvo management were worried about the future of Volvo car identity, technology and jobs, many foreign analysts wondered if Geely will be able to really benefit from the potential synergies of this acquisition.

Li Shufu has been quoted as saying, "Volvo is Volvo, and Geely is Geely", meaning that the two companies are entirely separate entities. The only thing they have in common is control by Li Shufu. In 2011, Geely and Volvo were planning to build assembly plants in China to make Volvo cars, in a bid to realize the dream of selling 300,000 vehicles a year. One assembly plant would be in Chengdu where Volvo would produce Volvo S60. Geely wants to build on the perception of Volvo in China as a premium brand, comparable to Mercedes-Benz or BMW.

Chengdu, the capital of the populous Sichuan province, is among many Chinese cities aspiring to become a major automobile manufacturing hub. It is also one of the country's biggest inland markets and investment in Chengdu is more than welcome by both provincial authorities and the central government in the framework of the China Go West policy.

Li Shufu also said in October 2010 that he hoped to sell China-made vehicles in Europe in a later stage, but that it would not be through Volvo's distributor network.

Source: J.-P. Larçon (HEC Paris, 2011) and company data.

Chapter 2

China's "Belt and Road" and Business Perspectives

Li Donghong and Tang Lingling

Tsinghua University School of Economics and Management

In September 2013, inspired by China's ancient Silk Road, Chinese President Xi Jinping proposed the "Silk Road Economic Belt" (SREB) and the "Maritime Silk Road" (MSR) initiative in order to promote the common development of all countries. In March 2015, China's National Development and Reform Commission (NDRC), Ministry of Foreign Affairs and Ministry of Commerce co-issued the "Vision and Proposed Actions Outlined on Jointly Building Silk Road Economic Belt and 21st Century Maritime Silk Road" (referred to as the "Belt and Road" or "B&R"). The Chinese government has determined that the "Belt and Road" initiative would cover 18 provinces in China. Among them, Xinjiang and Fujian have been designated as core areas, while the strategic positioning of other provinces will be determined by geographic location and region. Abroad, Chinese experts think that the B&R initiative will cover 65 countries in Asia, Africa and Europe (Central and Eastern Europe countries), with a population of about 4.4 billion (Table 2.1). This area accounts for 63% of

Table 2.1   The China + 64 = 65 countries along the "Belt and Road"

Regions	Countries
East Asia and ASEAN (11 countries)	China, Singapore, Malaysia, Indonesia, Myanmar, Thailand, Laos, Cambodia, Vietnam, Brunei and Philippines.
West Asia (18 countries)	Iran, Iraq, Turkey, Syria, Jordan, Lebanon, Israel, Palestine, Saudi Arabia, Yemen, Oman, the United Arab Emirates, Qatar, Kuwait, Bahrain, Greek, Cyprus and Sinai Peninsula in Egypt.
South Asia (8 countries)	India, Pakistan, Bengal, Afghanistan, Sri Lanka, Maldives, Nepal and Bhutan.
Central Asia (5 countries)	Kazakhstan, Uzbekistan, Turkmenistan, Tajikistan and Kyrgyzstan.
The Commonwealth of the Independent States (7 countries)	Russia, Ukraine, Belarus, Georgia, Azerbaijan, Armenia and Moldova.
Central and Eastern Europe (16 countries)	Poland, Lithuania, Estonia, Latvia, Czech, Slovakia, Hungary, Slovenia, Croatia, Bosnia and Herzegovina, Montenegro, Serbia, Albania, Romania, Bulgaria and Macedonia.

Source: China International Trade Institute (2015).

the global population and economic aggregate of about US$21 trillion, or 29% of global GDP (Chongyang Institute for Financial Studies Renmin University of China, 2016).

The Chinese government attaches great importance to the B&R, a global development concept proposed by Xi Jinping after he served as President of China. In order to promote the B&R initiative, the Chinese government has introduced some policies for domestic construction and development on the one hand, and pressed ahead with international bilateral and multilateral cooperation on the other (Figure 2.1). In the future, the Chinese government hopes to focus on "Five Connections"[1] and

---

[1]China will focus primarily on promoting cooperation in five major areas: policy coordination, facilities connectivity, unimpeded trade, financial integration and people-to-people bonds between the B&R countries and China. See NDRC (2015). Vision and Actions on

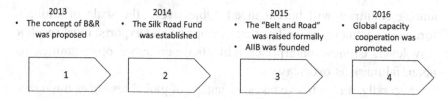

Figure 2.1 The progress of international cooperation in the "Belt and Road"
Source: Authors.

strengthen foreign cooperation in order to promote the common prosperity and development of all countries covered by the B&R. To maintain the open stance that China takes towards the outside world, partners of the B&R include but are not limited to those countries covered by the ancient Silk Road. The B&R is an open and collaborative initiative in which any country or region not covered by the "Belt and Road" is also allowed to participate.

1. China's Proposed Aim for the B&R

The "Belt and Road" is designed to promote both economic globalization and Chinese economic development.

1.1. *Deepening China's foreign economic and trade cooperation*

First, this project creates opportunities for markets. As the route chart of the B&R demonstrates, the route covers Central Asia, South Asia, West Asia, East Asia and the Middle East, including many developing countries or transitional economies. Compared with these countries, China is more advanced and experienced in infrastructure, manufacturing and smelting. The B&R initiative will help countries along the route advance economic development and strengthen trade cooperation among these countries. Generally, the depth and breadth of cooperation

Jointly Building Silk Road Economic Belt and 21st-Century Maritime Silk Road. Available at http://en.ndrc.gov.cn/newsrelease/201503/t20150330_669367.html.

among countries will be enhanced. Objectively, the scale of China's foreign investment, as well as that of imports and exports, must reach a new level; Chinese enterprises will also gain more opportunities to potential markets overseas.

Secondly, this initiative takes advantage of global resources through a range of channels. In 2014, the main imported energy sources in China included crude oil, refined oil and natural gas. With the rapid development of China's economy, the consumption of energy resources in China will continue to rise. In addition, data from the US Department of Energy, Energy Information Administration (EIA) indicates that China is poor in per capita resources, as its per capita crude oil reserves in 2015 were only 18 barrels.[2] According to the World Trade Organization (WTO), the main imported products for Asia were fuels, which accounted for 6.3% of the total imports (WTO, 2015). China is also one of the largest crude oil importers in the world. In the future, the gap between supply and demand of China's energy will continue to expand. In addition, based on the data from the US EIA, we find that oil reserves in countries covered by the B&R make up 57.1% of global oil reserves in 2016 (EIA, 2016).[3] Therefore, by cooperating with countries and regions along the route, China can easily acquire energy abroad. It was the case of the acquisition of DostykGazTerminal (DGT) by CEFC in Kazakhstan in 2015 (Case 2.1). There is a similar situation for other resources required by economic development. Thus, the common development concept, the B&R, can diversify and stabilize developing countries' use of global resources, and remove trade barriers between China and countries with various resources, reducing the cost of trade and investment.

---

[2]In order to calculate the latest results, we combined data from two countries. China's latest data about crude oil reserves was merely updated in 2014 while the US Energy Information Administration (EIA) has data from 2015. The data on oil reserves comes from the US Department of Energy, EIA (2015). The data on Chinese population is from the National Bureau of Statistics of the People's Republic of China — Statistic Bulletin of National Economy and Social Development (2016).

[3]Data comes from the US EIA. The actual ratio is likely to be higher as the data available on crude oil proved reserves in 2016 covers only 17 countries (EIA, 2016).

1.2. *Promoting economic development in neighboring areas*

First, the B&R anticipates achieving economies of scale from all countries. A country can establish a complete market. However, the domestic market of any country, including China, is small compared with that of 65 countries. Thus, the ability to realize economies of scale while depending only on the domestic market is very limited. If all countries can establish a large common market, then they can benefit from trade with other B&R countries. According to the evaluation results of the industrialization among countries along the route, the industrialization of the 65 countries differs greatly, and these countries are highly complementary (Huang, 2015). To some extent, by joining in the B&R initiative, these countries can achieve the construction of low technology, capital and personnel as well as improve industrialization. Also, the B&R initiative can expand the scale of markets that enterprises in these countries serve, thus reducing production and circulation costs due to economies of scale.

1.3. *The non-economic significance*

The B&R initiative can also play a role in maintaining world peace. Conflicts among countries may arise because of differences in levels of economic development and uneven distribution of resources or benefits. The B&R initiative can form some interest alliances by strengthening economic cooperation among countries. While frequent economic cooperation may increase trade friction, it can reduce the likelihood of military and political conflicts. Thus the B&R initiative can promote world peace and move the world economy toward a virtuous cycle of development.

2. Measures the Chinese Government is Taking to Promote the B&R Initiative

Implementation of the B&R initiative must depend on individuals, that is, enterprises in the countries along the route. When participating in construction, these enterprises should follow market laws. From the perspective of the Chinese government, the government can work hard to create and maintain a sound market environment on the one hand, while guiding and pushing enterprises to join in the B&R initiative on the other. To make this happen, the Chinese government has taken the following measures in recent years.

2.1. *Establish a framework for cooperation at the national level*

The implementation of the B&R initiative requires the joint effort of countries along the route. Any misunderstanding, from the perspective of government, enterprises or residents in participating countries, is likely to create risks. It is essential for participants to sign the cooperation agreement for foreign investments at the national level, in order to protect the legitimate rights and interests of enterprises in foreign investments and establish a framework for secure cooperation mechanisms.

According to the Ministry of Commerce of the People's Republic of China (Xinhua, 2016), China had signed the "Belt and Road" cooperation agreement with more than 30 countries in 2016. It is reported that China plans to promote the construction of six major economic corridors, including China-Mongolia-Russia, New Eurasian Land Bridge, China-Central Asia-West Asia, China-Indochina, China-Pakistan and China-India-Myanmar-Bangladesh with some relevant governments in the following five years.

In addition, China's Ministry of Commerce and China Development Bank has delivered *Guidance of General Office of the State Council on Financial Support for Economic Restructuring and Upgrading, 2013* in order to provide strong support for the construction of foreign trade and cooperation regions in order to shorten the cycle of transforming and upgrading economic structures, ensure that economic restructuring proceeds as planned and reduce the chance of "going along the indirect route". This initiative not only guides Chinese enterprises as they develop their business in cooperation regions, but also provides financial support for enterprises that will promote the development of new cooperation regions and support existing cooperation regions. According to the public service platform for "going global" of the Ministry of Commerce, [4] there

---

[4] For more details, please browse http://fec.mofcom.gov.cn.

are 13 overseas economic and trade cooperation regions that have passed the examination.

2.2. Establish a common financial system

The Chinese government has been endeavoring to work together with countries along the route to establish a well-regulated international financial system in order to fundamentally support global economic development. The lack of financial resources is one of the key factors restraining the development of countries along the route. The B&R initiatives at the initial stage are focused on "infrastructure connections" (Lin, 2015). The relevant projects must be large-scale projects, which require large initial investments and a slow return of capital. Therefore, current financial institutions should innovate in financial services in order to meet the needs of enterprises from all countries for large, long-term and stable funds. This is one of the issues that the G20 group has long been discussing. Other topics include establishing a new, globally unified capital framework, solving problems involving systematically important financial institutions and supervising over-the-counter derivatives trading.

Therefore, since 2013, the Chinese government has promoted the establishment of several B&R financial institutions, including the Silk Road Fund (SRF), Asian Infrastructure Investment Bank (AIIB), the Fund for Cooperation of China-Latin America Production Capacity, the "Belt and Road" Fund of China CITIC Bank, China's Insurance Investment Fund and China-Africa Fund of Industrial Capacity (Table 2.2). Over the same period, China has signed a currency swap agreement with 35 countries and RMB Qualified Foreign Institutional Investors with 17 countries. The Chinese renminbi (RMB) has also been included in the basket of currencies that comprise the IMF's Special Drawing Rights. Meanwhile, China has also built a Cross-border Interbank Payment System in order to provide capital settlement services for cross-border circulation of RMB and offshore RMB business. At present, China has built offshore RMB settlement centers in 17 countries. Thus, the Chinese government has encouraged domestic banks to increase loans for overseas large-scale investment projects and reduce financing standards.

Table 2.2   List of the "Belt and Road" thematic funds

Date of foundation	Name of organization	The basic situation
December 2014	The Silk Road Fund	Joint-contribution made by foreign exchange reserves, China Investment Corporation, Export-Import Bank of China (Exim Bank) and China Development Bank (CDB). The capital amount is US$40 billion. The received initial capital is US$10 billion. Among them, foreign reserves, China Investment Corporation, Exim Bank and CDB take up 65%, 15%, 15% and 5% respectively.
February 2015	Asian Infrastructure Investment Bank (AIIB)	The authorized stock is US$100 billion. The contribution proportion of domestic members and foreign members is 75:25. The initial goal of China's subscribed capital is about US$50 billion. And the prospective founding members agree to take economic weight by GDP as the basis of share distribution among countries. The contributed capital of the first phase as a trial in 2015 accounts for 10% of the initial goal of subscribed capital. China contributes US$2.5 billion.
June 2015	China Latin American Industrial Cooperation Investment Fund (CLAI Fund)	Joint-contribution made by foreign exchange reserves and CDB. The initial capital reaches US$10 billion. By calculating based on the principles stipulated in the agreement, China is now the first major shareholder of AIIB and has the highest proportion of voting rights, with a subscribed stock of US$29.7804 billion and 26.06% of voting right. India and Russia are the second and the third major shareholders.
June 2015	"The Belt and Road" Fund by CITIC Bank	The initial capital reaches 20 billion yuan. The fund is issued and managed by wholly-owned Zhenhua (Beijing) Private Equity Fund Management Co., Ltd. subordinated by CITIC Bank.
July 3, 2015	China's Insurance Investment Fund	Limited Partnership. China's Insurance Investment Co., Ltd. acts as a general partner. Insurance institutions and other qualified investors serve as the limited partner. The total fund reaches 300 billion yuan. The initial capital is 100 billion yuan and the duration is about five to ten years.
January 7, 2016	China-Africa Fund of Industrial Capacity	Foreign exchange reserves and Exim Bank. The initial capital is US$10 billion.

Source: Authors.

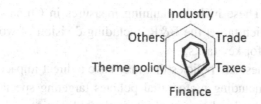

Figure 2.2   The profile of Chinese government's support policy to the "Belt and Road" (2013–2016)

Source: Collected from National Development and Reform Commission, Ministry of Foreign Affairs, and Ministry of Commerce, People's Republic of China. Authors' analysis.

2.3.   Promulgate the support policy

To promote cooperation among countries, China's central government and local government departments have implemented different policies as part of the "Belt and Road". The Chinese government's support for the "Belt and Road" mainly involves six aspects (Figure 2.2).

(1) Industrial policies. These include a policy for resolving overcapacity, a plan for the development of emerging industries and a support policy for Chinese enterprises' overseas investment;

(2) Trade policies. These include the plan for free trade zones, the management plan for foreign trade cooperation and the regional customs clearance integration reform in China's coastal areas. This mainly aims at facilitating foreign trade, reducing customs procedures and lowering difficulties of customs clearance for enterprises (General Administration of Customs, People's Republic of China, 2015);

(3) Tax policies. The main purpose of these policies is lowering corporate tax rates and tax services for the B&R. China has reduced the import and export tax rates and adjusted the management of the tax department so that enterprises can avoid paying high taxes, as well as the problem of paying taxes both at home and abroad;

(4) Financial policies. The aim of these policies is to meet the need for financial services after an enterprise goes global. The problems include financing difficulties, high cost and high risks;

(5) Theme policies. These include planning measures in China's major coastal areas, which target the B&R, including division of work and overall planning for key tasks;

(6) Other policies. These are policies that may have a direct impact on the B&R initiative, including preferential policies targeting special areas and planning for the development of international logistics.

2.4. *Measures of peripheral support*

First, the "Belt and Road" establishes various platforms for cooperation. Encouraged by the Chinese government, cooperation platforms for the B&R emerge, including the platform for cultural exchange and forums, which is designed to increase opportunities for cooperation between global enterprises and encourage collaboration between organizations from various countries. For example, the International Culture Expo for the Silk Road will be held annually, and participants will include international organizations and countries along the route.

Secondly, this initiative encourages leading companies to play an exemplary role. Though the opportunities for investment will increase through the B&R initiative, risk and financing constraints will also increase. Thus, the Chinese government hopes to encourage leading domestic companies to take the lead in guiding more companies to participate in the B&R initiative.

Thirdly, the initiative encourages monographic study. The Chinese government is working to encourage various research institutions to focus on the B&R initiative and set aside some money as research funds for special subjects. By doing so, the Chinese government aims to combine theory with practice to advance research in the field and provide reference value and guidance for enterprises and governments.

3. The B&R from the Perspective of Business

3.1. *New opportunities for enterprises among countries*

The Chinese government knows that cooperation at the national level only plays a facilitating role. Essentially, the B&R initiative aims to create investment opportunities for enterprises globally.

First, this program increases the development space for buildings and infrastructure. In order to promote facilities connectivity between neighboring countries, the primary task of the B&R is improving infrastructure in 65 countries, including transportation, telecommunications, electricity and housing. In this way, the development of infrastructure will expand. Engineering contractors in various countries will receive more opportunities for investment. They will be able to expand overseas markets by completing infrastructure projects, such as railways, harbors, airlines and power stations.

Secondly, the B&R initiative speeds up the development of industries for raw materials and advanced manufacturing equipment. The growth of infrastructure will drive the development of upstream and downstream industries in the value chain, for example, the raw materials and engineering machinery of infrastructure. The increase of market demand will accelerate the growth of supporting enterprises.

Third, this program expands the range of investment in financial services. For enterprises, financing and insurance play an important role in international investment, especially for large, long-term investment projects. Thus, the B&R initiative will bring more businesses to various financial institutions along the route. Meanwhile, in order to satisfy the need of enterprises for guarantees and financing, these institutions will be more motivated to develop new products.

Finally, the B&R promotes the development of tourism. As countries along the route move toward more openness, visa procedures have been simplified. The connection of roads improves the accessibility among countries and increases the convenience of transportation. Tourism, transportation and accommodation will become key areas for investment.

3.2. *The cooperation model of enterprises among countries*

The Chinese government has become more willing to encourage enterprises in different countries to make overseas investments by "gathering together". This phenomenon can be seen in developed economies in the world. Although Europe, America and Japan possess strong markets, enterprises in these countries are always allied with each other and work together to establish trade associations and coordinate corporate behavior in order to support sound and sustainable development of whole industries. In the process of internalization, these enterprises often compete with each other, but they cooperate with each other as well. They reach a tacit understanding when developing business in the overseas market, thus reducing the potential of destructive competition among enterprises due to the monopoly of individual enterprises. In Asian countries, Japanese companies are famous for a high degree of cooperation. In Japan, different enterprises have co-established many collaborative regional and professional organizations which are responsible for providing social services, circulating products and engaging in technical guidance and promotion.

This collaboration offers many advantages. First, it helps enterprises avoid low price competition, guarantees income and maintains sustainable development. In addition, enterprises can receive technical guidance, technical promotion and management references. Trade associations generally have an organization which provides technical guidance and operates testing fields and training centers in order to do research and develop technology. Collaboration also reduces default risks. From the amount of subject participation, the default risk of multi-cooperation is lower than that of mutual cooperation. Finally, working collaboratively can spread investment risks in a more scientific way, improving an individual company's ability to resist risk and reduce losses. As risk sharing is an investment responsibility, spreading risks properly incentivizes the development of enterprises. Therefore, the Chinese government has made a great effort to encourage enterprises in various countries to attach more importance to the positive effect by "gathering together" and participating in the construction of international industrial parks, trade and economic cooperation zones and other platforms for cooperation.

In order to realize the investment by "gathering together", the Chinese government has established many cooperation platforms for enterprises in different countries, that is, trade and economic cooperation zones overseas (See Case 2.2). Thanks to the efforts of the Chinese government, 13 new overseas cooperation zones have been approved (Table 2.3).

Table 2.3   The directory of trade and economic cooperation zones overseas

Name of cooperation zones	Name of domestic enterprises
Confirmed programs	
Cambodia Sihanoukville Special Economic Zone	Jiangsu Taihu Cambodia International Economic Cooperation Zone Investment Co., Ltd.
China-Thailand Luoyong Industrial Park in Thailand	Holley Group Co., Ltd.
Vietnam Longjiang Industrial Park	Qianjiang Investment Management Co., Ltd.
Pakistan Haier-Ruba Economic Zone	Haier Group Household Appliances Industry Co., Ltd.
Zambia-China Economic & Trade Cooperation Zone	China Nonferrous Metal Mining (Group) Co., Ltd.
Egypt-Suez Economic & Trade Cooperation Zone	China-Africa Taida Share-holding Co., Ltd.
Leckie Free Trade Zone in Nigeria	China-Africa Leckie Investment Ltd.
Russia-Ussuriysk Economic & Trade Cooperation Zone	Kangji International Investment Co., Ltd.
China-Russia Tomsk Timber Industry and Trade Cooperation Zone	AVIC Forestry
Ethiopia Oriental Industrial Park	Jiangsu Yongyuan Investment Co., Ltd.
China-Russia Agricultural and Industrial Cooperation Zone	Huaxin Group in Heilongjiang
Lung Yeuk Forestry Economic & Trade Cooperation Zone in Russia	Lung Yeuk Economy and Trade Co., Ltd. In Mudanjiang City, Heilongjiang
China-European Commercial Logistics Park in Hungary	Shandong Dihao International Investment Co., Ltd.
Programs under negotiation	

- Regional Comprehensive Economic Partnership
- China-GCC Free Trade Zone
- China-Norway Free Trade Zone
- China-Japan ROK FTA

(Continued)

Table 2.3   (*Continued*)

Name of cooperation zones	Name of domestic enterprises
• China-Sri Lanka Free Trade Zone	
• China-Maldives Free Trade Zone	
Upgrading cooperation	
• The Negotiation of the Upgrading of China-Singapore Free Trade Zone	
• The Negotiation of the Second Phase for China-Pakistan Free Trade Zone	
• The Follow-up Negotiation of Cross Strait Economic Cooperation Framework Agreement	

Source: Collected from Ministry of Commerce of the People's Republic of China Department of Outward Investment and Economic Cooperation (2016).

Conclusion

Though the "Belt and Road" initiative was proposed by China, its value is that, in the coming decades, the development of countries along the route will be a potential impetus for global prosperity, welcomed by countries around the world. Given future trends in global development, the B&R initiative is very promising. It can provide historic opportunities for relevant countries and regions, as well as enterprises in various sectors around the world.

As the world's second-largest economy, China, which has proposed the B&R initiative, needs to take the responsibility for it and establish global platforms for cooperation and communication with regard to the B&R. In addition, China needs to make greater contributions to investment capital, technology and talent, promoting bilateral and multilateral exchanges as well as creating a sound cooperation climate and mechanisms for all countries. Through this process, the Chinese government and investors from different enterprises should remain committed to the principle of "mutual benefit and win-win cooperation". They should work together with governments and enterprises from other countries as well as various global forces to participate in the B&R initiative and share the development achievements in order to achieve common prosperity. In the process of working for the B&R initiative, all sectors from China must abandon self-centered thinking and focus instead on common development. They must also avoid transferring excess low-end capacity and low-end capacity that is inimical to environmental protection and long-term development. Instead, they should focus on providing high-quality technology, talent and capital that can support the long-term development of those countries.

The countries and regions along the route seek to develop their own national economies. Undoubtedly, this is a common goal for government and enterprises. The B&R initiative proposed by China provides a new platform for cooperation and connection. From the perspective of national economic development and social progress, if countries and regions participating in the B&R are guided by the principle of "mutual benefit and win-win cooperation", they can promote their development better. The B&R initiative is not free economic aid among countries. It must follow market rules and be implemented in accordance with the rules of international trade and investment as well as common principles. Thus, countries and regions along the route should take an active role in the B&R initiative.

Other countries and regions, especially Europe, America and Japan, should also actively participate in the B&R initiative, taking into consideration the responsibility for global development, shared results from the economic growth of countries along the route, and new global business opportunities for local enterprises. Over the past few decades, both developed countries and their transnational companies have accumulated a great deal of experience in international economic cooperation. Thus, they have the ability to make contributions to forming new cooperation mechanisms as part of the B&R initiative.

Therefore, the B&R initiative represents a new engine of growth and business opportunity for the world. If all countries can participate in this initiative, new prosperity will await countries along the route as well as in other areas of the world. If countries cannot trust and respect each other, nor establish a mechanism for cooperation and communication, nor follow the principle of "mutual benefit and win-win cooperation", the value of this opportunity will be greatly reduced.

References

Chongyang Institute for Financial Studies Renmin University of China (2016). *The Belt and Road and New Pattern of International Trade*. Beijing, China: China CITIC Press.

General Administration of Customs, People's Republic of China (2015). No. 9 *Announcement on Customs Clearance Integration Reform in Customs Areas of Silk Road Economic Belt, March 31*. Retrieved August 11, 2016, from http://www.customs.gov.cn/publish/portal0/tab49564/info735387.htm.

Huang, Q. H. (2015). *Blue Book of Industrialization Progress Report*. Beijing, China: Social Sciences Academic Press.

Lin, Y. (2015). "One Belt One Road" and special tradezones: China's new external opening-up strategy (*"Yidaiyilu" yu zishangqu: Zhongguo xinde duiwai kaifang zhanlue*). Lin Xifu. *"One Belt One Road": National Strategic Top-level Design and Action Plan ("Yidaiyilu" Guojia dingceng zhanlue sheji yu xingdong buju)*. Beijing, China: *Zhongguo wenshi chubanshe*, 3–7.

Ministry of Commerce of People's Republic of China. *The 7th International Infrastructure Investment and Construction Forum in Macao, June 2 in Chinese*. Retrieved August 11, 2016, from http://www.mofcom.gov.cn/article/ae/ai/201606/20160601331773.shtml.

Ministry of Commerce of People's Republic of China (2013). No. 1016 *Notice of Ministry of Commerce and National Development Bank on Relevant Problems of Supporting the Development of Trade and Economic Cooperation Zones Overseas, December 19*. Retrieved August 11, 2016, from http://www.mofcom.gov.cn/article/h/redht/201312/20131200430374.shtml.

Ministry of Commerce of People's Republic of China (2015). No. 408 *Notice of Ministry of Commerce on Publishing the Copy of Service Guidance for Trade and Economic Cooperation Zones Overseas, August 4*. Retrieved August 11, 2016 from http://hzs.mofcom.gov.cn/article/zcfb/jwjmhz/201511/20151101153854.shtml.

Ministry of Commerce of the People's Republic of China Department of Outward Investment and Economic Cooperation (2016). Retrieved from http://fec.mofcom.gov.cn/article/jwjmhzq/article01.shtml.

National Bureau of Statistics of the People's Republic of China — Statistic Bulletin of National Economy and Social Development (2016). *China Population 2015*. Retrieved from http://www.stats.gov.cn/tjsj/zxfb/201602/t20160229_1323991.html.

The State Council, People's Republic of China (2013). No. 67 *Guidance of General Office of the State Council on Financial Support for Economic Restructuring and Upgrading, July 5*. Retrieved August 11, 2016, from http://www.gov.cn/zhengce/content/2013-07/05/content_1929.htm.

United States Department of Energy, Energy Information Administration (2015). *International Energy Statistics: Crude Oil Proved Reserves 2015 — China*. Retrieved from https://www.eia.gov/beta/international/data/browser/#/?pa=0 00000000000000000008&c=00000002&ct=0&tl_id=5-A&vs=INTL.57-6-CHN-BB.A&cy=2016&vo=0&v=H&start=1980&showdm=y.

United States Department of Energy, Energy Information Administration (2016). Crude Oil Proved Reserves in 2016, China's Key Energy Statistics. Retrieved from https://www.eia.gov/beta/international/country.cfm?iso=CHN.

Wang, L. G. (2015). *On One Belt One Road By Worldwide Major Think Tanks*. Beijing, China: Social Science Academic Press.

World Trade Organization (2015). *World and Region Merchandise Export Profiles 2015*. WTO Secretariat.

Xinhua (2016, September 26). China's Belt and Road Initiative makes significant progress: research report. Available at http://news.xinhuanet.com/english/2016-09/26/c_135714905.htm.

Zhong, F. T., Pu. Z. H., Liu, X. M., & Teng, Z. Y. (2015). *The Blue Ocean For Going Abroad, Investment Attractiveness Evaluation of One Belt One Road Countries for Chinese Enterprises*. Beijing, China: Social Science Academic Press.

Case 2.1   The purchase of DostykGazTerminal in Kazakhstan by CEFC International Holdings

On April 28, 2015, CEFC International Holdings Co., Ltd., an investment company in China, issued The Announcement of CEFC Anhui International Holdings Co., Ltd. about Foreign Investment of wholly-owned subsidiaries, which formally shows that CEFC Natural Gas (a wholly-owned subsidiary of CEFC International) will acquire DostykGazTerminal LLP (hereinafter referred to as DGT) by purchasing 40% of its shares and increase investment in DGT.

The original shareholders of DGT are TCO and Ropiton, each of whom holds 50% of the share. DGT serves as one of the companies which are qualified for developing its business in liquefied petroleum gas in Kazakhstan. Its logistics service target and trading partner are mainly petrochemical enterprises in China. DGT has previously signed a long-term memorandum of liquefied petroleum gas supply with many petrochemical enterprises in Xinjiang, China. As Kazakhstan can provide important energy logistics and intersection for trade along the B&R, the acquisition of DGT has a great significance for global strategic plans of CEFC International.

This time CEFC Natural Gas provides a fund of US$36 million which is used to purchase 40% of the shares from the two original shareholders, each of whom holds 20% of the shares. Apart from the acquisition plan, CEFC Natural Gas, together with the two original shareholders will increase investment in DGT, with the total amount of US$60 million. Besides, the original shareholder of DGT, Ropiton Holding B.V., will entrust 10% of DGT shares to CEFC Natural Gas. That said, CEFC Natural Gas will replace Ropiton Holding B.V. to exercise the right to vote. By the time, CEFC Natural Gas will possess 40% of DGT shares and 50% of the right to vote.

This cross-border acquisition has a great significance for CEFC International as well as energy logistics and trade in Kazakhstan. Firstly, CEFC International changed the purpose of funds to cross-border acquisition, thus improving the capital use efficiency. Furthermore, as DGT has already signed memorandums with many enterprises in Xinjiang, China, the expected returns of DGT must be positive. Secondly, Kazakhstan serves as a junction of the B&R, it must play a strategic role. This cross-border acquisition is also conducive to DGT and the development of the oil and gas industry in Kazakhstan.

(Continued)

Case 2.1 *(Continued)*

Sources:
http://www.allbrightlaw.com/info/f39e2c3d8f7941f7815d9b71e8371
bdfALLBRIGHT LAW OFFICES provides legal services for the purchase of
DGT in Kazakhstan by CEFC International Holdings Co., Ltd.

http://www.caiku.com/stock/002018/news/0000000000000b9jz2.html "The Anno-
uncement of CEFC Anhui International Holdings Co., Ltd. about Foreign
Investment of Wholly-owned Subsidiaries". Sec Code: 002018; Securities:
CEFC International Holdings Co., Ltd.; Notice 2015-041.

Case 2.2   Guangxi State Farms and China-Indonesia Economic and
Trade Cooperation Zone

Guangxi State Farms

Guangxi State Farms is a large state-owned group in Guangxi province, which
mainly engages in trading of agricultural products. Guangxi State Farms
responds to the state appeal and actively implements the "going global"
strategy. It successfully implemented the foreign projects of sisal processing
plant in Venezuela, logistics and processing center for agricultural products in
Russia, and substitute plantation of sisal in China and Myanmar.

Recently Guangxi State Farms has carried on the project of which is one of
19 economic and trade cooperation zones overseas and the first one that China
establishes in Indonesia. Now the first phase of cooperation zone has been put into
use, with an investment of 113 million yuan. 29 foreign and domestic enterprises,
including China XD Group and Schlumberger, have set up in the zone, thus
promoting the economic and trade cooperation between China and Indonesia.

China-Indonesia Economic and Trade Cooperation Zone (CIETCZ)

The industrial park of China-Indonesia economic and trade cooperation zone
adopts the developer-oriented management model. The developer is mainly
responsible for positioning, construction content and scale of industries in
order to make the overall layout. The overall structure of the cooperation zone
is "One Axis and Three Groups". "One Axis" refers to a main road that covers
the whole park and links to major service facilities and landscape belt in the

(Continued)

Case 2.2 *(Continued)*

park, thus forming the primary axis of the park. "Three Groups" refer to three industries, including household appliances, manufacturing and processing of agricultural products, all of which are distributed along the primary axis. The management model is conducive to professional development and management of the park in order to improve operational efficiency. It is also good for enhancing enterprises' sensitivity to the market so that these enterprises can keep up with the market.

It is very convenient for enterprises to settle in the industrial park. Firstly, an enterprise needs to sign a Cooperation Intention after visiting the industrial park. Then it needs to register a company in Indonesia, sign a land transfer contract and apply for a construction license. In this way, a company can be under construction and under preparation. Furthermore, the lease of plant and office service is available in the industrial park.

The policies of the industrial park

There are six policies that an enterprise can enjoy after it settles in the industrial park.

(1) Generalized Scheme of Preferences (GSP) tariff relief. Enjoy the treatment of GSP from the EU.
(2) Import duty exemption. Production materials, mechanical equipment, accessories, auxiliary equipment and other basic material for a company's private use can be exempt from import duty.
(3) Convenient taxes. Lower 30% of income taxes within six years; accelerate the depreciation and amortization; carry forward the loss within ten years.
(4) Export rebates. Luxury products and raw materials that are purchased in Indonesia can be exempt from value-added tax and sales tax.
(5) Bonded area. For enterprises in the bonded area that are approved by the Indonesian government, they can enjoy preferential treatment in import duties, tariffs on imports, withholding tax and excise tax.
(6) Foreign exchange control. Indonesia does not belong to a country under foreign exchange control. Therefore, the foreign exchange investment and after-tax profits that are made in Indonesia can be remitted abroad freely.

(Continued)

Case 2.2   (*Continued*)

China is one of the largest importers for Indonesia. Indonesia plays an important role for the Economic Belt of the MSR and Indonesia is implementing the "Strategy of Strong Marine Country". The completion of the project will become a common and substantive result for both the B&R initiative and the "Strategy of Strong Marine Country".

Source: http://www.kitic.net/ PT. Kawasan Industri Terpadu Indonesia China.

Chapter 3

The Baltic Sea Region and China: Economic Environment and Strategy of the Firms

Jean Paul Larçon

HEC Paris

Rold Jens Brunstad

NHH — Norwegian School of Economics

The Baltic Rim countries — Nordic Countries, Germany, Poland, the Baltic States and Western Russia — are characterized by a strong diversity from a historical, cultural and political point of view. However, these countries are closely connected between themselves, as well as with their neighbors of Central and Eastern Europe. They have a very different resource base, industrial structure and development level, which creates a need for more economic cooperation and integration in the broad region, as well as a strong interest in cooperation with foreign partners. The Baltic Sea Region is well connected to China through both the Silk Road Economic Belt and the Maritime Silk Road, and its economic cooperation with China is growing rapidly.

This chapter focuses on the business environment of the countries of the Baltic Rim and the collaboration with China. Special attention is dedicated to the business strategies of leading Chinese and European companies operating in the region.

1. The Baltic Sea Region: Towards Economic Integration

The main political forum for inter-governmental cooperation at the regional level is the Council of the Baltic Sea States (CBSS) founded in 1992. The Council associates eleven states: the five Nordic countries (Denmark, Finland, Iceland, Norway and Sweden), the three Baltic States (Estonia, Latvia and Lithuania), Germany, Poland and Russia, plus a representative from the European Union (EU). Belarus, among other countries, has observer status. The Council has defined three long-term priorities: "fostering the Baltic Sea Region identity, developing a sustainable and prosperous region, and enhancing the societal security and safety" (CBSS, 2014). R&D policy, low carbon economy, infrastructure, transport, communication and an integrated maritime policy, are among the key objectives.

The EU is the major driver of regional economic integration. Among countries of the Baltic Sea Region (BSR), Germany is one of the six signatory countries of the Treaty of Rome creating the European Economic Community in 1957, and a founding member of the EU. Denmark joined the EU in 1973, Finland and Sweden in 1995, Estonia, Latvia, Lithuania and Poland in 2004. The eight EU Member States bordering the Baltic Sea account for some 150 million inhabitants representing 30% of the total EU population. Norway, which joined the European Economic Area (EEA), together with Iceland and Liechtenstein in 1994 is almost fully integrated into the EU inner market for all practical purposes.

The economic cooperation between the eight EU Member States bordering the Baltic Sea and the Federation of Russia depends on the evolution of the overall EU-Russia cooperation. It also differs from one country to another according to the history of the bilateral relationship with Russia at the political, economic and cultural level.

1.1. The European Union initiatives in the BSR

Since 2009 the EU has built a specific institutional framework for the BSR in order to promote the economic and social integration of this EU "macro-region". The EU BSR framework includes six states (Denmark, Finland and Sweden, Estonia, Latvia and Lithuania) and two regions, the

Northern provinces of Poland and Germany bordering the Baltic Sea. Four neighboring countries, that are non-EU members, are formally associated with the work of the BSR: Belarus, Russia, Norway and Iceland (Map 3.1).

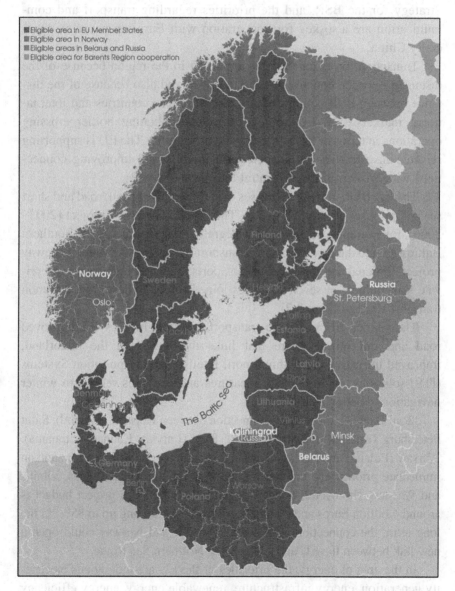

Map 3.1   The EU Baltic Sea "Macro-region"

Source: The Interreg Baltic Sea Region program, European Territorial Cooperation, EU Commission.

This EU organization for the macro-region aims at facilitating the definition of common goals, elaborating strategies and operational programs, and making choices in terms of fund allocation to specific projects. To connect the region is one of the major overall goals of the EU Strategy for the BSR, and the priorities regarding transport and communication are also key for cooperation with Eurasian partners, especially China.

Transportation is particularly important in the region because of the distances between countries within the BSR, and also because of the distance between BSR countries and other European countries and international markets. The EU strategy aims at facilitating border crossing operations in terms of infrastructure and procedures. The EU is supporting selected investments in transport infrastructure and improving connections with Western Europe, Central Europe and Russia.

The EU BSR strategy addresses the efficient use of rail, road and short sea shipping services in the region. The "Baltic Gateway" project (2003–2006), for example, was aimed at integrating the seaways of the Southern Baltic Sea into the pan-European Transport System. In the Baltic Gateway project, regional and local authorities, ports, transport authorities and private stakeholders in seven countries joined forces to develop a common transport strategy (Map 3.2).

The general EU vision for transport corridors focuses on "improved road and rail infrastructure that links the port with the hinterland, improved infrastructure within a port, Intelligent Transportation Systems (ITS) solutions, environmental measures and activities related to winter navigation" (Bodewig, 2015).

"Rail Baltica", the railway connection between Helsinki (Finland), Saint Petersburg (Russia), Tallinn (Estonia), Riga (Latvia), Kaunas (Lithuania), Warsaw (Poland) and Berlin (Germany) is an urgency for the region, and an immediate priority: the connection between Tallinn, Riga, Kaunas, Vilnius and Warsaw. The overall budget for the EU Rail Baltica project budget is around 4 billion Euros and could benefit from EU funding up to 85%. In the long term, the connection via Finland, Sweden and Norway could open a new link between the EU and Asia via the Northern Sea Route.

In the area of energy, the priorities of the EU are indigenous electricity generation, energy infrastructure, renewable energy, energy efficiency

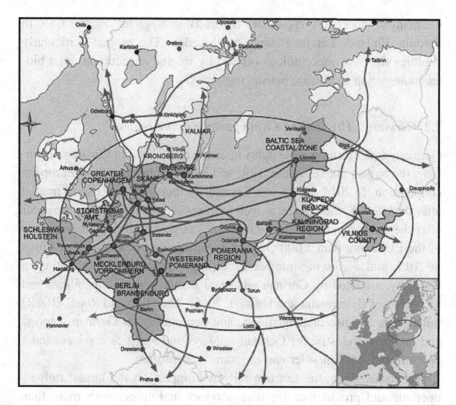

Map 3.2   The Baltic Gateway
Source: Baltic Gateway Quick Start EU Programme.

and ensuring the security of supply at affordable prices. The region, which has a great development potential for Offshore Wind Energy (OWE) has only 15% of the EU's offshore wind parks. Thus the EU is supporting OWE projects in the BSR-associated government agencies, research centers, utility providers and companies such as Siemens, the European leader in offshore wind industry.

The EU priority for innovation is to develop "the ability to innovate and to commercialize innovation" in the BSR. The EU supports projects aimed at capacity-building for "smart specialization" (EU Commission DG Regional Policy, 2012). The project "Smart Blue Regions: Smart specialization and blue growth in the Baltic Sea Region", for example, is led by the Ministry of Economic Affairs of Schleswig-Holstein (Northern

Germany), and covers six other "Smart Blue Regions" of the BSR in Estonia, Finland, Latvia, Poland and Sweden. The project particularly explores the new opportunities offered by marine aquaculture, blue biotechnology and food from marine resources.

1.2 *Germany: The leading China partner in the region*

Germany (80.7 million inhabitants in 2015) is the leading European economy, the largest market in the BSR, and a major player in Sino-European cooperation. In 2014, China was Germany's fourth biggest export market after the US, UK and France, as well as their second highest import partner after the Netherlands; China is Germany's largest trading partner outside of the EU. More than 5,000 German companies were operating in China in 2015, and a growing number of Chinese companies are investing in Germany, attracted by German advanced manufacturing capabilities and technologies (Hanemann and Huotari, 2015). The "Belt and Road" (B&R) initiative is an immediate challenge and opportunity for German seaports and maritime industry, for German railways and logistics services, and a new stimulus for Sino-German economic cooperation.

Deutsche Bahn, the German railway company, is the largest railway operator and provider of logistics services in Europe, with more than 300,000 employees. In 2016, Deutsche Bahn announced the development of its cooperation with China Railways in three directions: rail freight transport, high-speed train maintenance and infrastructure projects in third countries (Case 3.1). The two companies are hoping to triple the number of containers transported by rail along the Trans-Eurasian Land Bridge, by 2020, connecting China to Germany via Kazakhstan, Russia, Belarus and Poland (Map 3.3).

Maritime industry and international trade are key for Northern Germany: the federal states of Schleswig-Holstein and Mecklenburg-Vorpommern, the city-states of Hamburg and Bremen. According to DCW German-Chinese Business Association, in recent years, Schleswig-Holstein's exports to China have regularly recorded double-digit increases and economic collaboration has been growing rapidly, especially with Zhejiang province. Bremen is an attractive location for Chinese import- and export-based companies, and some 200 companies from Bremen are doing business with China.

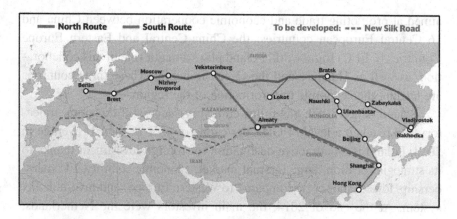

Map 3.3   The Trans-Eurasian Land Bridge: A transport alternative
Source: Deutsche Bahn, March 2016.

There are 400 Chinese companies headquartered in Hamburg such as Shanghai Baosteel and Shanghai Automotive Industry Corporation (SAIC). The seaport of Hamburg, located at the mouth of the Elbe River, is Germany's largest port and Europe's third largest; it is not only the most important port in Germany but also for Hungary and the Czech Republic (Merk and Hesse, 2012). China is Hamburg port's leading trade partner, with a share of its total container throughput of almost 30%. In 2014 the marketing campaign of Hamburg Port Authority put forward the image of the "smart PORT" on the "Maritime Silk Road".

Duisburg, the world's largest inland port, is located in the German federal state of North Rhine-Westphalia, the heart of the Rhine-Ruhr region. Duisburg port gives access to a regional market of 30 million consumers over a radius of 150 kilometers (km) and offers a unique combination of transport connections: river-sea vessels on the Rhine River, trains to over 80 national and international destinations, five autobahns and proximity to Düsseldorf Airport.

1.3. *Poland: A key partner in central Europe*

Poland (38 million inhabitants in 2015), which is a bordering country of the Baltic Sea, has the largest economy in Central and Eastern Europe. Since 2012, China has developed a specific mechanism of collaboration aimed at promoting trade and economic cooperation between China and 16 Central European countries: the China-Central and Eastern Europe Countries (CEEC) framework. Poland plays a major role in this collaboration, as well as Hungary and the Czech Republic. These three countries are leading the economic transformation of the region.

Poland, since 1989, has followed a very successful transition trajectory and reached a level of GDP per capita of 68% of the EU average in 2014. Poland is an attractive destination for foreign investment thanks to its strategic location, large internal market, economic stability, EU membership, lower labor cost (compared to Western Europe) and favorable tax system. At the end of 2014, the main investors were the Netherlands, Germany, Luxemburg and France, with investments mainly in the manufacturing, finance and trade sectors. Germany is Poland's leading trade partner followed by other EU countries such as Italy, France, UK and the Czech Republic.

The two priorities of the Polish authorities, in the cooperation with China, are to attract investment into Poland and to develop Polish exports to China in order to reduce the current trade deficit between the two countries (Skorupska and Szczudlik-Tatar, 2014). China's B&R initiative creates new opportunities for cooperation in the field of transport infrastructure and logistics. The Polish government is investing in the infrastructure of the seaport of Gdańsk on Poland's northern Baltic coast, in particular. Gdańsk is one of the largest ports of the Baltic Sea, and, thanks to its rail connections, could be a major cargo hub for Central and Eastern Europe. Poland is the second largest rail freight market in the EU after Germany, and has, since 2013, been developing a direct connection to China for container trains between the city of Łódź, Poland's third-largest city, and Chengdu, China through Kazakhstan, Russia and Belarus, which takes 15 days.

2. Russia, China and the Saint Petersburg Region

The Baltic Sea, the Black Sea and the Far East Basin, are the three major gateways to Russia, of which the Baltic Sea is the most important, representing more than 50% of the total Russian container market in 2014. Saint Petersburg, the second largest Russian city after Moscow (5.1 million

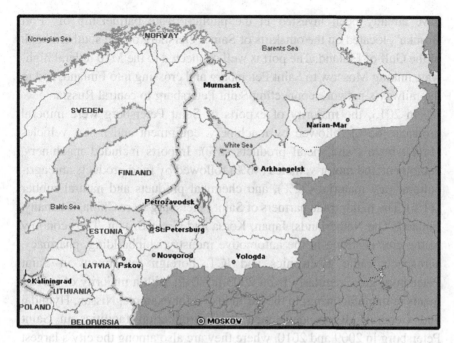

Map 3.4   The Northwestern Federal District of the Russian Federation

Source: Government of the Republic of Karelia, Russian Federation.

inhabitants in 2014), is situated on the Neva River, at the head of the Gulf of Finland on the Baltic Sea. The city is also the administrative center of the Northwestern Federal District of Russia, a Russian "macro-region" created in 2000, which is the only Russian region with a long border with the EU (Map 3.4). The economy of the district is based on natural resources: oil and gas, iron and non-ferrous metals, as well as extensive forest resources on a vast territory of 1,686,968 km² with a population of 13.7 million inhabitants (2012).

Saint Petersburg, a hot spot for Russian tourism which attracts a number of visitors each year (6.5 million in 2015, of which 40% were foreigners), is also the largest container port in the Baltic Sea and the European gateway of Russia, handling containers, cars, machinery, metal pipes, extra-heavy and oversized goods, wood, coal, grain, etc. The construction of a new multi-functional deep-water port started in 2015 in order to handle the new generation of ultra-large container vessels. 400 million Euros have already been invested in the public-private partnership of "Port Bronka", located on the outskirts of Saint Petersburg on the southern bank of the Gulf of Finland. The port is well connected to the M10 federal highway, linking Moscow to Saint Petersburg and crossing into Finland, and to the railway's network connecting Saint Petersburg to central Russia.

In 2013, the majority of exports of Saint Petersburg were mineral products (65%) followed by machinery, equipment and motor vehicles (11%), metals and metal products (8%). Imports included machinery, equipment and motor vehicles (46%) followed by food products and agricultural raw material (22%), and chemical products and natural rubber (11%). The major trade partners of Saint Petersburg were China, Germany, Finland, The Netherlands, Japan, Korea and Great Britain. The economy of the city is strong in the automotive industry, shipbuilding, pharmacy, aerospace, radio electronics and ICT. Foreign investment in Saint Petersburg grew regularly from 2003 to 2012, with a majority of investments in manufacturing. In the car industry, for example, Nissan, Hyundai and General Motors developed local production facilities in Saint Petersburg in 2009 and 2010, where they are also among the city's largest importers.

China is an important trade partner for Saint Petersburg but not a major investor, apart from a huge investment in real estate: the "Baltic Pearl" residential complex. The "Baltic Pearl" (Baltiyskaya Zhemchuzhina), includes housing for approximately 35,000 residents, shopping centers and public buildings in the southwest of Saint Petersburg. The project started in 2006 and suffered from some delays with the global financial crisis in 2008, but since its extension from 2013 to 2016, it has evolved very successfully. The "Baltic Pearl" is supported by the governments of Shanghai and Saint Petersburg. It was led in practice by Chinese Shanghai Industrial Investment (Holdings) Co. Ltd. (SIHL), acting as the lead investor and general contractor in partnership with other large Shanghai-based companies. SIHL, which is listed in Hong Kong, belongs to the Shanghai Municipal Government and the project was granted a loan by China Exim Bank, the Export-Import Bank of China. The total investment in a period of ten years was more than US$5 billion.

The EU-Russian cooperation in the region had been growing regularly from the mid-nineties up to the surge of the Ukraine crisis. The crisis started in November 2013 with the Ukrainian President Viktor Yanukovych abandoning a proposed trade agreement between the EU and Ukraine, instead of seeking closer cooperation with Russia. The conflict escalated into an armed confrontation between pro-Russia forces in Eastern Ukraine and the annexation of Crimea by Russia in 2014. The United States and the EU imposed sanctions on Russian banks, export of technology to Russia, as well as travel bans on some of Russia's personalities. Russia responded with import restrictions, especially on food products. A cease-fire accord was signed in Minsk in February 2015, with an agreement being reached between the Ukrainian and Russian foreign ministers in April. These events have strongly deteriorated the political climate and the economic cooperation between Russia and the EU. The situation resulted in a decline of EU-Russian trade and of FDI into Russia. On the EU side, there is no unanimity among the Member States about the policy to follow towards Russia. For example, The European Committee of the House of Lords (British Parliament) expressed at the same time a strong support in favor of the sanction policy, and the need to maintain the dialogue between the EU and Russia (House of Lords, European Committee, 2015).

The collapse in the price of oil from US$100 to US$60 per barrel in 2014 led to a financial and economic crisis because the Russian economy is highly dependent on the oil price. GDP growth which was 0.7% in 2014 contracted by 3.7% in 2015. Saint Petersburg's foreign trade suffered particularly from three negative factors: the Russian economic crisis, the Western sanctions as well as a decrease of containerized imports from China. The city is currently pursuing a policy of import substitute and development of foreign investment in manufacturing. Thus the government of Saint Petersburg is building an attractive environment for foreign investors, including tax benefits, especially those investing in Special Economic Zones.

Kaliningrad Oblast, which is part of the Northwest Federal District, is the most western territory of the Federation of Russia, located on the Baltic coast between Lithuania and Poland, with no land connection to the rest of the Russian territory. Kaliningrad, with a population of 1 million people, is an important strategic base for Russian defense and protection of national interests in the southern Baltic. It is the headquarters of the Russian Baltic Fleet and also includes three air bases. Kaliningrad Oblast also possesses about 90% of the world's amber deposits. A special economic zone (SEZ) with duty-free advantages, created in 1996 attracted foreign investment and contributed to increasing trade with neighboring EU countries, but the SEZ privileges expired in 2016. The tensions between the North Atlantic Treaty Organization (NATO) and Russia are bound to have a very negative impact on trade and economic cooperation.

3. Belarus, a Country at the Crossroads

The Republic of Belarus, independent since 1991, is situated at the crossroads of trade routes between the east and west. The territory of Belarus (207,600 km^2) is populated by about 9.5 million people, with an urban population of 70%. Belarus is a landlocked country bordering Russia in the east, Ukraine in the south, and three EU countries: Lithuania and Latvia in the north, and Poland in the west.

Belarus has no shoreline along the Baltic Sea but has good connections to the Baltic Sea ports of Lithuania and Latvia. Its strong infrastructure network of motorways, railways and air routes, as well as the fact that its capital city Minsk, is 700 km from Moscow, 500 km from Warsaw (Poland), 457 km from the Baltic Seaport of Klaipėda (Lithuania), and 1,060 km from Berlin, make Belarus a major hub for transport and trade between Western Europe and Russia, as well as between Western Europe, Central Asia and Asia.

Historically, politically, culturally and economically, Belarus is a close partner to Russia. Belarus was one of the founding members of the Commonwealth of Independent States (CIS) in 1991, linking Russia to 11 other sovereign states that were former members of the Soviet Union. Since its independence, Belarus has continued to receive financial assistance from Russia, and now also collects fees from the transit of Russian oil and gas across its territory. In 2011 Belarus, Kazakhstan and Russia signed the treaty founding the Eurasian Customs Union in Minsk. In May 2014 the three countries signed the treaty founding the Eurasian Economic Union (EEU) in Astana, followed by two other countries — Armenia and Kyrgyzstan — who joined the EEU in December 2014.

According to the transition indicators of the European Bank for Reconstruction and Development (EBRD), in 2013 Belarus was among the least advanced of the former Soviet Union's successor states in the transition towards a market economy (EBRD, 2014). However between 1991 and 2011 the economy grew rapidly, seeing an increase in foreign trade which is quite geographically diverse. Belarus' imports include oil and natural gas, raw materials and components for manufacturing equipment, while its exports include oil products, chemicals, agricultural products, machinery and textile. Russia is Belarus' main trade partner, accounting for almost 50% of its total foreign trade in 2014, with the EU being its second largest trading partner ever since 1995, constituting 30% of Belarus' exports and 20% of its imports. Their main partners in the EU are Great Britain, Netherlands, Germany, Lithuania, Italy, Poland, Latvia, Belgium and the Czech Republic. Belarus wants to expand its cooperation in transport, logistics and transit with Latvia and Lithuania in order to promote its exports through the Baltic ports. Furthermore, the joint projects between the three countries are eligible for EU financial support.

Without departing from its existing ties with Russia, Belarus has begun strengthening links to other European countries and is also opening the door to China. The economic cooperation with China started in 2007, with the creation of the joint venture producing microwave ovens. The joint venture was founded by Midea Group, China's top manufacturer of household appliances, and Horizont, one of the CIS' top manufacturers of household appliances and electronics. Midea owns 55% of the shares, while Horizont owns 45%. The joint venture produces microwave ovens and other home appliances in the free economic zone of Minsk. It employs some 150 people and exports 80% of its production to the CIS, including Russia and Kazakhstan.

In 2011 Chinese automaker Zhejiang Geely established a plant in Belarus for assembling cars from semi-knocked-down kits. Car parts are exported via container to the Belarus assembly plant near Minsk. The Belarusian-Chinese joint venture BelGee founders are Belarusian truck maker Autoworks (BelAZ), a major world manufacturer of mining dump trucks (50%), Zhejiang Geely (32.5%) and Soyuz, a Belarusian-Chinese automobile parts manufacturer (17.5%). The first cars were sold in 2013, and a new assembly plant is being built in 2016. Geely, which is already present in Russia, plans to use the Belarus plant to supply Russia's auto market.

Another very significant Chinese project in Belarus in the framework of the B&R initiative is the China-Belarus Industrial Park "Great Stone". "Great Stone" is a special economic zone located near Minsk. It is well-connected to the railway networks, the Moscow-Berlin highway, the airport and less than 500 km from the Klaipėda Baltic Sea port in Lithuania. The China-Belarus industrial park is one of the key junction points of the B&R: a logistics hub at the western leg of the transport corridor which starts from Khorgos at the Sino-Kazakh frontier and connects Europe and China (Case 3.2).

4. The Baltic States and China

4.1. *Economy of the Baltic States*

The Baltic States, Estonia, Latvia and Lithuania, are located on the eastern coast of the Baltic Sea. The three countries, which were independent during the period 1918–1940, have been occupied by the Soviet Union and incorporated as soviet republics of the former Union of Soviet Socialist Republics (USSR) in 1940. Latvia (2 million inhabitants), Estonia (1.3 million inhabitants) and Lithuania (3.2 million inhabitants) differ in terms of population, history, culture and international orientation, but share a common need to protect their identity from powerful neighbors. The three countries, which regained their independence in 1991, made the same two fundamental choices: joining the EU and becoming members of NATO.

The admission of Estonia, Latvia and Lithuania into the EU in 2004 was a recognition of their well-functioning democratic political system and competitive market economies. Estonia joined the eurozone in 2011, Latvia in 2014 and Lithuania in 2015. The three countries, which had the same economic system in 1990, have followed different paths for economic transition, with Estonia moving more quickly than Latvia and Lithuania. Today, all of them have liberalized their economy, privatized state-owned enterprises (SOEs), and opened the door to international trade and inward foreign investment.

The Baltic States are not rich in terms of natural resources but have a strong cost advantage compared to Germany and Nordic countries: their GDP per capita in 2013 was around 65% of the EU15 average and around

55% of the level in neighboring Sweden. They have strong capabilities in terms of R&D, education and research, as well as an entrepreneurial tradition and international culture. In terms of foreign direct investment, they have been especially attractive for Nordic and German firms. In terms of export, they operate both in the EU markets, especially Germany, as well as in the Russian market.

Port activities are important for the economies of the South Baltic region, and especially the Baltic States. The large ports operating all along the coasts of the Baltic Sea are well connected to the largest European ports, such as Rotterdam, Antwerp and Hamburg, which are located by the North Sea. The largest container port in the Baltic Sea is Saint Petersburg (Russia), followed by Gdańsk (Poland), Göteborg (Sweden), Gdynia, on the western coast of Gdańsk Bay (Poland), Hamina Kotka and Helsinki (Finland), Aarhus (Denmark), Klaipėda (Lithuania), Riga (Latvia) and Kaliningrad (Russia). The ports in the Baltic States are the main transshipment points for Russian container cargo. According to the Russian maritime information agency IAA Port News, containers bound for Russia made up 80% of Tallinn's total containerized trade, 65% of Klaipėda's and 60% of Riga's in 2014.

Russia's economic slowdown and the EU economic sanctions on Russia have a particularly negative impact on port activity in Saint Petersburg, Finland and the Baltic States. On the contrary, the development of Sino-European trade is generating new transit from China to Russia, and ports are in competition to capture the market of container cargoes coming from places like Hamburg to the Baltic States, ports and Russia. The key success factors for these sea ports are the overall cost of delivery, the quality of railway networks to the hinterland and the distance to the core EU markets. Thus the seaports of Finland, the Baltic States and Poland, in particular, need to invest in both port infrastructure, to welcome bigger ships, and in railway connection to the hinterland.

Estonia

Following the model of Nordic countries, Estonia has been the first to systematically promote the investment in innovation and the development of an information-driven society. Skype was created in 2003 by a team of

Swedish, Danish and Estonian entrepreneurs. The sale of Skype to e-Bay in 2015 contributed a lot towards stimulating entrepreneurship, raising Estonian government support, attracting financial resources from outside and recruiting high-tech talents internationally. Estonia is a leading country in terms of high-speed internet, Wi-Fi services and innovative e-solutions; the country is also a model of digital society and e-government, which uses the development of electronic solutions to facilitate the dialogue between citizens and government agencies, as well as education, healthcare, utilities, etc. This includes e-residency created to facilitate people outside of Estonia who want to establish an e-residence, invest in Estonia, establish a company there and contribute to Estonian foreign trade. Estonia's top export destinations are Sweden, Russia, Finland, Latvia and Spain.

Estonian-Finnish cross-border cooperation is very active, both in terms of trade, digital cooperation and transportation infrastructure. There is intense traffic between the two countries' capital cities, Tallinn and Helsinki, which are among the most active supporters of the Rail Baltic project connecting the three Baltic States to the European rail network.

Latvia

The key sectors of Latvian economy are the agricultural and forest sector, the chemical and pharma industry, the trade sector and the logistics sector. Latvia is rich in terms of ports, rail and road network connecting the west and east. Riga airport was the main hub for air transportation in the Baltic States in 2016. Latvia exports the products of its agriculture and forest: grain and dairy products, raw lumber and wood products. Latvian companies are very successful in the life sciences, health care, eco-friendly chemicals and biocosmetics sectors. The ICT sector is also growing rapidly. Latvia's biggest trading partners in 2014 were Lithuania (18%), Estonia (10%), Germany (9%), Russia (9%) and Poland (9%).

Lithuania

Lithuania's economy is strong in agriculture, food processing, dairy products, chemical products, furniture, etc., while German firms, which are the largest foreign direct investors in manufacturing, are present in the oil, chemicals, pharmaceutical and automobile industries. The economy is still not sufficiently oriented towards a knowledge-based economy, even if it has distinctive competencies, for example in biotechnology and laser technology. Lithuania Ekspla is a manufacturer of lasers, laser systems and laser components for R&D and industry; the company, which has some 100 employees, exports 90% of its production and claims more than half the global market for scientific picosecond lasers used in university research centers and corporate research laboratories.

4.2. *Chinese companies in the Baltic States*

Estonia

In 2011, Estonian Railways, the Port of Tallinn and Alekon — a leading Estonian company specialized in handling equipment for ports, signed a cooperation agreement with Sinotrans and CSC Group, China's logistics company. On the Estonian side, the objective was to enable Tallinn to become Sinotrans' hub in the Baltic, for delivering goods from Asia to Russia and CIS countries. Sinotrans, a state-owned company, is the largest Chinese logistics company, shipping agency and freight forwarding company covering all aspect of logistics, including ocean transportation, air transportation, trucking, freight forwarding, storing and warehousing business, etc. Sinotrans, which has cooperation agreements with some 400 logistics companies around the world, became a wholly-owned subsidiary of China Merchants Group (CMG) in 2016. The objective of the merger was to create synergies between the activities of the two companies in shipping, logistics, property development and marine engineering.

Chinese logistics firms are developing alliances with local logistics partners and local SOEs to learn how to adapt to local legislation, local competition and local consumer needs. Alibaba, China's biggest e-commerce operator, announced its objective to quickly develop its presence in the UK, France, Italy and Germany in 2015. However, there is no doubt that after an already long overseas journey by ship, train, truck or plane across Eurasia, Alibaba and other e-commerce giants will find ways to successfully face the challenges in the last leg of their delivery.

In September 2015, the state-owned Estonian postal company, Omniva, signed a memorandum of understanding with S.F. Express, China's largest private-capital-funded courier company, to set up a joint venture called Post 11. This includes warehouses in Estonia to make the import and export of goods between China and Europe faster and more efficient.

Latvia

Latvia is also looking for opportunities in terms of Chinese trade and investment. The first priority is to attract new cargo flow from Asia and the Far East in Latvian ports, which have good connections to both Russia and Europe (Bulis and Skapars, 2014). Riga International Airport is a specific asset for Latvia, as the main regional air hub in the Baltics for both cargo and passengers. Direct flights between Riga and Chengdu were planned in 2016. Kreiss International, one of the largest fleet operators in the Nordic-Baltic region with some 1,200 trucks and 1,400 refrigerated container trailers, is looking for partnerships with Chinese logistics firms to manage the potential new cargo flow expected from China. Latvian authorities are interested in developing agricultural exports to China, such as dairy and meat products, and in attracting Chinese investors in the country. Tongyu Communication, the first base station antenna manufacturer in China participating in the National Torch Plan of the Chinese Ministry of Science and Technology, has chosen Latvia to establish its first manufacturing project overseas. Tongyu's Latvian subsidiary is an assembly plant making microwave antenna products, with components imported from the group's leading factory in Guangdong province.

Lithuania

In 2015, CMG — one of China's largest state-owned enterprises and a leading port operator — signed several agreements in Lithuania with the Klaipėda port authority, Lithuanian Railways and the free economic zone of Kaunas. Kaunas is Lithuania's second largest city and is located between the seaport of Klaipėda and Minsk, the capital city of Belarus.

The objective on the Lithuanian side is to attract Chinese investors to the Klaipėda container terminal and the Kaunas Free Economic Zone, and to develop a joint venture to handle freight transportation between Lithuania and the China-Belarus Industrial Park "Great Stone" near Minsk.

Thus far, the Baltic States are in a very good position in terms of logistics to contribute to China-Europe trade, but have to invest rapidly in order to compete effectively with alternative solutions.

5. The Nordic Countries and China's B&R Initiative

The Nordic countries are Denmark (5.6 million inhabitants), Finland (5.4 million), Iceland (300,000 inhabitants), Norway (5 million) and Sweden (9.5 million). Three of them (Denmark, Sweden and Finland have an immediate shoreline along the Baltic Sea, while the other two (Norway and Iceland) have close economic, political and cultural ties with their Baltic neighbors. The Nordic countries are performing extremely well from a pan-European perspective in terms of economic performance, employment rate, investment in education and research, and development of renewable energy (Grunfelder, *et al.*, 2016).

China is the Nordic countries' largest trading partner in Asia, and the trade between them has been consistently growing since China's accession to the World Trade Organization (WTO) in 2001. FDI to and from China followed the expansion of trade, and in recent years Chinese companies have started investing in the region, recruiting talents and acquiring from Nordic firms.

5.1. *Nordic companies in China*

Swedish companies are sourcing in China, manufacturing locally, serving the local market and exporting globally. Swedish multinational companies especially have a very strong presence in China. ABB, the Swedish-Swiss multinational corporation headquartered in Zürich, which specializes in power and automation technologies, has 28,000 employees and 40 subsidiaries in China, its second-largest market worldwide in 2015. ABB has seven global R&D centers in China with some 2,000 employees and adheres to the vision of "In China, for China and the world". Swedish firms have developed a strong industrial and commercial presence in China in various sectors, for instance: Alfa Laval (energy and marine), Astra Zeneca (health care), Atlas Copco (construction and mining industry), Electrolux (home appliances), Ericsson (telecom), Husqvarna (machinery and machine parts), Sandvik Group (automotive, aerospace, mining and construction) and SKF (bearing and seals). In the retail business, China is the number one procurement country for IKEA, which has opened ten stores in China since 1998.

Danish companies, which are also well established in the Chinese market, are located primarily in Beijing, Shanghai, Shenzhen and Guangzhou, but some companies are beginning to Go West. One example of this is Carlsberg, which entered Western and Central Chinese provinces through a series of acquisitions and joint ventures. China is one of the biggest markets for Maersk Line, the world's largest container shipping company. Maersk Line is a division of Maersk Group which also includes: APM Terminals (one of the world's largest port and terminal operators), APM Shipping Services, Maersk Oil (an international oil and gas company) and Maersk Drilling (an offshore drilling contractor).

In 2016, the Chinese government decided to restructure its shipping industry, merging the container fleets of its two SOEs, China Ocean Shipping (Cosco) and China Shipping Group, to form a new national champion, China Cosco Shipping Corp, a serious challenger to Maersk along the MSR. The merger of the two Chinese firms also opened the way to new alliances between global shipping giants, such as the "Ocean Alliance", also created in Shanghai in 2016, and bringing together China Cosco Shipping (China), CMA CGM (France), Evergreen Marine (Taipei) and Orient Overseas Container Line (Hong Kong).

Finnish companies are doing business in China mainly in the ICT, forestry, paper and machinery industries, and engineering sectors. Among the largest investors are leading Finnish multinational companies: Nokia (ICT), UPM-Kymmene (the world's leading producer of printing papers), Metso (supplier of the mining, aggregates, recycling, oil, gas, pulp, paper and process industries), Stora Enso — the Finnish-Swedish multinational with headquarters in Helsinki — a pulp and paper manufacturer which has made huge investments in mega-plantations and manufacturing facilities in the Guangxi province and Kone (the world's largest manufacturer of elevators and escalators). Wärtsilä, a Helsinki-based global company manufacturing engines for the marine and energy markets, entered the Chinese market in Hong Kong in 1986. The company is a supplier to the Chinese ship building industry and established its activities through a mix of long-term licensing agreements, joint ventures and wholly-owned subsidiaries. Wärtsilä has a 50/50 joint venture in Zhuhai City, Guangdong province, with Yuchai Marine Power for manufacturing marine engines and a joint venture in Shanghai with China State Shipbuilding Corporation (CSSC). The joint venture is manufacturing diesel and dual-fuel engines targeting the market of offshore and LNG vessels, as well as the market for very large container vessels.

Political relations between China and Norway have been downgraded after the awarding of the 1989 Nobel Peace Price to the 14th Dalai Lama and to human rights activist Liu Xiaobo in 2010, but this did not prevent the increase of bilateral trade which reached record highs in 2015, and China is Norway's top trading partner in Asia. Norway is also among the founding members of the Chinese led institution, the Asian Infrastructure Investment Bank (AIIB).

Norwegian companies established in China operate mainly in the maritime sector (maritime equipment and shipping), environmental technology and manufacturing. In 2014, Norwegian company Statoil delivered its first liquefied natural gas (LNG) to China. The LNG was sourced from Statoil's gas liquefaction plant of Snøhvit, located in the Barents Sea in the Arctic Ocean. The gas traveled along the northern coasts of Norway, was sold to China National Offshore Oil Corporation (CNOOC) and finally delivered into CNOOC Zhuhai terminal in Guangdong province. Kongsberg Maritime is a Norwegian international company based in Kongsberg, developing software technology solutions for the maritime, oil, gas and aerospace industries. This technology includes systems for satellite positioning and navigation, marine automation, cargo handling, subsea survey and construction, etc. Kongsberg Maritime have some 600 employees in China, a wholly-owned foreign enterprise (WOFE), and a joint venture company in Zhenjiang, Jiangsu province, which is Kongsberg Maritime's largest production center outside of Norway.

5.2. *Chinese companies in Nordic countries*

Chinese companies have started investing in the region quite recently. The acquisition of Volvo cars in Sweden by Zhejiang Geely goes back to 2010 and was a real question mark: both the Swedish government and public opinion were anxious about the future of the company and especially the continuity of operations in Sweden. In fact, the Volvo-Geely deal success-fully opened the door of the Chinese markets to Volvo cars, in a way which would not have been possible under fully foreign management.

Chinese companies are also systematically exploring investment opportunities in natural resources, oil and gas as well as renewable energy, in the high-tech sector, real estate, hotels and consumer goods. In 2008 China Oilfield Services (COSL) acquired full control of Norwegian com-pany Awilco Offshore for US$2.5 billion. COSL, China's leading offshore oil and gas drilling services provider, is a majority-owned subsidiary of CNOOC Group, the largest offshore oil and gas producer in China, a lead-ing state-owned company operating directly under the State-owned Assets Supervision and Administration Commission of the State Council (SASAC).

In 2011 China Bluestar acquired Elkem from the Norwegian con-glomerate Orkla ASA for US$2 billion. Elkem is one of the biggest indus-trial corporations in Norway with a history going back to the first half of last century and linked to the development of hydroelectric energy in Norway. The transaction comprised silicon materials (including Elkem silicon business in Iceland: the second largest ferrosilicon plant in the world), foundry products, carbon and solar activities. Bluestar, an interna-tional chemical company, with a focus on new chemical materials and animal nutrition, is a subsidiary of China National Chemical Corporation (ChemChina). It is the largest enterprise in China's chemical industry, being a central state-owned enterprise which has more than 140,000 employees, 48,000 of which are outside China.

In 2016, another Chinese company, Sunshine Kaidi New Energy Group, was considering investing in a wood-based biorefinery in the city of Kemi, Northern Finland. Sunshine Kaidi New Energy is a high-tech investment company founded in Wuhan in 1992, already operating bio-mass plants in China and in Vietnam. Sunshine Kaidi said that the plant would employ around 4,000 people during its construction, and boost the regional economy, which is suffering from the closing of paper mills due to the increase of digital devices. It is an investment of 1 billion Euros and Sunshine Kaidi's Finnish subsidiary is looking for financial partners for this project as well as subsidies from Finnish governments or the EU. The project has the support of Tekes, the government funded organization in charge of promoting research, development and innovation in Finland. The government pays a great deal of attention to a project which could contribute to both the economic development of Lapland, and Finland's capabilities in the wood industry.

6. China and the Northern Sea Route

6.1. *Chinese firms and Iceland*

The Republic of Iceland is a Nordic island located between the North Atlantic and the Artic oceans with a population of 329,000 inhabitants (as of 2015) and a territory of 103,000 km². Iceland has been a founding member of the European Free Trade Association (EFTA) in 1970, and is a member, along with Norway and Lichtenstein, of the European Economic Area (EEA) founded in 1994, which links the three countries to the EU, of which Iceland is not a member. In 2013 China and Iceland signed a Free Trade Agreement (FTA), the first FTA signed between China and a European country; however, this agreement does not provide low-tariff entry for China's products into the EU market. Iceland is important for China because of the country's natural resources and experience in the field of geothermal resources, but also for its potential role as a Chinese partner in the development of the Arctic resources and routes.

In 2012 Orka energy, an Icelandic geothermal developer, signed an agreement with China's largest oil refiner Sinopec, to expand cooperation in developing geothermal resources. Sinopec Group is China's largest petroleum and petrochemical company and the fifth largest company in the world, and its objective is to develop a geothermal energy heating business in China. Sinopec and Arctic Green Energy Corporation from Iceland (formerly Orka energy) have a joint venture focusing on geothermal development for heating and power generation in and outside of

China. Sinopec Green Energy Geothermal Development Co., Ltd. provides geothermal district heating services: it operates 150 heating centrals, three waste heat and one geothermal heat pump projects. The company was founded in 2006 and is headquartered in Xianyang, China.

In 2014 CNOOC set up a joint venture with Iceland companies Eykon Energy and Petoro Iceland (with 60%, 15% and 25% share respectively), in an offshore petroleum exploration in the Dreki of Icelandic water. In 2015 Chinese group Geely, the owner of Swedish carmaker Volvo, said it had become a major shareholder of Carbon Recycling International (CRI), an Icelandic company founded in 2006 in Reykjavik, which produces renewable methanol from clean energy and recycled CO_2 emissions. Geely Group and CRI intend to collaborate on "the deployment of renewable methanol fuel production technology in China and explore the development and deployment of 100% methanol-fueled vehicles in China, Iceland and other countries". Geely said it would invest 41 million Euros over three years in CRI.

6.2. *China cooperation in the Arctic*

China shows great interest in the natural resources of the Arctic and the Arctic shipping routes connecting China to Northern Europe (Lantaigne, 2014). Since 2012, China's Artic specialists and official representatives refer to China as a "near-Arctic state" and China, as well as four other Asian countries, gained observer status at the Arctic Council in 2013. The Arctic Council, created in 1996 by Canada, Denmark, Finland, Iceland, Norway, Russia, Sweden and the United States, is the leading intergovernmental forum promoting cooperation among the Arctic states and local communities; it focuses particularly on sustainable development and environmental protection (Map 3.5).

China has many interests in the Arctic: scientific research, exploitation of natural resources (hydrocarbons, water, minerals and fish) and new shorter shipping routes as that region warms due to climate change. The Northern Sea Route could significantly reduce the distance between Europe and China and thus provides an interesting alternative to the route via the Suez Canal: shorter trips, lower cost, and potentially more security and limited cost of transactions with fewer countries.

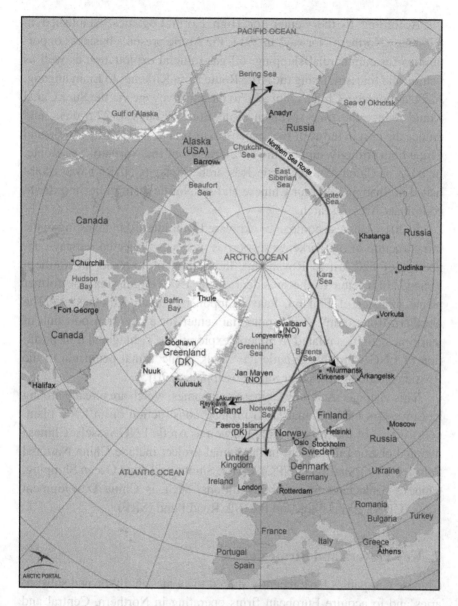

Map 3.5   The Northern Sea Route

Source: Arctic Portal.

According to the Center for High North Logistics established in Kirkenes (Northern Norway) in 2011, the Arctic presents business opportunities for commercial shipping, oil-gas-mineral exploitation as well as fishing and tourism. Using the Artic Route from Kirkenes to Lianyungang, Jiangsu province, China, compared to the same voyage via the Suez Canal would reduce the time spent on route from 40 days to 22.5 days, and reduce the cost in terms of fuel expenses, insurance and tariffs. Russia and China both strongly support the development of the Northern Sea Route. In 2013, a China-Nordic Arctic Research Center (CNARC) was established in Shanghai by four Chinese and six Nordic institutions in order to coordinate Artic research.

In 2015, Chinese companies expressed their interest in investing in the infrastructure of the Kirkenes seaport as well as a projected railway connection of 520 km to Rovaniemi, the capital of Lapland, in northern Finland. In a letter to the president of the EU Commission, the former prime minister of Finland, Paavo Lipponen, named Kirkenes as "The Northern Rotterdam". It is a potential center for a new transport hub of maritime activities related to mineral explorations, fishing and transportation of LNG from the gigantic gas fields of the Yamal peninsula to the Russian Arctic in northwest Siberia (Lipponen, 2015).

This vision is shared by Chinese companies, which are already among key investors in the Yamal LNG project: construction of an LNG plant, construction of the infrastructure, as well as Arctic LNG vessels. Chinese national champions present in the Yamal project include China National Petroleum Corporation (CNPC), CMG, Sinotrans, China Ocean Shipping, Chinese banks and financial institutions, such as China Development Bank (CDB), Exim Bank and the Silk Road Fund (SRF).

7. Key Players and Strategies

Chinese companies have recently started to create wholly-owned subsidiaries and to acquire European firms operating in Northern, Central and Eastern Europe. However, many projects linked to the B&R initiative cannot succeed without integrating the participation of local partners, government agencies and operators belonging to the different sectors: port authorities, national railway companies, shipyards, shipping, construction, engineering and logistics firms, energy companies, ICT and e-commerce companies.

On the Chinese side, the main actors are national champions, very large SOEs or private companies, such as China Bluestar, China Exim Bank, CDB, CMG, China National Chemical Corporation, CNOOC, China Railways, China Shipping Group, Cosco, Sinomach, Sinotrans, S.F. Express and Zhejiang Geely. Most of these firms already have a great international record and are investing actively along all the various "Silk Roads" connecting Europe, Asia and Africa. Company chairman Li Jianhong said that CMG plans to build key infrastructure projects, such as specialized marine terminals, in countries along the B&R initiative — including Djibouti, Sri Lanka and Belarus — during China's 13th five-year plan for 2016 to 2020 (Zhong Nan, 2016).

Their counterparts in Europe are also leading large private companies or public agencies. Prominent actors are among the top European port authorities, such as Antwerp, Hamburg, Rotterdam and Saint Petersburg; leading national railways companies such as Deutsche Bahn and Russian Railways; energy giants such as Norway's Statoil; and shipping leading firms such as Maersk Line. Thus the successful development of China's initiative depends on the quality of collaboration between these diverse actors, the integration of the projects in the local economic and cultural environment, and the art of managing complementary capabilities between firms.

Europe's reaction to China's initiatives have always been rather fragmented, with each country negotiating separately according to its national interests, regional interests, or the opportunities linked to a specific economic sector or leading firm. The initiative remains in the hands of Chinese firms that have both a strong international experience and the capacity to leverage Chinese and international financial resources. Chinese firms, financial institutions and governments have a proactive and coordinated approach giving them a competitive advantage over their European partners.

In the transport and logistics sector, China is financing a high-speed railway connection between Budapest (Hungary) and Belgrade (Serbia), as well as the Athens-Hungary railway connections. These investments and the acquisition of Greece's largest container port of Piraeus by Cosco are offering Chinese and other firms working with Asia a faster route from Asia than traditional Northern Europe alternatives. Meanwhile, the EU, which needs more time for internal concertation between the EU Member States, moves less quickly in the implementation of its pan-European transport corridors policy.

Conclusion

Intermodality is the key. The countries, regions or cities that are able to rapidly create the best intermodal connections between their sea ports, railway networks and the main EU transport corridors will gain a long-term comparative advantage.

Germany's role as a magnet for Sino-European cooperation, trade, investment and logistics will continue to grow. According to Hansakul and Levinger (2014), "Germany is particularly well placed to benefit from an intensification of bilateral trade … German exports to China could grow by 60% in the next decade, and if the (EU-China) FTA comes into being exports could double". This situation should also benefit neighboring BSR countries, which can take advantage of China's initiative, by attracting Chinese investments that are aiming for the pan-European market. In doing this, BSR countries will be able to develop their exports to China and co-invest with China in innovation-driven business ventures.

China's B&R opens new opportunities both for Chinese and European companies in the BSR. Even at this early stage of its development, China's initiative acts as a stimulator and accelerator in terms of trade opportunities, infrastructure development and collaboration between partners belonging to different institutional environments.

References

Baltic Gateway Quick Start Programme (2006, June 8). *Promoting Maritime Related Intermodal Transport in the South Baltic Sea Area.* Final Report, Karlskrona, Sweden: Region Blekinge.

Bodewig, K. (2015, May). *Baltic-Adriatic Work Plan of the European Coordinator.* Brussels, Belgium: European Commission, Directorate-General for Mobility and Transport.

Council of the Baltic Sea States (2014*). Declaration of the Council of the Baltic Sea States on the Implementation of the Vilnius Declaration on a Vision for the Baltic Sea Region by 2020.* Stockholm, Sweden: Council of the Baltic Sea States Communique.

Dastanka, A. A. (2015). Multilateralism in foreign policy of Belarus European and Eurasian dimension. *Regional Formation and Development Studies, 16* (2), 16–23. Doi http://dx.doi.org/10.1787/5k97g3hm1gvk-en.

European Bank for Reconstruction (2014). *Transition Report 2013: Stuck in Transition?* London, UK: European Bank for Reconstruction.

European Commission, DG Regional Policy (2012, March). Guide to research and innovation strategies for smart specializations.

European Union Commission (2012). Smart specialization: the driver of future economic growth in Europe's regions. DG Regional Policy, *Panorama Inforegion, 44*, Winter.

European Union Commission (2015, June 15 Version). *Action Plan for the European Union Strategy for the Baltic Sea Region.* Commission Staff working document. Brussels, Belgium: EU Commission.

Government of the Republic of Karelia. Map of Karelia. The Official Web Portal of the Republic of Karelia. Retrieved from http://www.gov.karelia.ru/ Different/Federal/map_e.html.

Grunfelder, J., Rispling, L. & Norlén, G. (Eds.) (2016). *State of the Nordic Region 2016.* Nordregio Report. DIGI-02.

Hanemann, T., & Huotari, M. (2015, June 26). *Chinese Companies in Europe and in Germany (2015). Preparing for a New Era of Chinese Capital.* Berlin, Germany: MERICS.

Hansakul, S. & Levinger, H. (2014, July 31). *China-EU relations: Gearing up for growth.* Frankfurt am Main, Germany: Deutsche Bank Research.

Hellström, J. (2014). *China's Political Priorities in the Nordic Countries.* Report FOI-R—3879-SE. Stockholm, Sweden: Swedish Defence Research Agency (FOI).

House of Lords, EU Committee (2015) *The EU and Russia: Before and beyond the crisis in Ukraine.* Technical report. House of Lords, European Union Committee, 6th Report Session 2014–15, HL Paper 115. London, UK: House of Lords. Available at http://dx.doi.org/10.1787/5k97g3hm1gvk-en.

Lantaigne, M. (2014). *China's Emerging Arctic Strategies.* Reykjavík, Iceland: Institute of International Affairs, Center for Arctic Policy Studies (CAPS).

Lipponen, P. (2015). *For an ambitious EU Arctic and Northern Policy.* Memorandum to European Commission. Arctic Finland.

Merk, O., & Hesse. M. (2012), *The Competitiveness of Global Port-Cities: the Case of Hamburg,* OECD Regional Development Working Papers, 2012/06, Paris, France: OECD Publishing. Available at http://dx.doi.org/10.1787/5k97g3hm1gvk-en.

Purju, A., & Branten, E. (2013). The Economies of the Baltic Sea Region: Growth Patterns and Foreign Trade Now and in the Future, *Journal of East-West Business,* 19, 4–15. DOI: 10.1080/10669868.2013.779541.

Skorupska, A. & Szczudlik-Tatar, J. (2014). *Regional Cooperation Key to Polish-Chinese Strategic Partnership.* PISM Strategic Files, 25 (61). Warszawa, Poland: Polish Institute for International Affairs (PISM).

Zhong Nan (2016, June 2). China Merchants Group plans network of ports, terminals. *China Daily.* Retrieved from http://europe.chinadaily.com.cn/business/2016-06-02/content_25584474.htm.

Case 3.1   Deutsche Bahn expands collaboration with China

"The People's Republic of China is an important market for us and will remain so in future. In view of the plans to invest more than 300 billion Euros in transport infrastructure, we wish to benefit from the growth and potential in China. Our expertise is in high demand and our successful international activities also strengthen our position in our home market of Germany." Dr. Rüdiger Grub, CEO of Deutsche Bahn AG, (Beijing, June 2016).

Rail freight transport between China and Germany: DB Schenker, the freight logistics subsidiary of Deutsche Bahn (DB), has been a pioneer in developing rail logistics solutions from and to China since 1981. It runs its operations in 2015 in over 60 key Chinese cities, employing more than 5,000 people. DB Schenker uses two main rail routes between China and Europe: the Northern route (based on the Trans-Siberian rail route in Russia) for transport with origins or destinations in Northeast China, and the Southern route through Kazakhstan for traffic from Central and Western China to Europe. The first freight train from Beijing arrived in Hamburg in 2008. In 2011 DB Schenker organized for German car manufacturer BMW regular rail shipments of completely knocked down (CKD) kits on the Northern route from Leipzig logistics center in Germany to BMW's joint venture assembly plant in Shenyang, northeastern China. In 2012 DB Schenker opened a weekly service on the Southern route from Chongqing to Duisburg for IT manufacturers based in Chongqing.

DB's consulting services for CR relating to high-speed train maintenance: China Railway (CR), the national railway operator, operates a roughly 19,000 km high-speed rail (HSR) network with over 1,400 trains, accounting for 60% of the world's tracks. China's train manufacturers have entered a very active phase of internationalization since 2013: Turkish high-speed train in 2014, contract with Russian companies in 2015 for the Moscow-Kazan line, and China-Indonesia joint venture agreement on the Jakarta-Bandung HSR, also in 2015. In 2016, the overseas large projects under construction included railways links between China and Laos, China and Thailand, and the Belgrade-Budapest high-speed train. DB intends to make its knowledge available for servicing and maintenance support.

DB engineering expertise: China wants to support infrastructure activities in over 65 countries with the B&R. The partners are planning to collaborate on the development of infrastructure projects, and DB will contribute its engineering expertise.

(Continued)

Case 3.1   (*Continued*)

DB's procurement office in Shanghai: In November 2015, DB opened an international procurement office in Shanghai to purchase rail vehicle replacement parts and infrastructure materials from Chinese manufacturers.

Sources: Deutsche Bahn, www.bahn.com, DB Schenker, www.dbschenker.com and China Railway Rolling Stock Corporation (CRRC), www.crrcgc.cc/en.

Case 3.2   China-Belarus Industrial Park "Great Stone"

The idea of creating the China-Belarus Industrial Park was launched during a visit by Vice President Xi Jinping (now head of state) to Belarus in 2010, followed by the signature of an intergovernmental agreement on the joint project in 2012. The Park is established in the Smolevichy district, 25 km from Minsk, the capital of Belarus, on a territory of some 9,000 hectares. The Belarus government has created a special legal status for the economic zone with attractive financial and administrative conditions for potential investors. The project is based on the successful experience of China and Singapore in the development of the China-Singapore Suzhou Industrial Park.

A joint venture, the China-Belarus Joint-Stock Closed Company "Industrial Park Development Company", founded in 2012, is in charge of designing and building the infrastructure, real estate management, maintenance and consulting services, and attracting investments to the Park. On the Chinese side, the main shareholders are China National Machinery Industry Corp (Sinomach) (32%), China Merchants Group (20%), China CAMC Engineering Co., Ltd. (CAMCE) (14%). CAMCE, affiliated to Sinomach, is specialized in engineering procurement construction (EPC) projects in China and abroad. Minsk region and Minsk city authorities, representing Belarus national interests, own 32% of the joint venture. China's interest in the Minsk region to develop a logistics hub is due to its unique strategic location in the center of Europe and at the interface of the EEU and the EU. The region is offering excellent transport connections: the Berlin-Moscow highway, a rich network of railroad tracks, Minsk International Airport and an easy connection with the Baltic Sea port of Klaipėda at a distance of 500 km.

Chinese companies plan to build large production facilities and R&D centers focusing on machine building, electronics and health care for export.

(*Continued*)

Case 3.2 *(Continued)*

Sinomach announced in early 2016 that eight companies had already registered their admission to the Park: China Merchants Logistics Holding Co., Ltd., YTO (farm machinery and construction equipment), Zoomlion (construction machinery and sanitation equipment), ZTE (telecom equipment), Huawei (telecom equipment), Chengdu Xinzhu Corporation (machinery and electronic products), Gansu Juxin (malt production) and Belarus Nano Pectin Corporation. ZTE considers manufacturing telecommunication equipment and components for automobile transport, small-scale power engineering and communications. Huawei would set up an R&D center.

Sources:

Republic of Belarus official web site.
Belarus News (2015, November 21). Belarus ready for all-round cooperation with China's Xinjiang, Ningxia.
China Daily (2015, December 28). Sinomach, China Merchants build 'a pearl on Silk Road' in Belarus.
Sinomach Today (2016, March). China-Belarus Industrial Park Ready for Admission, 35 (1): 18–19.

Chapter 4

Nordic-Baltic Countries and China: Trends in Trade and Investment

Joné Kalendiené, Violeta Pukeliené and Mindaugas Dapkus

Vytautas Magnus University, Faculty of Economics and Management

The "One Belt One Road" (OBOR) program, launched by the Chinese Government with the intention to promote economic cooperation, is realized mainly through various forms of trade and investment among regions. This chapter aims to give an overview of the development and trends in trade and investment between China and the Baltic Sea Region. Providing a general view on economies, we decided to analyze countries as units and to leave the regional approach aside. Therefore, we concentrate only on the three Baltic States (Lithuania, Latvia and Estonia) and the four Nordic countries (Denmark, Finland, Sweden and Norway).

In this chapter, the official statistical data on bilateral trade and investment is used. International trade is very well documented in the UN Comtrade database. The export and import reports of China, Latvia, Lithuania, Estonia, Norway, Sweden, Denmark and Finland are used. The bilateral investment flows are not documented so well and there are many inconsistencies in data in different databases. UNCTAD database on bilateral foreign direct investment (FDI) is used as the main source of investment data. The additional information was retrieved from Eurostat,

China's national statistical office and various reports and surveys that are listed in references.

1. Trends in Investment between the Nordic and Baltic Countries and China

The fast growth of the Chinese economy, its rapid industrial development and increasing foreign trade has made China one of the most attractive destinations for foreign investment. On the other hand, the world has experienced the vast Chinese expansion in FDI. At the end of 2014, China became the third largest investor in the world. Nevertheless, Chinese FDI stock is mostly concentrated in Asia. The European Union (EU) gets only 8% of it. Thus the global share of Chinese investment in the Nordic and Baltic countries is even smaller.

1.1. *China's outward direct investment in the Nordic and Baltic countries*

In general, Chinese investment activities in Europe started around 2002. A number of new establishments in EU have been spurred since 2005, an indication of the increasing investment. According to the ESADEgeo database, Chinese investment in Europe grew by 177% in 2014 and reached an all-time high at US$20.170 million (Casaburi, 2016). The sectoral distribution of Chinese investment in EU is not wide. Seven sectors (energy, real estate, manufacturing, agriculture, financial sector, transportation and telecommunications) got 95% of total FDI into the region from 2010 to 2014 and the energy sector became the leading one. Nevertheless, the sectoral distribution of Chinese investment is changing. It is moving from manufacturing to service at an increasing rate. This trend was positive for the majority of the European countries as they were also included in the Chinese FDI map.

This is also the case of the Nordic and Baltic countries. According to Rhodium Group, most of the Chinese investment goes to the core European countries, to the exclusion of the Nordic and Baltic countries. However, the sectoral changes of investment that were mentioned above helped the region to attract more FDI and since 2010 the investment flows from China have achieved dramatic and sustainable growth. Denmark and

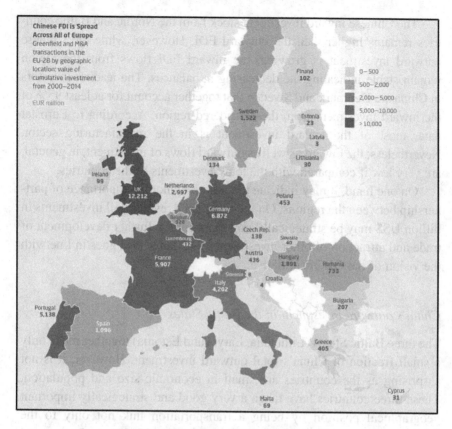

Map 4.1 Chinese FDI in the EU-28

Source: Hanemann, T. & Huotari, M. (2016, February). A New Record Year for Chinese Outbound Investment in Europe, MERICS/RHG Report. Retrieved from http://www.merics.org/fileadmin/user_upload/downloads/COFDI_2016/A_New_Record_Year_for_Chinese_Outbound_Investment_in_Europe.pdf.

Sweden are the most important partners as on average they get 90% of the Chinese investment in the region (Map 4.1). Huge investments in Sweden overstated the importance of Denmark and since 2007 the gap is increasing. It is partly due to the deal between the carmaker Zhejiang Geely (China) and Ford Motor to buy Volvo Cars (Sweden) in 2010. This agreement is a rare example of acquisition as a form of Chinese investment in the Nordic and Baltic countries. In general, greenfield projects dominate in the region (Hanemann and Huotari, 2015, 2016).

The Chinese inward investment stock from the Nordic and Baltic countries remains higher than the outward FDI. However, while the Chinese outward investment is growing, the inward FDI flows from the region remain stable indicating the decreasing imbalances. The leading investors in China are Denmark and Sweden that together account for at least 95% of the inward investment from the considered region. According to Eurostat data, most of the inward investment is in the manufacturing sector. Nevertheless, the inward as well as outward flows of investment, in general, are very low if compared with the total investments of the countries.

On one hand, it may indicate the minor economic importance of partnership between the regions. On the other hand, even small investments in billion US$ may be strategically important for the further development of trade and attraction of other investments. The latter idea goes in line with the vision of the OBOR initiative.

China's outward investment in the Baltic States

The three Baltic States (Lithuania, Latvia and Estonia) together make only a small fraction of China's total outward investment. However, it is not surprising as the countries are small in economic size and population. These three countries have taken a very good and strategically important geographical position by being a transportation link not only to the European and Scandinavian markets but also to the East: Russia and the former Soviet Union. Therefore, Chinese investors have been using the region as a springboard for expansion. For example, in 2012 China's largest producer of ATM machines, GRG Banking — that accounts for 23% of the Chinese market, made its first big investment in Lithuania. The company considered choosing Vilnius as a location for its European headquarters. Therefore, the three Baltic States pay great attention to China's "Belt and Road" (B&R) initiative that promises new investment projects in the region.

The largest recipient of China's outward investment during the recent years was Lithuania — the biggest country of the Baltic States. It accounts for more than 75% of Chinese outward investment in the Baltic States (Table 4.1). According to national statistics, at the end of 2014 China was 41st in the ranking of top investors in Lithuania.

Table 4.1   China's outward investment in the Baltic countries, million US$

	2007	2008	2009	2010	2011	2012	2013	2014
Latvia	0.57	0.54	0.54	0.54	0.54	0.54	0.54	0.54
Lithuania	3.93	3.93	3.93	3.93	3.93	6.97	12.48	12.48
Estonia	1.26	1.26	7.5	7.5	7.5	3.5	3.5	3.5

Source: Statistical bulletin on China's outward direct investment.

Since 2004 China's investment in Lithuania has tripled. Most of it is concentrated in manufacturing and technical services. However, the situation is changing.

The B&R initiative, or OBOR project aims to create distribution links. Thus, the transportation sector becomes very attractive for investments too. Klaipėda — the largest container port with its biggest retail chain in Lithuania and the Baltic States — is one of the important factors that attract Chinese investment in Lithuania. One of the best examples of the importance of the transportation sector is S.F. Express investment and cooperation with Lithuanian Post, the state-owned postal and shipping services company (Case 4.1). This investment of S.F. Express is also one of the top ten Chinese outward investments in the transport and communications sector in EU. This cooperation agreement and investment were a good injection into the state-owned company that had problems in sustaining profitable activities and maintaining a competitive edge with private courier companies.

Moreover, the development of transport infrastructure is multidimensional. According to the Lithuanian Confederation of Industrialists (2015), China Merchants Group and Lithuanian Railways are going to set up a joint Lithuanian and Chinese company which will take care of freight forwarding services between Lithuania, Belarus and China and will provide logistics services. This will enable China's outward investment in Lithuania to increase and continuously strengthen its position. For Lithuanians, it means support for the sector that is considered a competitive advantage for the country, and it dominates in service exports. So, continuous Chinese investments in transporting services should lead to the faster development of Lithuanian economy.

China's outward investment in the other two Baltic States (Latvia and Estonia) remains fixed for several years. Estonia is among the leading countries in Eastern and Central Europe regarding FDI per capita. It was also the leading country in the Baltics to attract Chinese investment. However, in 2012 China's outward FDI fell from US$7.5 million and remains at US$3.5 million indicating about zero net investment flows from China to Estonia. Despite a good geographical location and favorable infrastructure for maritime roads (there are nearly 30 ports in Estonia), there have been only a few initiatives for China's investment in the transport sector. Most of the Chinese outward investment in Estonia is concentrated in electrical machinery manufacturing and business service sectors.

Estonia is a leader in a number of start-ups among the Baltic States. This young business is usually very promising and needs funds. Chinese investors may find an opportunity here as some of them already did by supporting Estonian start-up Testlio — a global community of test engineers focused on bug-finding and quality assurance. More cooperation opportunities between China and Estonia in educational, medical and health issues were confirmed in 2015.

China's outward investment in Latvia is quite poor. It stands at US$0.54 million since 2009. China ranks 51st among the foreign investors and 44th by the contributions to the share capital in Latvia. At the beginning of 2016, 166 companies had Chinese capital in the country. Latvia's strength is its geographical and economical position. It is a natural transport hub with three of the largest ports and the biggest airport in the Baltics. Therefore, there are more negotiations taking place between China and Latvia under the framework of the OBOR initiative.

In general, China's outward investment is a great opportunity for companies in the Baltic States. They may be funded to develop their ideas, to strengthen competitive advantages, to expand to other European markets, etc. Sometimes one initial kick is needed to generate massive flows from company to company, from sector to sector. China's OBOR initiative provides a big opportunity for the Baltic countries to get integrated into the global trade-investment-transport network that could generate many benefits for their economies.

The Baltic States are still under negotiation with China on long-term investment projects related to the B&R initiative. One of the biggest threats is the competition among Lithuania, Latvia and Estonia. Being a very integrated and small region, they should put more effort on cooperation and only then can all three benefit.

China's outward investment in the Nordic countries

China's investment stock in the Nordic countries (Denmark, Finland, Sweden and Norway) has recently seen an increasing trend but their market share remains quite stable since 2010. In 2005 only 0.2% of Chinese outward investment went to the Nordic countries. Since 2010 the share increased and remains at 0.5% of China's total investment abroad. Looking from the European perspective, the Chinese investment stock in the Nordic countries makes 8% of total investment in the region.

Most of China's outward investment in the Nordic countries is concentrated in Sweden. It gets almost 90% of the investment in the region and the investment stock stands at US$2.4 billion. It is mainly because of the few big mergers and acquisitions in the Swedish automotive industry. In 2010 Chinese Zhejiang Geely Holding Group bought the Swedish car manufacturer Volvo Automobile Company for US$1.5 billion. It was also the biggest Chinese investment in the European automobile industry. Another big increase in China's outward investment in Sweden was recorded in 2012 when National Modern Energy Holdings Ltd. operating from Hong Kong established National Electric Vehicle Sweden AB (Nevs) in Sweden. This transaction aimed to buy the main assets of the other Swedish car producer Saab Automobile.

Despite the monetary injections into the Swedish economy, Chinese investments play an important role in promoting research and development as well as the technological advance of the receiving country. Swedish firms have substantial technological capacities and know-how, so Chinese funds were used to promote R&D in Sweden. Geely Auto established a R&D center in Göteborg. Moreover, Nevs transformed Saab Automobile into a company ready for development and manufacturing of electric cars.

Denmark was one of the first Nordic partners of China's outward investment. It was a leader in the region with US$97 million Chinese investment in 2005 (80% of the market). However, in 2007 the situation changed. Now China's investment accounts for US$53 million and that makes almost 1% of total foreign investment in Denmark. Again, China's investment in Denmark flows to high-tech, knowledge-intensive sectors such as electronics, healthcare and biotechnology, industrial equipment and informational technology. It is also the energy sector that is on the top of Chinese investment in Denmark. Renewable energy is also an issue that is of much interest to China.

China's investment in Finland has an increasing trend. It tripled in 2010 compared with the previous year and it still continues to grow. However, in total terms, the investments are not big. It stands at US$34 million that accounts only for 1% of China's investment in the Nordic countries. Most of the investment is in the information technology, healthcare and biotechnology sectors. In order to enhance the existing relationship, Finland and China entered into a new agreement on expanding bilateral cooperation between the countries on technological innovation, clean energy, urbanization and sustainable energy in 2013. The trade and investments between the countries are expected to increase in the future.

To sum up, China's outward investment in the Nordic countries is not high in monetary terms. China is not one of the leading investors in the region nor is the region one of the key markets for China. However, China's investment in Sweden, Denmark, Finland and Norway follows a similar pattern. It is an example of cooperation for R&D, for technological advance when Chinese financial funds are used to support the know-how accumulated in the Nordic countries. Such a partnership favors both of the parties and the global world in general.

1.2. *Trends in China's inward investment from the Nordic and Baltic countries*

The inward FDI flow into China remains quite stable during the past 6 years (KPMG, 2016). It performs a moderate growth of 1%–2% per year and in 2014 the flow was US$119.6 billion. Even though the Chinese economy was showing signs of slowing down it is still one of the most attractive markets in the world ranking among the top three of the largest FDI destination countries. Most FDI stock is concentrated in manufacturing as it was Chinese policy to allocate investment into export-led manufacturing sectors and to promote economic development. Even so, the situation is changing in the economy and FDI flows. In 2014, the service sector attracted US$66.2 billion in FDI and now service takes a greater share of FDI than the manufacturing sector. These changes go in line with the shift in China's policy towards the consumption-led economy. Therefore, the demand to finance qualitative healthcare and education services is increasing.

The breakdown of China's FDI by country shows that the largest investor is Hong Kong and more than half of FDI in China belongs to it. The EU countries account for 8% of China's FDI but the share of the Nordic and the Baltic countries is very small (0.4% of China's FDI stock). According to the Chinese report in the UNCTAD database, the Baltic States (Latvia, Lithuania and Estonia) and Norway have made no investment in China so far.

The biggest investors from the region are Sweden and Denmark (each has 0.16% of FDI stock in China). As was mentioned above, the outgoing investment flows from Sweden and Denmark to China are higher than the incoming flows meaning that Swedish and Danish investors have been more active in the Chinese market. 5% of the total Danish outward FDI stock and 2% of the total Swedish outward FDI stock are in China. That makes China an important partner.

Denmark is among the European countries that have the largest investments in China per capita. About 40 cities are engaged in direct cooperation. It was one of the first developed countries to establish political and economic relations with China. For quite a long time the investment flows were one-sided: from Denmark to China. Danish firms invested much in manufacturing in different regions in China to take advantage of the cheap labor force and to sell their products in the Chinese market. From 2004 there was the spurious growth of Danish investments in China and it continued till 2009. At that time about 80% of all investment was in energy and food sectors. After the global recession, the investment growth slowed down but it still remains quite moderate.

One of the prevailing trends is the investment in renewable energy. Denmark is one of the global leaders in the production of renewable energy and the related services. The demand for energy and renewable energy increase together with economic progress in China. So Danish firms exploit this opportunity and invest in various types of renewable energy. According to the Danish Climate Investment Fund, Danish companies produce and promote biofuel in China, and are involved in wind power and other areas (KIF, 2014).

According to the Swedish Trade and Invest Council, today there are more than 500 active Swedish companies in China. The majority of these companies are still oriented to manufacturing but there is an increasing trend of inflow investments in the service sector. The aim of these investments is usually to sell services in the Chinese market that is growing rapidly. Most of the Swedish investment flows in China focuses on the life science, environmental technology, retail and vehicles industries.

China is a minor investment partner for Finland. Only 0.1% of the total Finnish outward investment stock is in China. The investment was growing rapidly until 2010 and since then has experienced a negative flow. This might be related to a poorer performance of Finnish companies in China or to the investments really leaving the country. There are approximately 300 Finnish firms established in China. Nearly half of them are involved in manufacturing. Machinery, electronics, information technology, forestry and chemicals are the industries where Finnish companies invest most in China. Traditionally most of the investments were located in coastal areas of China. As the production costs started to increase there, Finnish companies decided to move their production to inland areas or other countries (like India or Pakistan). There were some companies, such as Biolan (fertilizers) and Cencorp (automation), which announced the relocation of manufacturing back to Finland.

Despite these tendencies, the total investment in manufacturing in China is still increasing. As in the case of Denmark, the government incentives towards sustainability have made way for Finnish innovations in cleantech. Finnish companies working in healthcare, telecommunications and gaming have great potential in China too. This could promote a new wave of Finnish investments in China but more in high-tech industries.

Summing up the findings about China's inward investment from the Nordic and Baltic countries, a few conclusions can be drawn. First of all, it is clear that China's inward investment flows from Denmark, Sweden, Norway and Finland are higher than China's outward investment to these countries both in nominal and per capita basis. It suggests that from the Nordic perspective the Chinese market is more important as an economy to place investment than a possible investor or partner for development. Moreover, the situation has been changing recently.

Secondly, the Nordic investors have changed their attitude and purpose of investing in China. It is closely related to government policies and orientation. China used to be a cheap labor country with the market oriented towards exports. Thus most of the Nordic investment focused on manufacturing. Recently the Chinese government has introduced plans for technological upgrading and is trying to orientate the economy towards domestic consumption; the Nordic investments benefit from it once again and this makes them change their industrial orientation.

Lastly, China is a minor investment partner of the three Baltic countries. The FDI flows from the Baltics to China are very scattered and do not show any clear trend. In most cases the investments are incidental. These countries are more likely to be recipients rather than donors in investment partnership with China.

2. Trends in Trade between China, and the Nordic and Baltic Countries

China is one of the major countries in global trade that promotes export-led economic growth. Its fast expansion started in 2002–2003. Trade in goods and services between China and the Nordic and Baltic countries is moderate both ways. The aggregate bilateral statistics on export and import indicates very small but increasing flows. The Nordic and Baltic economies are small; their domestic market is not big. This is the major reason for low bilateral trade. In 2015 the Nordic and Baltic countries received 1.2% of Chinese export and sold 0.8% of Chinese import (Table 4.2). Most of the trade is with the Nordic countries. The market share of the Baltic countries is minor. The biggest China export partner is Norway, which receives 28% of China's export to the region. The main Chinese import partner is Sweden (37% of imports from the region).

One of the biggest threats to the Nordic and Baltic countries while trading with China is big imbalances. On average, the exports to imports ratio in the Nordic and Baltic countries is about 40%. It is higher in the

Table 4.2   The share of the Nordic and Baltic countries in China's exports (%)

Year	Denmark	Sweden	Finland	Norway	Nordic	Estonia	Latvia	Lithuania	Baltic	Nordic and Baltic
2011	0.354	0.361	0.160	0.437	1.311	0.075	0.022	0.033	0.130	1.441
2012	0.313	0.323	0.287	0.394	1.317	0.069	0.022	0.033	0.124	1.441
2013	0.298	0.304	0.220	0.374	1.196	0.066	0.020	0.034	0.120	1.316
2014	0.304	0.311	0.211	0.361	1.187	0.064	0.020	0.038	0.122	1.309
2015	0.279	0.306	0.191	0.351	1.128	0.055	0.020	0.035	0.111	1.239
Average	0.309	0.321	0.214	0.383	1.228	0.066	0.021	0.035	0.121	1.349

Source: UNCTAD data, own calculations.

Nordic countries and much lower in the Baltic countries. The exports to imports ratio is the highest in Sweden (about 80%) whereas the smallest is in Estonia (about 13%). Norway also has a ratio lower than 50% as do the Baltic countries. This means that imports from China in the region is much higher than exports. The Nordic and Baltic countries are not able to sell in China's domestic market; however, they import many goods from there. It seems likely that as income level in the countries become more even, the Nordic and Baltic countries' export to China will grow faster.

Looking from the balance of payments perspective the imbalances in trade in goods in the Baltic countries and Norway are partially compensated by positive inflows of investments from China. This is what we have mentioned in the previous section. China's investment inflow in the Baltic countries and Norway overstates the outflow at a high rate. However, this is not the case for the other three Nordic countries: Sweden, Denmark and Finland. The net flows from these three Nordic countries to China are negative, suggesting that countries should generate positive net flows from other trading and investment partners.

2.1. *China's perspective on trade: Chinese export to the Nordic and Baltic countries*

At the beginning, the Chinese government took policies to promote the export-led growth of the economy. Thus China's export was constantly growing at high rates and only in 2015 did it record an annual decrease of 2.6% in nominal values. The export expansion made China look for new markets, consequently, in 2002 the statistics recorded the start of a trade boom between the Nordic and Baltic countries and China. However, the flows were not big and as indicated in Table 4.3, China's export market share in the region remains moderate (increased to 6.7% in 2015).

In the Nordic and Baltic region, the biggest Chinese export market is Norway that gets almost 30% of the total Chinese exports. The biggest export market share of China is in Norway too. In 2015 it reached its highest level — 10.4%. The second biggest export market of China in the Nordic and Baltic region is Sweden, though China's export market share here is lower (5% in 2015). This suggests that China has the possibility to increase its exports into the region even more.

Table 4.3 China's exports market shares in the Nordic and Baltic countries (%)

	Denmark	Sweden	Finland	Norway	Nordic	Estonia	Latvia	Lithuania	Baltic	Nordic and Baltic
2011	6.97	3.87	3.62	9.13	5.56	7.47	2.68	1.98	3.09	5.32
2012	7.01	4.02	7.73	9.25	6.44	7.03	2.78	2.11	3.06	6.05
2013	6.78	4.18	6.26	9.20	6.22	7.25	2.66	2.16	3.09	5.85
2014	7.14	4.49	6.45	9.48	6.50	7.45	2.79	2.51	3.31	6.13
2015	7.48	5.06	7.26	10.42	7.14	8.01	3.32	2.86	3.58	6.76

Source: UNCTAD data, authors' calculations.

Estonia is an example of a small economy where China on average exports only 0.07% of its global exports. Nevertheless, from the Estonian perspective China's export makes more than 8% of total imports in the country, making Estonia the second biggest Chinese export market share in the Nordic and Baltic countries. Thus China might be an attractive partner for very small markets too (Estonia is the smallest economy in the Nordic and Baltic region). China's export market share in the other two Baltic countries — Latvia and Lithuania — is the lowest. In 2015 imports from China made up 2.8% of total imports in Lithuania and 3.7% of total imports in Latvia.

Taking a sectorial perspective on bilateral trade, we can see that imports from China dominate in several sectors in almost all the Nordic and Baltic countries. China's exports lead in the textile industry. China gets half of the export market of apparel and clothing in Norway, one third of the export market in Denmark and Finland and about 25% of the market in Sweden and Estonia. China's exporters of man-made staple fibers are leading in Estonia. Their export market share is about 40%. However, the imports of the textile industry from China make about 10% of the total Chinese imports in the Nordic and Baltic countries.

Most of China's exports in the Nordic and Baltic countries is electrical and non-electrical machinery and equipment. They contribute to about one third of Chinese exports into the region and most of it goes to Norway and Finland. However, the demand for imports of these goods has a slightly decreasing trend. Nevertheless, China's producers were able to keep their market share constant or even increase it in Norway and Finland. These facts suggest the high competitiveness of Chinese exporters.

There are two more sectors left to mention when we talk about China's export concentration and its market share in the Nordic and Baltic countries: toys and furniture. Although the nominal value of toys, games and sports requisites exports is not big (only about 3% of total export into the region) its market share is significant. Chinese exporters have 50% of the market in Norway and Estonia, 40% of the market in Finland, 35% of the market in Denmark, 25% of the market in Sweden and Lithuania, and 10% of the market in Latvia. The export market share of Chinese furniture producers is smaller, ranking from 27% of the market in Denmark to 10% of the market in Lithuania.

The Nordic and Baltic countries put together are a minor export partner for China. They all receive only 1.3% of the total Chinese exports (where the Nordic countries receive 1.2% and the Baltic countries receive 0.1% of total exports). However, for several Chinese sectors the region is more important. 5% of the exports of the manufacturers of apparel and clothing accessories go to the Nordic and Baltic countries where Denmark receives about 2% of China's apparel export. The region receives about 2.5% of Chinese toys export and 2.25% of Chinese furniture export. Nevertheless, the importance of the region is decreasing in both industries. Exports of electrical and non-electrical machinery and equipment to the Nordic and Baltic countries also make about 2% of China's export and the share remains stable suggesting that for at least five years Chinese producers have not been able to find better or new ways to the Nordic and Baltic markets.

Summing up the trends of China's export to the Nordic and Baltic countries, we can see that it has been constantly increasing. However, China's market share remains comparatively low as the main trading partners of the Nordic as well as the Baltic countries are from the EU single market; and thus they enjoy a more favorable environment for trade. Nevertheless, we can identify a few industries where Chinese imports dominate, i.e. textile and toys. Both of the industries are low-tech and labor-intensive. This suggests that labor costs are still one of the main competitive advantages of Chinese exporters in the Nordic and Baltic countries.

Electric and non-electric machinery and equipment are the only significant Chinese high-tech export to the Nordic and Baltic countries. It remains stable for at least five years. This implies that it is difficult for Chinese manufacturers to find other competitive advantages apart from labor costs.

2.2. *China's import from the Nordic and Baltic countries*

In order to evaluate the importance of the Chinese market for the Nordic and Baltic countries, we should look closer at China's import from the region. First, it is worth to mention that imports from the Nordic and Baltic countries have a minor share in China's market. Altogether the seven countries import 0.7% of China's total import. The market share remains quite stable as well as the imports in nominal value. It has not performed any growth since 2010 and decreased by 5% since 2010. It may be treated as a loss of exporters in the Nordic and Baltic countries especially having in mind that the foreign demand was increasing whereas the domestic market and consumption in China went up during the same period (Table 4.4).

The biggest importer from the Nordic and Baltic countries to China is Sweden, which takes almost 38% of the import from the region. Its export market share in China is 0.3%. The second biggest exporter in the list is Finland (22% of imports from the region). Imports from all three Baltic countries together make only 0.02% of China's imports and that is 3% of the Chinese imports from the region.

However, the importance of imports from the Nordic and Baltic countries is much higher in particular sectors in China. Firstly, we should start from fur skins and artificial fur and manufactures thereof where half of the imports is from the Nordic and Baltic countries (55% on average during 2011–2015). All fur pelts imports come from two countries — Denmark and Finland. The other is the pulp and paper industry, where imports from the Nordic and Baltic countries (mainly Finland and Sweden) make 14% of the total imports in this industry in China.

Trends of the Nordic countries' exports to China

The four Nordic countries (Finland, Sweden, Denmark and Norway) export 97% of goods from the Nordic and Baltic region to China. On average one third of all the exports from the Nordic countries to China are electrical and non-electrical machinery and equipment. The share of these goods in the exports of the Nordic countries to China has decreased from 38% in 2011 to 30% in 2015. The cause is the decreasing nominal value of the exports from the Nordic countries in this sector that on average records 6% decrease annually. There was a big decline in exports recorded in Sweden and Finland since 2011 (30% and 45% respectively) that is related to changes in manufacturing in these countries. In aggregate data, the decline of Swedish and Finnish export was partly covered by the increasing exports of electrical and non-electrical machinery and

Table 4.4   The Nordic and Baltic countries' exports market share in China (%)

	Denmark	Sweden	Finland	Norway	Nordic	Estonia	Latvia	Lithuania	Baltic	Nordic and Baltic
2011	0.136	0.325	0.195	0.157	0.812	0.016	0.003	0.004	0.024	0.836
2012	0.130	0.280	0.167	0.122	0.699	0.007	0.003	0.004	0.014	0.714
2013	0.139	0.285	0.170	0.131	0.725	0.007	0.005	0.006	0.018	0.743
2014	0.149	0.274	0.158	0.156	0.738	0.010	0.007	0.006	0.023	0.760
2015	0.178	0.291	0.153	0.164	0.787	0.009	0.006	0.006	0.022	0.809
Average	0.146	0.291	0.169	0.146	0.752	0.010	0.005	0.005	0.020	0.772

Source: UNCTAD data, authors' calculations.

equipment in Norway. These changes in exports in this sector are the main reason why the exports from the Nordic and Baltic countries to China remain almost stable for five years.

The decreasing trend of exports of electrical and non-electrical machinery and equipment was compensated by the fast growth of the nominal value of exported fur skins and artificial fur and manufacturers thereof (import almost doubled from 2010 to 2015) and pharmaceutical products (export increased by 57% since 2010). These two sectors account for about 10% of China's total imports from the Nordic countries.

Sweden, which is the leader of exports to China in the Nordic region, is losing its export market share in China. Its exports to China decreases on average by 3% annually. This is mainly because of the decreasing trend of exports of electrical and non-electrical machinery and equipment discussed above. Sweden is also the leader in exports to China in the chemical industry. It mainly sells pharmaceuticals (15% of exports to China) and organic chemicals (4% of exports to China). The Swedish export market share of pharmaceutical products is 4% in China.

After the Chinese company had acquired Saab Automobile (Swedish manufacturer of automobiles and other vehicles), the exports of vehicles from Sweden to China started to grow more rapidly. The annual growth rates of exports almost doubled from −19% in 2012 to 19% in 2015. This break in trend increased the importance of the vehicles sector in Swedish exports: it increased from 7.9% in 2011 to 14.3% in 2015 of the total Swedish exports to China. The example illustrates how national economies take advantage of foreign investment and how it helps to reach distant locations. Thus the Eurasian Land Bridge can be an opportunity for Sweden (Case 4.2).

The Finnish exports to China also keep a clearly decreasing trend. Its exports to China shrank by 23% from 2011 until 2015 and this is the biggest decline recorded. About half of Finnish exports to China was concentrated in one sector — electrical and non-electrical machinery and equipment. A decline in manufacturing caused the exports of this sector to decrease too. However, Finnish companies are successful in exporting fur skins and artificial fur to China. This industry's exports increase on average by 16% annually. China's market is very important for Finnish exporters of fur skin as 45% of their exports are sold in the Chinese market.

Finland is also a regional leader in exporting pulp and paper to China. The exports of this industry make up almost a quarter of all Finnish goods sold in the Chinese market.

Denmark had the fastest growth of exports to China during 2011 to 2015 in the region. Despite the decrease in exports of the leading industry — electrical and non-electrical machinery and equipment, the exports went up by 29% in five years. Danish companies are successful in exporting food products to China, namely meat and fish products. This industry contributes 16% of the total Danish exports to China. Fur skins and artificial fur make 14% of the Danish exports to China. However, the export growth was recorded not only in low-tech industries. Exports of pharmaceutical products (10.4% of exports) were growing by 10% per year on average and exports of the optical industry (8.7% of exports) increased by 4%.

Norway's exports to China had a slowly increasing trend mainly because of the growing exports from the industry of electrical and non-electrical machinery and equipment that exports about 25% of Norwegian goods to China. The second highest exporting industry is fish and its products (15% of Norwegian exports to China) and it experienced a severe decline in exports to China in 2015. The industry with the fastest growing export to China is organic chemicals, which also contributes about 15% to the Norwegian export to China.

We should conclude by noting that the Nordic countries are twofold in their exports to China. On the one hand, high-tech industries, such as electrical and non-electrical machinery and equipment, pharmaceuticals, and optics are among the biggest exporting sectors. However, on the other hand, quite a big share of exports is in the food processing, fur, pulp and paper industries, which are considered as low-tech sectors. These low-tech industries outperform the high-tech industries by their significance for China's imports, as their export market share is much higher.

Trends of the Baltic States' exports to China

The Baltic States' economies are very small, thus their trade with China disappears in the aggregate data. Therefore, we decided to take a closer look at the development of Latvian, Lithuanian and Estonian exports to China. The distribution of exports from the region among the countries is almost even: Estonia's export makes up 40% of the total export of the Baltic countries to China whereas Latvia's and Lithuania's export make up 30% each. However, the relative importance of the Chinese market differs. It is higher in Estonia and Latvia than in Lithuania where the Chinese market gets only 0.4% of global exports of the country.

The Baltic countries' exports to China are not so concentrated on electrical and non-electrical machinery and equipment, though the industry is still important for exports from Latvia and Estonia. Although none of the Baltic countries is rich in oil, there are oil refineries. This causes a moderate share of fuels in total exports of these countries. In the trade with China, fuel makes up 10.7% of exports in Estonia, 11.6% of exports in Latvia and 6.6% of exports in Lithuania.

The geographical and biological location of the countries makes them rich in forests. It explains the high exports of wood from the Baltic countries to China. In export flows from Latvia to China the wood industry (40%) dominates as it is also an important part of trade in Estonia and Lithuania (about 10% of exports to China in each country). The metal industry mainly concentrated on copper makes up about 14% of exports to China from Latvia and Lithuania.

The structure of Estonia's export to China is similar to that of the Nordic countries. However there is a higher concentration in Estonia's exports on electrical and non-electrical machinery and equipment, as well as a few other high-tech industries. Latvia's and Lithuania's export to China is mainly concentrated in primary and low-tech industries. Such an export orientation was more favorable during the recent five years for it helped Latvia and Lithuania to increase the scope of trade as well as their export market shares with China.

Conclusion

The scope of monetary and goods flows between the Nordic and Baltic countries and China historically has always been moderate. For China, the region is too small because of its economy size and population so this is one of the most serious obstacles preventing the development of bilateral relationships. Therefore the cooperation between the Nordic and Baltic countries should be even more welcome. The Nordic and Baltic countries are integrated within the EU's market whereas the Chinese market is a distant destination in the geographical, political and cultural sense. A number of agreements and projects, including negotiations on a new investment agreement, Junker plan, "New Silk Road", the creation of new institutions such as Asia Infrastructure Investment Bank (AIIB) and New Development Bank (NDB), should help to intensify the communication and cooperation between the regions (Casaburi, 2016).

The gains of all the initiatives, including the OBOR initiative promoted by the Chinese government, are already visible. In 2015 the investment from China to the Nordic and Baltic countries increased. As the example of Sweden suggests, bigger investment should lead to the growth of trade flows in the nearest future. As China's investment flows move from manufacturing to services, the orientation of foreign trade should also change. It is expected that the importance of low-tech manufacturing industries in foreign trade between the Nordic and Baltic countries and China will decrease and be compensated with the growth of trade in services. It is likely to bring this cooperation to a qualitatively new level, especially in the Baltic countries.

References

Casaburi, I. (2016). *Chinese Investment in Europe 2015–16*. Barcelona, Spain: ESADE Center for Global Economy and Geopolitics (ESADEgeo).

Chan, L. (2016, March 21). *Lithuania: A Maritime Link between East and West*. Hong Kong: HKTDC Research. Retrieved from http://beltandroad.hktdc.com/en/market-analyses/details.aspx?ID=473744.

Chan, L. (2016, April 30). *Estonia: Market Profile — Major Economic Indicators*. Hong Kong: HKTDC Research. Retrieved from http://china-trade-research.hktdc.com/business-news/article/One-Belt-One-Road/Estonia-Market-Profile/obor/en/1/1X000000/1X0A3GWS.htm.

Glitterstam, T. (2016). *Business Sweden in China*. Stockholm, Sweden: Business Sweden. Retrieved from Business Sweden http://www.business-sweden.se/china/.

Glitterstam, T., Portén, P., Zhao, J. & Scheibenpflug, A. (2016). *Redefining Success Strategies in China: How to Win in the New Normal in Chinese Industry*. Stockholm, Sweden: Business Sweden. Retrieved from Business Sweden Website:http://www.business-sweden.se/contentassets/6271258852 1f4068aeb031124c23251b/redefining-success-strategies-in-china-ny.pdf.

Hanemann, Th. & Huotari, M. (2015). *Chinese FDI in Europe and Germany.* Berlin: Germany: Mercator Institute for China Studies (MERICS), Rhodium Group.

Hanemann, Th. and Huotari, M. (2016). *A new record year for Chinese outbound investment in Europe.* Berlin: Germany: Mercator Institute for China Studies (MERICS), Rhodium Group.

KIF (2014 Oct 21). *Climate Investments in China.* Copenhagen: Denmark. The Danish Climate Investment Fund (KIF). Retrieved from http://www.ifu.dk/en/service/news-and-publications/publications/kif-climate-investments-in-china.

KPMG Global China Practice (2016). *China Outlook 2015.* KPMG International. http://www.kpmg.com/ES/es/Internacionalizacion-KPMG/Documents/China-Outlook-2015.pdf.

Lithuanian Confederation of Industrialists (2015). 11 Cooperation Agreements between Lithuanian-Chinese Businesses Have Been Signed, 2015-11-23 http://www.lpk.lt/en/11-cooperation-agreements-between-lithuanian-chinese-businesses-have-been-signed/.

Martyn-Hemphill, R. & Morisseau, E. (2015, May 2). Small Step for China — Giant Leap for the Baltics? *The Baltic Time.* Retrieved from http://www.baltictimes.com/small_step_for_china_-_giant_leap_for_the_baltics_/.

Case 4.1   China-Baltic States cooperation in postal and shipping services

The rapid development of e-commerce in China increases the need for shipping the goods to other countries. One way to do this is to send it by mail. But it requires the mailing company to have agreements with particular institutions abroad. China's largest private-capital-based courier company S.F. Express meets a high need for collaboration in postal activities as it serves much of e-commerce trading in China. S.F. Express operates 39 transport aircraft, 19,000 vehicles, and they have 12,260 service points throughout the world. S.F. Express has been operating since 1993 in China, Hong Kong, Macao and Taiwan, expanding internationally to operate in the US, Japan, Korea, Singapore, Malaysia, Japan, Thailand, Vietnam and Australia. The company has more than 240,000 employees.

The other and faster way to serve e-buyers overseas is to establish a logistics center somewhere closer to the customers. This is the intention of Alibaba Group. Since launching its first website helping small Chinese exporters, manufacturers and entrepreneurs to sell internationally in 1999, Alibaba Group has grown into a global leader in online and mobile commerce.

The main agreements in shipment between S.F. Express and Baltic companies

There are three major agreements in the shipment industry between China and Baltic countries. All of them were initiated by Chinese companies S.F. Express and Alibaba group. One of the first agreements in the area was signed by Lithuanian public-owned company AB "Lietuvos paštas" (Lithuanian Post) and Chinese S. F. Express. AB "Lietuvos Paštas" is the biggest company delivering postal services in the country. The company provides mail, shipping services, as well as logistics, financial intermediation and electronic services. At the end of 2015, its capital was 71 million Euros, and it had 4,800 employees. In 2015 the company received about 1 million Euros of net profit. The company started to cooperate with Chinese Clevy and S.F. Express in 2014. The companies cooperate on the delivery of items from China to European Union countries, Russia and Belarus.

The next step of S.F. Express in the Baltics was an agreement with Estonian Omniva in 2015 to establish a new joint enterprise called Post11 aiming to transport goods between China and Europe faster and more efficiently. Estonian

(Continued)

Case 4.1 *(Continued)*

state-owned postal company Omniva is an international logistics company that transports goods and information. The company currently employs about 2,500 employees throughout Estonia, Latvia and Lithuania. The Omniva group consists of the state-owned AS Eesti Post (Estonia Post) as the parent company, and AS Eesti Maksekeskus as a subsidiary, along with subsidiaries UAB Omniva LT in Lithuania and SIA Omniva in Latvia. Omniva operates in all three Baltic markets using parcel machines.

A slightly different cooperation scheme was suggested to Riga Airport (Latvia) by Alibaba group in September 2016. This Chinese e-commerce company wants to use Latvia as a transit point when shipping its goods to Northern Europe. Earlier expected to be aimed at setting up a comprehensive logistics facility at Riga Airport, Alibaba Group now seems to be looking purely into using the airport as a transit point if attractive handling and other charges can be obtained. Riga Airport is the busiest airport in the Baltic countries with the highest number of passengers, aircraft movements, freight and mail tons.

Effects of collaboration on Lithuanian postal company

The collaboration between Chinese and Baltic companies can bring many advantages for both sides. The effect of such collaboration can be seen best when analyzing AB "Lietuvos paštas". As stated in the Company's annual report, in 2015 the company's flow of services provided increased over 11%, and this increase was mostly caused by the growth of the amount of services originating from Chinese shipment. On the whole, the discovery of China's direction allowed the volume of shipments to increase by more than 20. The shipping business is currently associated with e-commerce development and this sector accounts for about 10% of the total retail sales volume in China and has a tendency to grow. In the middle of 2016 half of the total postal items received by AB "Lietuvos paštas" was from China.

Sources: Lithuanian Post Financial report for 2015; postandparcel.info; The Baltic Course, http://www.baltic-course.com.

Case 4.2   The Karlshamn-Klaipėda ferry and China-Sweden trade

The port of Karlshamn (Southern Sweden)

The seaport of Karlshamn is the largest industrial and commercial port in southeastern Sweden. The port is a full-service port and mainly handles oil products, storage, and distribution of dry, liquid and refrigerated cargoes.

The Port is strategically situated in one of the most industrial areas of south Sweden and is in an ideal position for the new trade routes between Scandinavia and Eastern Europe, the Baltics and Russia. Most of the capital cities of the Baltic region can be reached within 12 hours. A ferry route between Karlshamn and Klaipėda (Lithuania) allows easy travel between Scandinavia and Eastern Europe which could take days by road. The ferry is operated by Danish company DFDS — the largest integrated shipping and logistics company in Northern Europe.

The regional business environment

The Småland-Blekinge region covers four counties in the southeast of Sweden; Kalmar, Jönköping, Blekinge and Kronoberg, which include three universities Blekinge Institute of Technology, Jönköping University and Linnaeus University. The area is known to be one of the most business-friendly parts of Sweden, with several innovation-orientated clusters, such as "Smart housing Småland" focusing on the industrialized production of housing based on timber.

The world's largest furniture retailer, IKEA, originated in Småland, The region is rich in international oriented companies such as Absolut Vodka, Dynapac (compaction and paving equipment), Kalmar Industries (heavy duty materials handling equipment to ports, intermodal traffic, terminals), Sapa (extruded aluminium profiles), ProfilGruppen (aluminium extrusions and components), and Volvo Construction Equipment.

The China-Sweden trade via Karlshamn-Klaipėda

Sweden is the country in Scandinavia which has the most trade with China. The competitive advantage of Karlshamn is the daily ferry connection with the port of Klaipėda. From Karlshamn, operators can distribute by rail all over Sweden and to Norway, within a few days, shipments from Eastern Europe

(Continued)

Case 4.2 (*Continued*)

and Eurasia. When transporting a Swedish container by rail to China via for example Germany, the container must be reloaded in east Poland, due to different rail gauge in West Europe and the former Soviet Union, but from Lithuania, which has Russian rail gauge, containers from Scandinavia may be transported directly to Kazakhstan and China. The New China-Europe Land Bridge is serving the needs of Swedish multinationals and their foreign partners.

Sources: OECD (2012) and Karlshamns Hamn AB.

Chapter 5

Logistics along the "New Silk Road": The East-West Transport Corridor in the Baltics

Algirdas Šakalys

Vilnius Gediminas Technical University, Competence Center of Intermodal Transport and Logistics

The European Union's (EU) infrastructure and transport policy aims at strengthening the social, economic and territorial cohesion of the EU and contributing to the creation of a single European transport area which increases the benefits for its users and supports inclusive growth, as well as at promoting the Trans-European transport network policy into third countries. The attention of decision makers is focused on building the core network corridors which are the strategic heart of the EU Trans-European transport network (TEN-T) (Map 5.1).

At the same time, on-going globalization and European integration lead to a rapid increase in transport of goods and people in all directions across Europe. Transport flows between the Black Sea Region, Central Asia and China and other parts of the Far East on the one hand, and Europe on the other are about to increase again in the current post-crisis period. This will result in the growing demand for reliable, efficient, fast and innovative transport and logistics solutions.

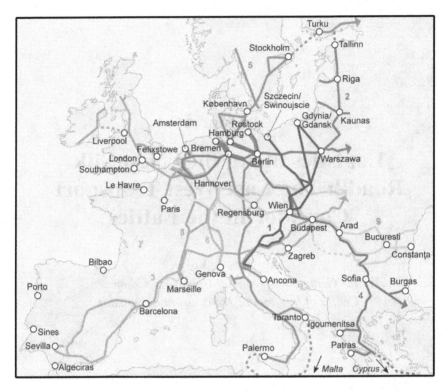

Map 5.1   Trans-European Transport Network (Ten-T Corridors)

Source: Trans-European Transport Network (TEN-T). Mobility and Transport.

This is especially important for the East-West Transport Corridor (EWTC) in the Baltic Sea Region (BSR) and beyond it, due to its physical nature interchange points, multi-language and cross-border interaction. The EWTC has evolved as the backbone of the Pan-European transport corridor IXB (Klaipėda-Minsk-Kiev-Odessa/Ilyichevsk) with the recently added links with Danish, German and Swedish seaports via Klaipėda seaport in Lithuania (Map 5.2).

It also includes (besides several TEN-T ports) motorways of sea, road and railway links. The EWTC forms the Baltic section of the global supply chain with the links to China, Russia and the Black Sea Region in the

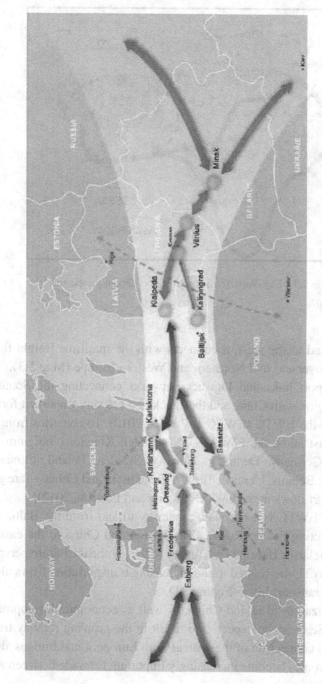

Map 5.2   Baltic East-West Transport Corridor: Regional perspective

Source: EWTC II, 2012.

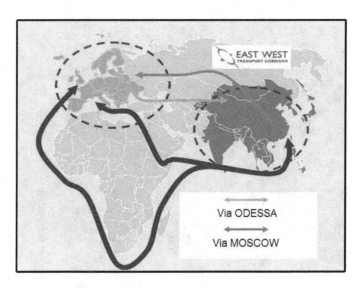

Map 5.3   East-West Transport Corridor: Global perspective
Source: EWTC, 2007.

eastern end, and to the west, it connects with the maritime freight flows coming from overseas and Northern and Western Europe (Map 5.3).

The transport links and logistics networks connecting the Southern Baltic Sea Region with China and the Black Sea are very important for the functioning of the EWTC (EWTC II Project, 2012). 16 countries from the west to the east along the EWTC — the United Kingdom, Belgium, the Netherlands, Germany, Denmark, Norway, Sweden, Poland, Lithuania, Latvia, Russia, Belarus, Ukraine, Turkey, Kazakhstan and China — are generating transport flows in the EWTC (Troeng and Larsson, 2012).

Thus, the EWTC is a promising gateway to and from the Baltic Sea Region connecting it with Russia, Kazakhstan and China to the east, as well as with Belarus, Ukraine and Turkey to the southeast. Future perspectives of the EWTC are related to the increasing transportation flows along Asia-Europe transport links (Figure 5.1).

Industrialization of inland China, as well as economic developments in the Black Sea, can be expected to result in the growing railway transport flows and connection of these areas with Europe. Land bridges along the New Silk routes become increasingly important for trade between Asia and Europe.

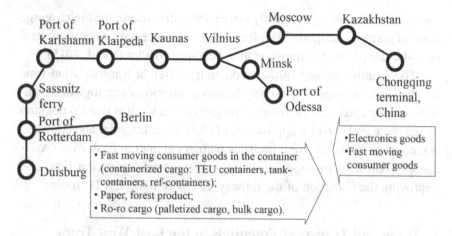

Figure 5.1   Potential transportation flows along the EWTC

Source: VGTU, 2014.

In the global context, it is not yet clear which routes will be attractive in the future since some of them still need development. As Chinese manufacturing is moving further to Central and Western China (due to lower manufacturing costs and congestion closer to the Chinese coast), the land routes to Europe become more attractive, especially for higher value cargo. Different routes are already being tested or effectively used for transportation of cargo between China during the recent years.

Time is the most important advantage of railway transportation over maritime transportation on Asia-Europe transport connections. Thus, the key selling advantage of railway freight transportation over maritime transport on these connections is speed rather than cost. It takes about 40 days to deliver a container by sea; at the same time it can be delivered within 20 to 25 days on land (DB Cargo Russia, 2014). Moreover, according to specific examples of the container train Saulė (Transporter, 2012) and Hewlett-Packard, it is possible to achieve even higher differences in time, because in both cases, when transporting cargo from Chongqing to Europe via railway it is possible to reduce the transportation time twice compared to the time taken by maritime transport; of course, with higher (20% to 25%) transportation price (Donnan, 2014).

Although the surface transport routes along Asia-Europe links are in absolute terms shorter than maritime transport, not all surface transport routes constitute an economically viable alternative due to the high average costs of surface transport. Therefore, when it is necessary to cross several cross-border points, the transportation becomes costlier (Viohl, 2015).

The monitoring and further reduction of freight transportation time are the key challenges for railway transport operators and logistics companies along Asia-Europe routes. The use of block trains that do not stop on the route and corridor approaches of close organizational and commercial cooperation of different logistics partners along the East-West (Asia-Europe) corridors presuppose shortening cargo transportation time and improving the attraction of the railway transport along EWTC routes.

1. Trade and Transport Potentials in the East-West Trade Corridor

Transport flows in the Asia-Europe routes are generated by merchandise trade between the above-mentioned macro-regions. Despite the ongoing economic slowdown in 2013 to 2015, Asia recorded the fastest regional GDP growth and its seaport volumes grew faster than any other macro-region. Europe remained the largest exporter of merchandise trade in value, at the same time China has become the world's biggest merchandise trade partner (in value) with import and export in 2013 totalling US\$4,159 billion (WTO, 2014). The EU-28 countries and China have the strongest trade partnerships. China's export to the EU-28 accounted for US\$371.286 billion and at the same time import was at the level of US\$195.815 million in 2013 (Viohl, 2015).

It is also important to note that it is possible to make a specific assessment of the future transport flows along the EWTC in the BSR, and to estimate the potential for shifting cargo from the maritime transport to railway transport on Asia-Europe routes. We can make certain insights only based on the analysis of the current situation. The freight that we can expect will be driving future demand for long-distance railway services between macro-regions (consumer goods or intermediate goods for which the container freight trains can compete with maritime transport).

To successfully develop the Western leg of the "Belt and Road" connecting China to the BSR, it is necessary to adequately evaluate the potential transport flows in the EWTC generated by the Asia-Europe trade connections (both in the short-term and long-term perspective). Unfortunately, in this sphere, there are only fragmented studies pursuant to which it is difficult to reveal or define the potential of the EWTC. A welcome exception here is the contribution of Swedish engineering consulting company Sweco with the "Global Study on Trade and Transport Potentials of EWTC" aiming to evaluate the Baltic Sea Region (including Baltic-Black Sea route) from the perspective of the years 2030 and 2050 (Troeng and Larsson, 2012). According to the executors of the above study, in 2010 the total number of goods flowing in the EWTC was nearly 14 million tons. When converting from weight to monetary value in Euros, the flows of goods within the EWTC amount approximately to 12.7 billion Euros. Whereas the total trade value in the East-West routes from Asia/China to Europe with the potential to generate freight transport flows in EWTC was on the level of 552 billion Euros in 2010.

Thus, according to the evaluators of the *Sweco* study, the share of EWTC market in the global East-West transport/logistics chain in 2010 accounted for 2.3%. As has been mentioned above, since there are no extensive studies on transport potential in the EWTC, the Sweco study results should be used, although evaluations of transportation volumes of 2010 made by Sweco study authors are a bit doubtful. In 2010, the Klaipėda seaport, which is one of the most important hubs of intermodal transport in the EWTC, handled 31.27 million tons of cargo, mostly transported in the east-west direction. Considering that cargo in the BSR east-west direction was also transported by other routes, i.e. by land transport, it is safe to assume that EWTC's market share in the Sweco study was underestimated. At the same time, it is necessary to highlight that potential and perspectives of the EWTC in the Sweco study have been evaluated in detail and objectively.

According to the forecasts made in this study, the market share of the EWTC in serving Asia-Europe trade flows will double by 2030; the number of vehicle-kilometers undertaken by trucks is estimated to increase by 73% between 2010 and 2030. The increase of the vehicle kilometers per day will be most notable in Poland, the northern part of Germany and Sweden during this period. The international rail freight transport is estimated to increase by 43% in the BSR. The most significant growth is predicted in Germany, Lithuania, Poland and Sweden. Besides, in the maritime sector, a growth of 140% is anticipated.

At the same time, it is necessary to note that there are differences between the developments of the type of goods transported. The share of non-bulk cargoes handled in the BSR seaports accounted for approximately one third of the cargo in 2010 and this share is expected to grow up to 45% in 2030. Whereas the share of liquid bulk cargoes is expected to decrease from 40% to around 30% during the same period (Baltic Transport Outlook 2030, 2011; Troeng and Larsson, 2012). The study also provides guidelines for the key actions, the execution of which could help reach the market share 2030 targets and make the EWTC more competitive: enhance intermodal interchanges; ensure better hinterland accessibility; strengthen connection with the Eastern freight corridors; improve cooperation among main stakeholders (including authorities) along the EWTC; strengthen commercial connections between the EWTC transport and logistics hubs; and deploy ITS services. Most of the proposed actions are specified in the EWTC Strategy Action Plan (EWTC II, 2012).

2. Action Plan for the Baltic EWTC

The above action plan was prepared and launched in implementing the Interreg BSR Programme EWTC II project. The Interreg Baltic Sea Region Programme is an EU-funded program, aiming at facilitating transnational cooperation in the region. Partners from countries around the Baltic Sea, public agencies, education and research NGOs, and enterprises work together to address common key challenges and opportunities. The focus of the EWTC Strategy Action Plan on the identification and development of the main transport hubs having a major impact on EWTC competitiveness. Figure 5.1 provides the scheme/chain of ports and inland hubs/intermodal terminals the facilities of which have a vital importance on the attractiveness and efficiency of the EWTC.

At the same time, it is necessary to note that to ensure seamless transport flows along the transport corridors or global supply chains, we have to adequately evaluate the increasing role on their competitiveness. Their main functions are to ensure an efficient, smooth and synchronized freight handling along the corridor. It means that they need to operate with the same key performance indicators or standards and integrated information systems. This includes the flow of information across the national borders and between the single hubs/terminals as well as a smooth handling of imports and exports related to national legislation, customs, etc. Seaports and hinterland intermodal terminals/logistic centers along the EWTC were mapped in the handbook that describes the location, hub/terminal area, and facilities, organizational structure, cargo turnover and connections for every intermodal terminal/hub. The handbook addresses the need for a joint action program and proposals on how to remove the bottlenecks in the hinterland of the seaports, intermodal logistics centers and in the hub interconnections along the EWTC.

2.1. *Best practices along the EWTC*

Although the EWTC II project has been completed and implementation of the EWTC Action Plan commenced only in 2015, Klaipėda (Lithuania) and Karlshamn (Sweden) seaports, as well as Taulov Transport Center (Denmark) could be highlighted as good practice examples, where recommendations of the EWTC II project have been successfully realized to increase competitiveness of not only those transport hubs but also of the entire EWTC.

Klaipėda seaport (Lithuania)

The strategy for the Klaipėda seaport foresees the development plans of the marine infrastructure such as the access channel, harbour channel and quays, as well as terrestrial infrastructures such as roadside and railway side access. Following efficient implementation of the port infrastructure plans and the related development plans of the port handling companies, in 2015 the Klaipėda seaport handled 38.51 million tons of cargo and this is the best port achievement in the entire history of the port. Moreover, a project of strategic importance, the liquefied natural gas (LNG) terminal, was implemented during a short-term period. It provided the possibility for Lithuanian industrial companies and citizens (including the neighboring countries) to use gas from alternative sources.

In 2015 Klaipėda joined the ranks of seaports able to accommodate more than 9,000 Twenty Foot Equivalent Unit (TEU) container ships (Klaipėda Seaport, 2016). Having the possibility to accommodate both feeder and ocean-going container ships, Klaipėda seaport has the ambition to turn into a transshipments hub for the BSR. Besides, a bulk cargo transshipments center has already started its operation in the Klaipėda seaport. Technologically, terminals of the bulk cargo transshipments center are adapted both to export and import, having the possibility to perform cargo handling operations simultaneously in two directions; their technical possibilities allow them to perform the functions of a cargo transshipments center, i.e. to accommodate "Post-Panamax" size ships with a large amount of bulk cargo and to transship this cargo with smaller vessel among the Baltic seaports.

Karlshamn seaport (Sweden)

To expand the business and handle various types of goods, the EWTC Strategy Action Plan for Karlshamn seaport was focused on investment in port facilities and connecting the infrastructure such as roads and railways as key aspects in the development of the seaport. The beginning of the implementation of the investment program resulted (during a short-term period) in the doubling of the capacity of the Karlshamn seaport and created favorable conditions for this port to become Sweden's gateway towards the East and for the development of its market share along the EWTC. Having started its activity, the Kombi Terminal makes it possible to handle all kinds of goods (not only seabound or intermodal), therefore it also strengthens the position of the Karlshamn seaport as an important cargo handling node regionally and nationally as well as in the international markets (Baltic Transport Journal, 2016).

Taulov Transport Center (Denmark)

The Taulov Transport Center (TTC) in Denmark was established by the association of 23 local companies aiming to create more business opportunities and synergy effects using the same brand. Thanks to the EWTC II project the board of the association established a set of statutes and a business plan providing the guidelines for its business development. In its turn, the government has invested in infrastructure improvements. It is expected that the currently ongoing transformation of the TTC into Denmark's Multimodal Transport Center would transform it into Denmark's logistics center of nationwide importance, having an opportunity to combine the four transport modes: ship, train, truck and airplane; it also has a vision to become one of the most important logistics centers in Denmark. Moreover, it is ideally placed in the EWTC for trade with countries beyond Denmark's borders: it has prompt access to the Nordic and Baltic countries as well as good transport links with continental Europe via Northern Germany.

It should be noted that here we identified only three success stories, where important transport and logistics hubs (in implementing recommendations of the EWTC II project of the Interreg BSR Programme) increase their potential in the southern part of the Baltic Sea of the Western Transport Corridor, as well as competing opportunities in serving trade flows not only of this macro-region, but also the global (Asia-Europe) flows. It is understandable that development of transport and logistics capacities in this sub-region is carried out on a wide scale. Consequently, the EWTC stimulates the economic growth of the region through: creating the conditions for an increasing amount of goods moving toward the east-west (and reverse) direction in the South Baltic Region in serving trade needs of Scandinavia and the Baltic States with the neighboring and Far East countries; joining forces of stakeholders to enhance sustainable transport planning and innovative solutions in the field of transport and logistics, and establishing the networks and platform of researchers along the EWTC.

2.2. *The Transport system and European strategy in the Baltic Sea region*

Besides national, regional and sub-macro regional tasks and taking account of the current challenges, for the Baltic States, it is very important to reach agreement and to pursue joint actions facilitating a sustainable and efficient transport system in the entire macro-region. This system should efficiently serve internal trade within the BSR as well as the international trade between the BSR, neighboring countries and Eurasia.

A new Transport Action Plan of the European Strategy in the BSR is currently under development. Its final draft anticipates that the transport system in the BSR should be composed of:

- European-level (TEN-T core network corridors) and other transnational corridors for better external accessibility of the BSR, with well-developed cross-border sections to secure interoperability of national transport networks.
- National and regional transport links, to improve access from the European and transnational corridors to the local and regional production areas and to the customer's markets.
- Ports, airports and intermodal terminals acting as interfaces between the land, sea, inland waterways and air transport modes, well connected with their respective hinterlands.
- Efficient local and regional public transportation contributing to better mobility within the commuting areas and to more compact settlement structures.
- Innovative solutions in logistics and in traffic monitoring systems, development of infrastructure for alternative fuels and electro-mobility systems.
- Platforms for cooperation between the public administration, research and business sectors to identify potentials and pave the way for future investments.
- Compatible and consistent transport planning and management process between the government levels and across the administrative borders (EUSBSR, 2016).

Implementation of the above actions at the regional level would contribute to the increase of EWTC competitiveness (especially in the BSR segment) in serving both regional and global trade flows. Therefore, today it is very important to share best practice examples at the regional level in implementing innovative solutions and technologies in the sphere of transport and logistics. It should also aim at identifying the topics of shared interest, which can be deployed through new networking projects aspiring to increase institutional knowledge in designing and deploying smart freight transport and logistics solutions and technologies in the BSR.

According to the author and taking account of the current challenges, it is especially important to apply innovative and effective solutions and technologies such as:

- Innovative models and processes managing open type global transportation corridors and logistics networks.
- Integration of fragmented and different transport/logistics ITC (along the transport corridors and logistics network) aimed at forming a common open type information platform.
- Integrated solutions and technologies for long-distance and last-mile carriage.
- Introduction of the innovative concepts and technologies of interoperability and synchronization activities of multimodal (intermodal) terminals along the global transport corridors.

Here the main goal is to get transportation and supply networks that are operated as a whole, meaning full vertical and horizontal coordination and cooperation where new instruments and technologies are needed to maximize the resource utilization and manage events across the different stakeholders and systems.

2.3. *The Asia-Europe transportation-logistics chain*

Trade with East Asia

A new strong impulse to develop EWTC at the global level (as a chain of BSR in the global Asia-Europe transportation-logistics chain) is provided by the measures anticipated in the new BSR Strategy Action Plan over contributing to the development of BSR transport cooperation. Specifically, the final draft of the above document anticipates promoting a coordinated corridor approach to managing international trade exchange flows between the BSR and the Asian economies (including Central Asian countries and China) along land bridge connections. The development of the "Silk Road Economic Belt" entry to Europe via the BSR is foreseen and should be based on the implementation of new innovative intermodal supply chain solutions and green transport technologies that serve both as alternatives and complements to the traditional transport routes and means to deal with growing trade between Asia and Europe.

The adaptation of indicative TEN-T maps for third countries, and in particular the EU East Partnership countries, is an important step to ensure coherence in infrastructure and transport activities planning. Such an approach brings benefits both to the BSR transport system (ensuring the continuation of the infrastructure beyond EU borders) and neighboring countries, facilitating connectivity between the macro-regions as well as access to BSR and the entire EU market. It is also the way to secure or introduce new trade routes with the new potential BSR partners (TEN-T Corridors, 2016).

Trade from East Asia heavily relies on maritime routes. Maritime transport will keep its leading role in the external trade of the EU, including the BSR. The European ports are adapting their infrastructure to cope with bigger ships coming into the market. At the same time, this trade should be accommodated by the hinterland network in Europe. To ensure the sustainable development of transport in the EU, it is crucial to increase the capacity, quality, interoperability of rail and road connections to the ports.

China-Europe cooperation

One of the strategic partners, China, has taken a leading position in the development of land transport connections from Asia to Europe, the potential of which is promising. With shortened transit time in comparison with maritime routes and lower transportation costs in comparison with aviation, the railway connection seems to find its niche in the growing international transport market. There are already train services from China to European countries such as Germany, Benelux and Baltic countries.

The question which requires particular attention is the imbalance in the freight traffic Europe-Asia. Volumes of cargo leaving Europe using the railway to China represent only one third of the ones from China to Europe. One of the main reasons is that the type of goods that the EU could export to China does not correspond to the needs of the region where the trains go (consumers of the EU products are mainly located in the southeastern part of China, along the coastline).

Both China and the EU should develop cooperation to solve the above-mentioned and other emerging challenges.

Given that China and EU are at the beginning and the end of the Asia-Europe links (routes, connections), they both should develop transport initiatives with their neighbors. Coordination is essential to ensure compatibility and complementarity between relevant policies and plans. Such coordination must not only take place between the EU and China; it should definitely involve the countries which will be part of this new connection and which should also benefit from it. One of the key challenges of this approach is that the EU's expectations meet China's as well as the views of transit countries. The transit countries crossed by a new modern infrastructure should also benefit from it from their own development needs.

2.4. *Reducing supply chain barriers*

Transport between Asia and Europe is obstructed not only by physical bottlenecks related to geographical constraints and poor infrastructure but also by non-physical obstacles. Non-physical barriers cause significant delays, increase transport and logistics costs, and have a negative impact on visibility and reliability of the transport chain. These non-physical barriers are the result of the complex national legislation and regulations, lack of cross-border harmonization and collaboration, organizational inefficiencies, non-application of trade facilitation standards and practices, lack of trained human resources, and insufficient investment in modern infrastructure and IT equipment for processing and data exchange (Viohl, 2015).

Several studies showed that border crossing times on Asia-Europe transport links vary from several days to a few hours. Such waiting time ranges from 6.5 hours at Sarygash (Kazakhstan) to 42.7 hours at Alashankou (China) (Troeng and Larsson, 2012).

Activities at the border crossing for cargoes by rail include documentary checks for matching between the consignment notes, wagon lists and cargo documents, customs control and other operations such as classification and switching of wagons, locomotives and crew, marshalling and technical inspections and preparation of rail transfer documents (Viohl, 2015).

Break-of-gauge operations also involve trans-loading of wagons/containers and require specific facilities and equipment such as forklifts, cranes, etc. The equipage of the border crossing points with such equipment is spotty. For example, Alashankou on the Chinese side has four transloading centers, each equipped with the crane that can handle 36 tons, but Dostyk on Kazak side (where goods are trans-loaded then transported eastwards) has only one trans-loading facility (CAREC, 2013).

Temporary closures at border crossing points between the countries are also frequent in Central Asia, where the border crossing point between Tajikistan and Kyrgyzstan has been closed frequently in 2013 and 2014 because of border incidents, and Uzbekistan frequently closes its borders with Tajikistan in the Fergana valley for short periods (e.g. 10 days) for Independence Day festivities (CAREC, 2013).

This is happening even though there are multilateral frameworks in place that govern freight railway transportation along Asia-Europe routes.

2.5. *The cooperation between railways*

Most of the countries the territory of which is crossed by Asia-Europe transport links are members of the Organization for Cooperation between Railways (OSJD).

Other countries (mostly from Europe) are members of the Intergovernmental Organization for International Carriage by Rail (OTIF) which are developing the uniform system of law which apply to the carriage of freight along the international routes by rail. This system of law is known as COFIT/CIM. Some countries (Poland, the Baltic States, Ukraine and few others) are members of both the above-mentioned organizations.

As usual, when trains cross countries or regions where different legal regimes apply, it is necessary to rewrite the Consignment Notes to correspond with the applicable legal regime. To avoid reusing of transport documents and to simplify customs clearance, a common CIM/SMGS[1] consignment note has been developed. The use of the joint CIM/SMGS can significantly reduce delays in cross-border railway transport (Viohl, 2015).

---

[1]CIM/SMGS: CIM (Carriage of Goods by Rail)/SMGS (International Goods Transport by Rail)

The CIM/SMGS consignment note could also be issued as an electronic document. But not all customs administrations accept this document.

According to DB Schenker experts' estimation, CIM/SMGS consignment notes in both directions are only used in 26%–27% of cases (DB Cargo Russia, 2014).

It is evident that transport infrastructure bottlenecks and non-physical barriers along Asia-Europe surface transport connections increase transportation time and lead to comparatively high transport costs that prevent usage of the competitive advantages of surface transport over maritime transport. Finally, landlocked countries (primarily countries of Central Asia) along these transport links lose the possibility to effectively integrate into global trade flows.

Viohl (2015) highlighted that both spheres, quality of trade and transport infrastructure (e.g. ports, roads, railway, information technologies) and customs performance (speed, simplicity and predictability of formalities which have increasingly been recognized as important to the development of international trade) belong to the sphere of state institutions.

2.6. *Logistics performance*

According to practical experience, building trusted partnerships among the government agencies, and regular bilateral and multilateral consultation meetings can be very effective and allow interested parties to find common solutions corresponding to the emerging challenges. A good practice example where such partnership is reflected is infrastructure modernization, simplification of procedures and electronic processing; they come together to improve the quality of performance of transport and logistics operations and increase its competitiveness in the Viking transport corridor (the southern branch of EWTC) (Case 5.1).

At the same time it is necessary to note that infrastructure quality and customs performance issues are considered at the level of governmental institutions, whereas the remaining four logistics performance indicators (LPI) defined and annually announced by the World Bank (WB) — competence and quality of logistics services; ease of arranging shipments; ability to track and trace consignments; and timeliness of shipments in reaching destinations with the scheduled or expected delivery time

— depend highly on the operational effectiveness of transport and logistics companies operating in one specific international transport corridor.

Moreover, competitiveness of an international transportation-logistics chain depends on both the LPI of each country which is crossed by a specific international transport corridor, and on the level of key performance indicators (KPI) of a specific company involved in this international transportation-logistics chain, defining the quality of provided services. One or two partners with low KPI can severely restrict competitiveness of the entire global supply chain or international transport corridor.

In terms of the EWTC in the southern part of the Baltic Sea Region, it is necessary to note that countries the territories and territorial waters of which are crossed by this international corridor, have reached very high LPI global rates in 2016 — Germany (1), Sweden (3), Denmark (17) and Lithuania (29) — whereas the neighboring countries developing competing transport corridors have lower global LPI ratings: Poland (33), Estonia (38) and Latvia (43).

However, considering the EWTC at the global level as one of the potential Asia-Europe transport links, it must be said that only China (rated 27th) comes into the top list of 30 countries with the highest LPI rates. Other countries where the EWTC links are currently being planned or tested (between Asia and Europe) have considerably lower positions in the LPI 2016 rating: Kazakhstan (77), Ukraine (80), Iran Islamic Republic (96), Russian Federation (99), Belarus (120), Uzbekistan (118) and Turkmenistan (140) (WB, 2016).

It is obvious that trade facilitation performance across the countries along the global EWTC is unequal. It is therefore necessary to pursue innovative trade facilitation actions along this transport corridor, especially in both EU Eastern Partnership and the Central Asian countries, and strengthen macro-regional cooperation among transport and logistics stakeholders.

2.7. Cooperation between operators: the case of the East-West Transport Corridor Association

In this context, the EWTC is a challenging case to test innovative tools and cooperation models accommodating the goals of seamless freight flows, harmonized operational indicators and interoperability across the borders of countries with different political and economic goals and systems (EU Member States, EU neighboring and Asian countries). Besides, it is necessary to consider the expectations of the end-users of the services to achieve market integration along the corridor. The numerous parties involved in the corridor development and operations require coordination of their activities and, first of all, the development of trusted partnership between the traders, transport and logistics operators and government authorities. This led to the idea to establish the EWTC Association (EWTCA) as a cooperation platform of commercial, academic and public organizations interested in promoting commercial opportunities and ensuring high quality transportation and logistics services along the EWTC (Case 5.2). The main aim of the EWTCA is to reach a high level of mutual dialogue among the business, academic and public structures that would lead to the most efficient, sustainable, environmentally friendly and safest connection for freight transport in the East-West (Asia-Europe via BSR) intermodal transport corridor.

Since a transport corridor is a sum of facilities supplied and offered through the partnership, a core parameter of the corridor management is the quality of cooperation between the stakeholders and the ability to expand the activities (Interreg BSR Programme, 2014 —TransGovernance project). A very important feature of the EWTCA activity is assurance of regular feedback. Every two years the EWTCA partners are asked about operational priorities and expectations of the association and, based on these surveys, two-year plans of the association are prepared.

The development of the container train Saulė (Sun), operated by Lithuanian Railways, which is in principle in the midst of testing of its capacities, perspectives and viability, is an interesting case for the EWTCA. Saulė container train runs from Klaipėda (Lithuania) to Russia and Kazakhstan, and from Kazakhstan to Chongqing in China (Map 5.4).

In pursuing this project the EWTCA association partners face big challenges in the sphere of non-physical barriers. In the international space, the EWTCA acquires greater recognition for it provides a well-established corridor management supporting setup of services. It provides access to different modes of transportation and enhances cooperation and visibility of different actors involved, as well as a link to other international transport corridors (VGTU, 2015).

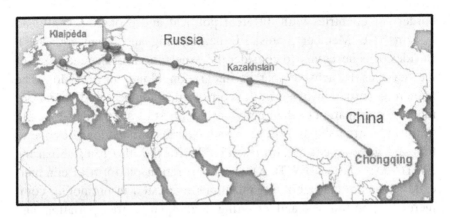

Map 5.4   The container train "Saulė" (Sun)

Source: Port of Klaipėda.

3. Innovation along the EWTC

It is also important to highlight the feedback (based on the outcomes of a specific survey performed in the framework of the EU TransGovernance project, 2014) of the main EWTC stakeholders concerning the integrated developments along the EWTC.[2] The main priorities for further development of 18 respondents from eight countries in Europe and Asia along EWTC include:

- Development of the monitoring system for KPIs by sharing performance data of logistics and freight transport services in the EWTC.
- Implementation of a co-modal transport information and management system increasing reliability and accessibility of intermodal freight transport solutions through one-stop-shop booking, reporting and payment services.
- Enhancement of the end-to-end supply chain security by ensuring the integrity of the entire transportation and supply network and prompt risk assessment through data sharing and single window services for interaction between the authorities and commercial stakeholders in the EWTC.

---

[2]The BSR TransGovernance project, developed in the framework of the EU Strategy for the Baltic Sea Region calls for coordination of national transport policies and actions to ensure a harmonized transnational development of the transport system.

Many EWTC partners require a single service provider to deliver a door-to-door service on time and at reasonable costs. This kind of integrated demand of transport demand for transport services motivates and urges maritime service providers such as ports and shipping companies to become more supply chain oriented. The seaport-hinterland interactions play an increasing role shaping supply chain solutions for shippers and logistics service providers along the EWTC (according to the outcomes of the specific survey). In terms of reliability of transport solutions, seaports and hinterland corridors take up a more important role in supply chains. Seaport hinterlands have become a key component for linking more efficiently more elements of the supply chain, namely to ensure that the needs of consignees are closely met by the suppliers in terms of costs, availability and time freight distribution. That is why it is important to ensure better information integration and exchange along all the EWTC. Due to all these issues, Vilnius Gediminas Technical University (VGTU) researchers carried out a EWTC pilot study (as part of EU FP7 programme eMAR project[3]) which was dedicated to investigate application to application integration across the EWTC and to propose an innovative architecture of interoperability of IT networks serving the entire transport corridor: the Corridor Single Window (Figure 5.2).

The Corridor Single Window is a facility that allows transport corridor parties involved in trade and transport along the corridor to exchange by Single Windows standardized information and documents with the single entry point to fulfill all import, export and transit-related requirements.

At the same time, a new EWTCA plan includes implementation of other innovations along the EWTC such as:

- Development of a smooth interaction between the transport hubs along the EWTC.
- Initiation of R&D activities and promotion of transport and logistics clusters development in the BSR and along the transport links connecting China with Europe via Baltics.

---

[3]The EU eMAR project aims to empower the European maritime sector in offering efficient quality shipping services fully integrated in the overall European transport system over an upgraded information management infrastructure. The eMar project received funding from the Framework Programme 7 (FP7) of the EU Directorate on Mobility and Transport.

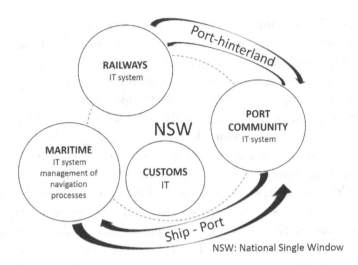

Figure 5.2   Corridor Single Window: integrating IT networks along the East-West Transport Corridor

Source: VGTU (2014).

- Promotion of integration of processes and technologies for long-distance carriage and last mile carriage.

Conclusion

In conclusion, it should be stated that the EWTC in the southern part of the BSR has great potential to become a competitive branch of the Silk Road connecting China with Europe via the Baltic with great impact on trade between the BSR and China. However, in order to achieve this goal, it is necessary to take new innovative intermodal and multimodal supply chain solutions based on "green" transport technologies. The efficiency of multimodal interchanges, the attempts to organize nonstop transshipment, one document service, one-stop (Single Window) information system architecture, as well as the establishment of a coordination mechanism among the related nations and enterprises under the agreed common principles should be included in the revised agenda of cooperation between Chinese and European partners interested in the development of this transport link. A newly prepared Transport Action Plan of the EU's BSR Strategy, as well as its provisions in developing transport connections with third countries, is a very important instrument in implementing the above tasks.

References

Baltic Transport Journal (2016, February 15). *Karlshamn port's doubled rail capacity.*

Baltic Transport Outlook 2030 (2011). *BTO Executive Report.* European Commission: Trans-European Transport Networks (TEN-T).

CAREC (2013). Corridor Performance Measurement Annual Report 2013 – Available at http://www.carecprogram.org/uploads/docs/CAREC-CPMM-Reports/CAREC-CPMM-Annual-Report-2013.pdf

DB Cargo Russia (2014, September 01). *Interview Hr. Hans-Georg Werner The Eurasian corridor: yesterday, today, tomorrow.* Available at http://ru.dbcargo.com/rail-russijaservices-en/News_Media/news/7832774/ interview_georg_werner.html.

Donnan, S. (2014, October 17). Geopolitics cast shadow over New Silk Road. *Financial Times.*

EUSBSR (2016, May 18). *Action Plan — Coordination Group final proposal.* European Union Strategy for the Baltic Sea Region. Policy Area Transport.

EWTC II (2012). *East West Transport Corridor II Strategy and Action Plan —* Final Report September 2012. Karlskrona: Region Blekinge.

Interreg BSR Programme (2014). *BSR Trans Governance project. Applying multilevel governance in transport planning and management in the Baltic Sea Region.* Interreg Baltic Sea Region.

Lithuanian Railways (2014). *The container train "Saulė".*

Notteboom, T. (2009), *The relationship between seaports and the intermodal hinterland in light of global supply chains: European challenges*, in Port Competition and Hinterland Connections, OECD Publishing, Paris.

Šakalys, A. (2015, November). *EWTCA as a best practice case or an instrument of interregional cooperation.* Presentation made at the BESTFACT Final Conference, Vilnius, Kaunas and Klaipėda, Lithuania. Available at http://www.bestfact.net/wp-content/uploads/2015/11/BESTFACT_Final_Conference_Sakalys.pdf.

Šakalys, A. (2014, May). *East-West transport corridor as a promising interregional transport link.* Presentation made at the EWTCA Conference, Paris. Available at http://www.bestfact.net/wp-content/uploads/2014/05/20140411_Conference_Paris_EWTCA_Sakalys.pdf.

Šakalys, A. & Greičiūnė, L. (2015). Innovative Measures Ensuring Integrity of the Entire Supply Chain or Transport Corridor. *Journal of Shipping and Ocean Engineering*. 5, 280–288.

TransBaltic (2015). *Macro-regional Transport Action Plan.* Available at http://www.ladec.fi/filebank/3157-TransBaltic_MTAP_2014_edition.pdf.

TEN-T Corridors (2016). *Forerunners of a Forward-looking European Transport System.* Issues Papers of European Coordinators. TENT-T Days 2016 Rotterdam The Netherlands. European Commission — Directorate-General for Mobility and Transport Available at- http://ec.europa.eu/transport/themes/infrastructure/news/doc/2016-06-20-ten-t-days-2016/issues-papers.pdf.

Troeng, U. & Larsson, P. (2012, March 30). *Global Study on Trade and Transports in the East West Transport Corridor. Sweco Infrastructure Report.* East West Transport Corridor II. Available at — http://www.ewtc2.eu/media/7371/S%20-%20Global%20study%20on%20trade%20and%20transports%20in%20the%20East%20West%20Transport%20Corridor%20-%20Sub-report%20task%206B.pdf.

Transporter, (2012, January). *East-West Transport Corridor Association.* 1/12 (Special Edition).

Viohl, B. (2015). *Euro-Asian Transport Links Transport Flows and Non-physical Barriers.* Informal document WP.5GE.2 (2015) No. 1. UNECE.

VGTU (2014). *EU FP7 eMAR Project.* Vilnius Gediminas Technical University.

VGTU(2015). *EU FP7 BESFACT Project. Best Practice Factory for Freight Transport.* Best Practice Handbook 3. Vilnius Gediminas Technical University.

WTO (2014), *World Trade Report 2014 — Trade and Development: Recent Trends and the Role of the WTO,* Geneva: WTO.

Case 5.1   The Viking Train

An example of good practices where effective international cooperation, infrastructure development and modernization, simplification of procedures and electronic processing come together to improve the performance of the activity of a transport corridor is the Viking train project. Viking train offers regular intermodal freight transport services from Klaipėda seaport (Lithuania) to Odessa/Ilyichevsk (Ukraine). These railway services are based on cooperation between the railway's operators and freight forwarders of Lithuania, Belarus and Ukraine (many of them are EWTCA members), as well as the partners from Bulgaria, Moldova and Turkey who joined recently.

The duration of traveling 1,734 km with regular weekly scheduling from Klaipėda to Ilyichevsk is 56.5 hours. After Turkey joined the project, the Viking connection from Turkey to China via Iran, Turkmenistan and Kazakhstan has become very promising. It is expected that the Viking corridor could become a branch of the Southern Silk Road to the Baltic Sea Region.

The Viking train project has demonstrated how the railway corridor can become a backbone of the new transport link. During the development of the Viking train project the below-mentioned obstacles of border crossing points between the countries from different political and economic spaces have been removed:

- Technology (lack of platforms for loading/unloading cars and trucks).
- Information system (variety of standards of integrated transaction control systems (ITC) and documentation).
- Organization (variety of interests and action instructions).
- Law (different legislation in separate countries).
- Policy (different economic and transport policy in the countries involved).

At the beginning of 2010, a pilot project, Single Automated Information System, was launched. Belarusian, Lithuanian and Ukrainian customs offices and transport companies implemented a New Computerised Transit System (NCTS) for the transportation of goods among these countries that facilitated the execution of customs procedure for freight transported by the Viking train.

(Continued)

Case 5.1   (*Continued*)

Currently, the Viking train needs 30 minutes to cross the Kena border station with Belarus. At the same time, it is necessary to note that only the communication between the various parties has improved in reaching such a result (which is so far the best in crossing the EU's border with third countries) but the modernization of the Kena station infrastructures also contributed to this achievement. Because of the modernization, Kena station is well prepared for the increased train traffic. In 2003, 1,777 TEU have been transported by the Viking train, whereas the freight volumes have increased to 38.173 TEU in 2013 (albeit with some decline in 2012).

*Sources:*Viohl (2015), VGTU (2015), Šakalys (2014, 2015).

Case 5.2   The East-West Transport Corridor Association

The EWTCA can be considered as a best practice example. So far (i.e. before implementing this solution) there was no similar tool to promote unified transportation and logistics solutions from Western European countries to the Far East of Asia.

The aim of the EWTCA is to establish and develop transportation and logistics networks between Europe and Asia (with a focus on the BSR). At the same time, the association is an innovative instrument of regional and interregional cooperation among business, academia and public sector.

Members of the EWTCA include forwarders, logistics companies and their associations; universities and research institutions; railways and maritime companies; and ports and public institutions. Currently, it has a broad representation of more than 30 stakeholders from ten countries, namely: Belarus, China, Germany, Kazakhstan, Lithuania, Mongolia, Russian Federation, Slovenia, Sweden and Ukraine. The association seeks to work out an optimum governance and management model for the EWTC that allows integration of different business and policy approaches, as well as the development of the joint corridor strategy.

The association assists in solving cargo transportation problems and catalyzing cooperation along the EWTC through:

- Enhancing intermodal interchanges
- Ensuring hinterland accessibility

(*Continued*)

Case 5.2 (*Continued*)

- Facilitation of BSR transport connections to third countries
- Keeping focus on shorter transportation routes between the countries around the Baltic Sea
- Closer cooperation between operators and authorities

Tightening commercial connections between the EWTC hubs

The EWTCA is commonly regarded as working successfully, e.g. facilitating the stakeholder's cooperation and business development such as Viking and Saulė (Sun) container trains. The Saulė (Sun) train (with 82 TEU container capacity) from Klaipėda (Lithuania) to Almaty (Kazakhstan) and through Doystik/Alatawshankou to Chongqing (China) operated by Lithuanian Railways has run bimonthly and on a flexible schedule since 2012. The travel time for 10,929 km is 13 days and the Sun train transported 1,260 TEU in 2013 (UNECE, 2015).Through an extension transportation by short sea shipping from Klaipėda to Antwerp, the total route becomes 11,068 km long and can be covered in 18 days. There are also opportunities for container transportation from Lithuania to Antwerp by railway through Poland, Germany and the Netherlands with approximately the same time costs.

Sources: VGTU (2015), Šakalys (2014, 2015).

Chapter 6

Central Asia, Global Value Chains and China's "Silk Road Economic Belt" Initiative

Richard Pomfret

University of Adelaide School of Economics,
and the Johns Hopkins University SAIS Europe

Since the start of the 21st century China has launched two major programs relevant to Central Asia's potential role in global value chains. The **Go West** policy was launched just before China's entry into the World Trade Organization in 2001.[1] Although China's western provinces have experienced at times stellar growth, they continue to lag behind the economic development of the eastern provinces, and one important reason is their weaker infrastructure, especially when complex global supply chains are involved. The second major program is the **One Belt One Road** program, which includes ambitious plans to improve China's global connectivity. The overland "Silk Road Economic Belt" (SREB) could be of great significance to Central Asia.

---

[1]Officially called the Western Development Program, it covers the municipality of Chongqing, the provinces of Gansu, Guizhou, Qinghai, Shaanxi, Sichuan and Yunnan, and the autonomous regions of Guangxi, Inner Mongolia, Ningxia, Tibet and Xinjiang.

1. Going West

The Go West program tackled a salient feature of China's economic development since 1979: although the national economy had grown rapidly, the benefits were unevenly shared between the booming eastern coastal provinces and the poorer western areas. Despite substantial infrastructure and other investment in the west, the coastal provinces continued to enjoy geographical advantages. Western suppliers faced extended and expensive supply chains: costly alternatives to the congested Yangtze River route, bonded cargo requirements for exporters, and lack of scale economies all add to supplier costs.

For western producers, logistic improvement came slowly. Shipping goods from inland factories to the coast along the Yangtze River, a journey normally taking five days from Chongqing to the container line in Yangshan port off Shanghai, offered the most attractive speed/cost combination. However, there are choke points, such as the Three Gorges Dam's five-tier ship lock that has seen significant congestion as traffic increased; according to the Three Gorges Navigation Administration, 44,458 vessels mainly carrying mining materials, ore and containers passed through in 2014 (Knowler, 2015). Alternatives to the river route were restricted and expensive. If an export cargo went by road it had to be in a sealed truck, and bonded and unbonded cargo could not be mixed. For freight sent by air from Western China, the first stop had to be Chengdu.

In 2010 a bonded train link between Chongqing and the Shenzhen terminals in Yantian was opened. This encouraged Hewlett-Packard and Foxconn to jointly invest US$3 billion to build laptop manufacturing bases in Chongqing, opening the prospect of Western China joining the boom in production in global value chains (GVCs). At the same time, exporters in Chongqing were searching for alternative export routes, and around this time the first rail services from Chongqing to Germany were essayed.

After some experimental starts in 2010 and 2011 with individual trains connecting Sichuan province and Chongqing Municipality with Germany, regular rail service between Chongqing and Duisburg was established in 2013, and routes from Chengdu and Zhengzhou to Europe were also being established (Summers, 2013). To electronics firms in

Western China (e.g. HP, Acer and Foxconn) supplying EU markets and to EU firms shipping parts to their operations in China (e.g. Volkswagen, Audi and BMW), the Eurasian Land Bridge rail link offered an attractive price/time option, taking 16 days which was faster than by sea (about 36 days) and at lower cost than by air.

2. China Looks Further West

Overland trade across the Eurasian landmass has a long tradition dating back at least to the "silk roads" connecting China and India to western Asia and Europe in the 2nd century BCE. Urban centers such as Samarkand and Bukhara flourished at the start of the second millennium. Improved ocean travel between Europe and South and East Asia after 1500 was associated with a long period of economic decline in Central Asia; the impoverished region was incorporated into the Russian Empire in the second half of the 19th century, and economic ties were increasingly directed north towards Russia. After the 1960 Sino-Soviet split, physical connections between Central Asia and China were broken. Only at the very end of the Soviet era were road connections reopened and the first rail link between Kazakhstan and China constructed.[2]

During the 1990s relations between China and the Central Asian countries gradually improved, first through joint efforts to demarcate and demilitarize borders and to build trust, and then the formalization of the group that was renamed the Shanghai Cooperation Organization (SCO) in 2001. The 21st century saw the rapid rise in importance of China as a trading partner and financer of infrastructure projects in Central Asia. China's growing economic presence was highlighted by President Xi Jinping's high-profile September 2013 tour when he visited four Central Asian countries before attending the SCO summit in Bishkek; President Xi met all five Central Asian presidents, and pledged over US$50 billion in Chinese funding for energy and infrastructure projects. At the summit he proposed a "Silk Road Economic Belt" as a way of integrating the region through new infrastructure, increased cultural exchanges and more trade. The

---

[2] For more details see Pomfret (1995), and on China-Central Asia relations in the 1990s and early 2000s, Pomfret (2006, 178-80).

Asian Infrastructure Investment Bank (AIIB), mooted at the same time and formalized in 2014 to 2015, stood ready to provide funding.[3]

The major components of China's economic relations with Central Asia are imports of minerals, oil and gas, and other primary products in return for exports of Chinese manufactures. An oil pipeline from the western Kazakhstan oil fields to China was constructed in stages between 2003 and 2009. A gas pipeline from Turkmenistan through Uzbekistan and Kazakhstan to China completed in 2009 provided the strongest demonstration of China's interest and potential role in Central Asia.[4] China has also been active in the poorer countries, Tajikistan and the Kyrgyz Republic, partly as an investor but also providing aid in the form of road-building and so forth (Kassenova, 2009). Politically China presents itself as a good neighbor, with similar concerns to Central Asian governments, especially with respect to extremism and splittism.

3. A Eurasian Rail Network?

The concept of a land bridge between China and Europe has entered the popular imagination, but there is little precision about the route. The long-standing link is the Trans-Siberian railway from Vladivostok through Moscow to Europe, with spurs connecting Mongolia and China to the mainline. This and the lines from Tashkent or Almaty to Russia are legacies of the Soviet rail network. In 1990 a line from Urumqi to Kazakhstan provided the first direct link between China and Central Asia, and in 1997 a rail link between Turkmenistan and Iran was completed, although it carried little traffic. The Kazakhstan-China rail line carried coal, minerals, and iron

---

[3]The 50 countries signing the AIIB's Articles of Agreement in June 2015 included Kazakhstan, the Kyrgyz Republic, Tajikistan, Uzbekistan, Iran, Azerbaijan and Turkey, as well as seven Arab states (Egypt, Jordan, Kuwait, Oman, Qatar, Saudi Arabia and UAE).
[4]Turkmenistan, Uzbekistan and Kazakhstan agreed on the pipeline route, on transit rates, and on options for Kazakhstan and Uzbekistan to export their own gas through the pipeline. Given the previous record of non-cooperation among Central Asian countries, this was a notable achievement by China. The pipeline from Turkmenistan is being expanded from 40 billion cubic meters (bcm) to 60 bcm annual capacity, and linked to the Kyrgyz system. The gas pipeline network could also be expanded to include Iran, further reducing China's dependence on maritime deliveries of gas.

and steel to China, and in some years it has also carried wheat. A trading zone, primarily for Chinese manufactured goods, has been established near the Khorgos border crossing point into Kazakhstan (Case 6.1).

The land bridge rail connections established since 2010 have almost all gone via Urumqi, Astana and Minsk to Europe.[5] However, Chinese commentaries on the SREB have been accompanied by maps showing an alternative main line through Tashkent and Tehran, with Moscow reduced to a spur (Map 6.1).These two routes have important differences, as the former includes Russia as a transit country, while the latter transits Iran and Turkey to Europe and is easily linked to the Arab world. Routes north or south of the Caspian Sea dominate multimodal routes that include a sea-crossing.[6]

Given the large fixed costs of upgrading a rail system, the two routes are likely to be mutually exclusive as mainlines between China and Europe, especially if the intention is to cut transport times by constructing a high-speed rail line. Chinese proposals for a high-speed rail service that would link Shanghai to Berlin in two days via Astana are not implausible given the speed with which China has constructed its domestic high-speed rail network.[7] On the Lanzhou-Urumqi high-speed line, completed in 2014, the 1,776-kilometer (km) journey takes ten hours. The train journey from Urumqi to Dostyk/Alashankou on the Kazakhstan border is 460 km. If a single high-speed rail line is to be constructed, a key issue for the two largest Central Asian countries is whether it passes through the capital of Kazakhstan, Astana (as in the current land bridge), or passes through Uzbekistan (as in Maps 6.1 and 6.2).

---

[5]Some China-EU rail traffic uses the Trans-Siberian line, but from most Chinese cities that is longer; from Shanghai, Duisburg is 13,000 km on the Tran-Siberian versus 10,300 km via Kazakhstan.

[6]In the 1990s the EU promoted, with little success, the TRACECA route from Central Asia and the Caucasus to Europe avoiding Russia by crossing the Caspian Sea from Turkmenistan to Azerbaijan. Kazakhstan has recently promoted a rail/ferry trans-Caspian route via Aktau and Baku, which may temporarily have advantages over the alternatives, but the sea crossing reduces its long-term attractiveness.

[7]Purpose-built track is required for high-speed freight that usually involves speeds of around 200 kilometers per hour (kph).

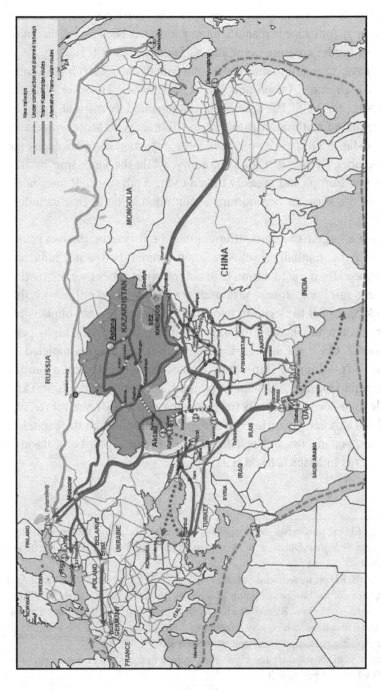

Map 6.1   Kazakhstan in the system of international transport corridors

Source: Kazakhstan Ministry for Investments and Development (2015)

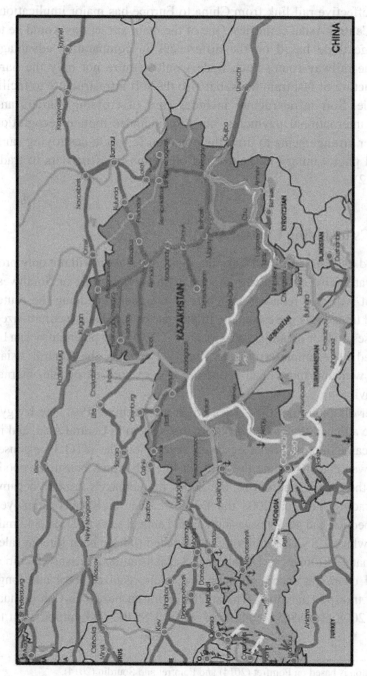

Map 6.2   International Transport Corridors crossing Kazakhstan

Source: Kazakhstan Railways KTZ

An effective rail link from China to Europe has major implications for the Central Asian countries. One of the main attractions would be to encourage trade based on the differences in comparative advantage along the railway route. Such trade would require not only the hard infrastructure of fast train lines, but also the soft infrastructure to facilitate trade. Soft infrastructure includes ease of crossing borders and making international payments, but also includes mutual recognition and other arrangements to limit the potential for trade-destroying sanitary and phytosanitary measures and other non-tariff barriers to trade (Case 6.2).

4. GVCs including Central Asia[8]

Improved overland transport links through Central Asia will not only provide an attractive cost/speed route from China to Europe or Southwest Asia, but will also reduce trade costs of the countries along the route. Reduced trade costs are especially important for small and medium-sized enterprises and for potential participants in GVCs. The potentiality can be illustrated by examples from the Kyrgyz Republic, the Central Asian country with the most open economic system and reasonable internet connectivity.

After dissolution of the Soviet Union in December 1991, the Kyrgyz Republic adopted the most open economic system in Central Asia, and in 1998 became the first Soviet successor state to join the WTO. One consequence was that it became the entrepôt through which consumer goods entered the region, and during the 2000s the country's bazaars became major trading hubs. In 2008 the Dordoi bazaar in Bishkek employed 55,000 people, had 40,300 sales outlets and annual sales of US$2,842 million, of which US$2,131 million are estimated to have been foreign sales (to ultimate customers in Uzbekistan, Kazakhstan and Russia); facilities included overnight accommodation and well-organized local and long-distance transport facilities. The smaller Karasuu bazaar in Osh (annual sales in 2008 of US$684 million, of which US$400-500 million went to

---

[8] This section is based on Pomfret (2014) and Pomfret and Sourdin (2014).

Uzbekistan) involved mainly ethnic Uzbek traders with family connections on both sides of the border.[9]

The logistics developed around the bazaars facilitated the development of production for export, notably the rapid growth since the early 2000s of an export-oriented clothing industry located primarily in Bishkek and to a lesser extent in Osh. At independence, textiles accounted for over 80% of light industry production in the Kyrgyz republic and clothing for 15%. Following disintegration of the unified Soviet economic space and the breakdown of supply chains, output of textiles and clothing collapsed in the 1990s. Re-emergence in the 2000s was based on clothing exports to Russia and Kazakhstan.[10] The clothing producers are mostly small and informal; official estimates are of exports of US$170 million in 2008 falling to US$155 million during the global recession in 2009, and of employment just over 100,000, but the actual numbers for exports and employment are believed to be three to four times higher. Material inputs are mostly imported from China, with a significant portion purchased at the Dordoi bazaar (Birkman *et al.*, 2012; Nurbek, 2014).

The open Kyrgyz economy has also had success in agricultural GVCs, importing know-how and inputs and benefitting from foreign intermediaries with knowledge of export markets. With the introduction of new bean varietals, primarily from Turkey, the land devoted to bean production in Talas oblast increased from 5,000 hectares in 1999 to 45,000 hectares in 2012, as small-scale farmers became competitive producers supplying export markets in Turkey, Bulgaria and Russia (Tilekeyev, 2013). A combination of forces may have been necessary to stimulate the technology transfer and investment from Turkey, but some degree of policy certainty related to WTO membership and liberal trade policies helped.[11] Tilekeyev

---

[9]Data in this paragraph are from surveys in summer 2008 (World Bank, 2009). On the operation of the bazaars, see also Kaminski and Raballand (2009) and Kaminski and Mitra (2010).

[10]Textile production has not recovered, and accounted for less than 10% of light industry production in 2010; the largest cotton textile producer went bankrupt in 2012.

[11] Geography mattered as bean production was concentrated in two of the four rayons, Kara-Buura (72% of cropland devoted to beans) and Bakai-Ata (87% of cropland devoted to beans), both located between 1,000 and 1,400 meters above sea level (the other two rayons are lower and higher) and with plentiful water and a hot-weather growing season

uses household survey data from May–June 2011 to show that households specializing in beans were significantly better off than non-bean producers. By 2011 bean production generated employment for 162,000 people in Talas, and although still a minor player in the global market the Kyrgyz Republic was one of the world's top 20 bean exporters.[12]

The significance of the value chain lies in the emergence of many small and medium-sized enterprises offering intermediary services. Several local companies have imported cleaning equipment, and they grade and pack the beans in standard 25-kilogram and 50-kilogram polypropylene bags and offer storage services. There is an active web-based market in transport services to Europe, Russia and China. A Bulgarian company, emphasizing the reliable quality of the Talas beans, is negotiating a contract to provide packaging and marketing services for the EU market. The basic lesson is that with good hard and soft infrastructure new products and markets can develop, including niches that previously did not exist and whose existence was not predicted.

5. Prospects for Agricultural Trade along a "New Silk Road"

The historical Silk Road was actually several routes whose relative importance ebbed and flowed, and the goods transported by caravans along the route also varied. In the prime of Baghdad and Damascus, melons from today's Uzbekistan were highly prized in those cities. Other cultivated crops, such as grapes, peaches, vegetables, spices and sugar enhanced their geographic distribution with the help of silk road merchants. The SREB could revive such mutually beneficially trade in agricultural products as long as the hard and soft infrastructure were improved.

(May-August). Before independence transport links from Talas went primarily to Dzhambul (now Taraz) in Kazakhstan, and better road links to Bishkek had to be developed in the 1990s.

[12]On the negative side, an export-oriented monoculture exposes Talas to market volatility, especially as domestic consumption is low, and to risks of land degradation and disease (Tilekeyev, 2013, 6). Hegay (2013) reports that due to poor markets farmers do not always have access to clean seeds, and this is responsible for the spread of pathogens and declining yields.

The main agricultural product traded along this route today is wheat from Kazakhstan. Kazakhstan is one of the world's leading wheat exporters, and its high quality wheat is well regarded, especially for making pasta-style noodles.[13] Important markets since independence have included neighboring countries in Central Asia, but also China, Iran, Turkey, Egypt and other Arab states. The quantities are, however, often small and highly volatile due to logistical difficulties. The wheat is grown in northern Kazakhstan and, apart from sales to China and Central Asia, mostly passes through Caspian or Black Sea ports. Kazakhstan's wheat exports face problems of accessing rolling stock, of low priority on the Russian rail network, and of access to space in grain elevators at the rail station and seaports; all of these are exacerbated in good harvest years. Kazakhstan is addressing the problems by upgrading Aktau port and buying or leasing facilities in Georgia and Azerbaijan. In 2014 a new rail line was opened along the Caspian to Turkmenistan and Iran. In 2015 Kazakhstan joined the World Trade Organization.[14]

Global wheat demand is projected to increase from 666 million tons in 2010 to 880 million tons by 2050, with increasing import demand primarily coming from Africa and the Middle East. Practically all of the increased exports will come from North America, the EU, Australia, Argentina, Kazakhstan, Russia and Ukraine (KRU). The KRU share of world trade is variable, but it has increased substantially over the last quarter century, from 3% in 1992 to 12% in 2010 (Burkitbayeva and Kerr, 2013), and 29% in 2015/2016. Kazakhstan has found markets in Southwest Asia (Turkey and Iran) and North Africa (Egypt and Tunisia), but is hampered by higher transport costs, e.g. in January 2013 wheat from the Black Sea was selling in the Gulf states at US$340 for Ukrainian wheat, US$355 for Russian wheat and US$425 for Kazakhstan wheat.[15] An efficient Eurasian rail or

---

[13] In 2015/2016, Kazakhstan, with 7.5 million tons, was the world's eighth largest wheat exporter.

[14] All Kazakhstan's wheat competitors are WTO members facing "most favored nation" (MFN) tariffs, while wheat importers often impose much higher tariffs on imports from non-members; e.g. both Turkey and China have bound MFN tariffs on wheat of 65%, but occasionally levy non-MFN tariffs of 180% and 130% respectively (Burkitbayeva and Kerr, 2014, 1).

[15] Five-year average market shares of Kazakhstan's wheat exports to the top ten destinations

multimodal transport network would allow China and others to tap these supplies more favourably when needing to import wheat.

More generally, a well-functioning SREB would allow efficient specialization and trade among the countries from the EU or from Southwest Asia to China. This prospect is especially important for agriculture because the great variation in geographical conditions can support production of a large variety of agricultural products and because reliable rail service is well-suited to handling perishable goods. Air freight services offer faster delivery, but are typically too expensive for any but the most highly demanded niche agricultural products or delivery to high-income countries. Maritime transport is cheaper but slower, and almost always has to be part of a multimodal network. Rail is well-suited to providing reliable service among land-linked countries. The vision of high-speed trains, i.e. over 200 kilometers per hour (kph) for freight, holds huge promise for linking Central Asia to the east and the west, and promoting agricultural production and trade across those countries.

6. Opportunities for Participation in GVCs

The striking failure of Central Asian countries to diversify their exports beyond a narrow range of primary products (oil and gas, cotton and minerals) has often been ascribed to high costs of international trade due to the region's landlockedness.[16] More recently, however, commentators have pointed to the benefits of location in a dynamic neighborhood and for the failure to become land-linked; high trade costs that have been as much due to poor policies and institutions as to geography. An ADB study on transport, trade and transit that was coordinated with a broader United Nations Development Program (UNDP) project on Central Asia highlighted the impact of poor hard and soft infrastructure and the welfare costs of foregone trade (UNDP, 2005; ADB, 2006). The coordinator of that project Johannes Linn (2004) highlighted the potential for Central

---

in 2008/2012 were Azerbaijan 17.25%, Turkey 13.58%, Tajikistan 9.52%, Iran 9.35%, Kyrgyzstan 8.15%, Egypt 7.48%, Uzbekistan 7.23%, Tunisia 4.89%, Georgia 4.85% and Turkmenistan 3.30%.

[16]On landlockedness, see Raballand (2003), Cadot *et al.* (2006) and Grigoriou (2007).

Asia to be land-linked to some of the world's most dynamic economies. Nevertheless, trade outside the major primary product exports has remained small, and Central Asia is notably absent from the development of GVCs which have flourished to the west in the EU and to the east in Factory Asia (Pomfret and Sourdin, 2014).

There is considerable anecdotal evidence of high trade costs in Central Asia, but little systematic research. An oft-cited example is export of Kyrgyz onions to Siberia, which had thrived in the early 1990s but disappeared by the late 1990s, because of the high cost of transiting Kazakhstan due to a mixture of border delays and frequent stops along Kazakhstan roads when official or unofficial payments were demanded before the truck could continue on its journey; by the time the onions reached Russia, the cost exceeded the value of the sale.[17]

The most frequently cited supporting evidence is from the World Bank's *Doing Business* database. In *Doing Business 2015*, the four Central Asian countries covered ranked between 77th and 166th out of 189 countries for overall ease of doing business, but they were among the seven worst places in the world for ease of conducting international trade (Table 6.1). Turkmenistan was not covered, but would probably have been lower than the other four Central Asian countries. In *Doing Business 2016*, which assessed performance in June 2015, the four Central Asian countries had moved to substantially higher ranks for both overall ease of doing business and ease of international trade. The figures in Table 6.1 are misleading for both years; the situation was not quite so bad as the June 2014 rankings imply and the scale of improvement between 2014 and 2015 is unbelievable. The relative positions of the four countries in June 2015 is plausible and corresponds to casual observation, but the *Doing Business* numbers tell us little about the real costs of international trade in Central Asia.[18]

---

[17] It is logical for each policeman or other agent along the route to take a cut, but when added together these cuts killed the trade, and everybody (Kyrgyz farmers and drivers, Kazakh policemen and border officials and Russian consumers of onions) ended up with nothing. This is a tragedy of the anticommons, in which too many people hold rights of exclusion leading to underuse of, say, the route (Heller, 1998; Buchanan and Yoon, 2000), in contrast to the tragedy of the commons where nobody has rights of exclusion leading to, say, exhaustion of deep-sea fisheries.

[18] The *Doing Business* methodology is based on asking informed people in national

Table 6.1   Ease of Doing Business, June 2014 and June 2015 (rank out of 189 countries)

Country	Overall Ease of Doing Business[a]		Ease of International Trade	
	June 2014	June 2015	June 2014	June 2015
Kazakhstan	77	41	185	122
Kyrgyz Republic	102	67	183	83
Tajikistan	166	132	188	132
Uzbekistan	141	87	189	159

Source: World Bank at http://www.doingbusiness.org/rankings.
Notes: a = overall rank based on unweighted average of scores in the ten areas. Turkmenistan not included.

The Corridor Performance Measurement and Monitoring (CPMM) program conducted by freight forwarders under the aegis of the Central Asian Regional Economic Cooperation Secretariat (ADB, 2014) provides the most convincing indicators of high trade costs in Central Asia and some neighboring countries. These indicators are based on a large number of trips, and provide a detailed picture of the difficulties of conducting overland trade in Central Asia.[19] Some of the physical infrastructure is good, e.g. the Tashkent-Beyneu corridor (part of the E40 route to Berlin) has been upgraded so that speeds of 100 kilometers per hour (kph) are possible in parts and 60 kph on most of it (a big improvement over the Kungrad-Beyneu section which was a rough dirt road seven years ago). In 2012, however, crossing the border took on average 30 hours at the Kazakhstan border crossing post (BCP) and 14 hours at the Uzbekistan BCP (CAREC, 2012, 24). This is typical of a general pattern of some improvements in roads but little improvement in trade

---

capitals about the cost in dollars and in time of shipping a container from the country's commercial center. This may be appropriate for a country like Singapore but is less appropriate for the Central Asian countries where a small share of trade is by container and where there is a large variance between what an observer in the capital city may hear and what happens on the ground.

[19] The 2012 sample consisted of 3,194 trips, of which 80% were by road, 17% by rail and 3% intermodal.

facilitation; indeed, for many BCPs delays have become longer, apart from those between Russia and Kazakhstan which have shortened since the establishment of the customs union in 2010. The longest delays are on the corridor with the highest volume of freight, the railway between China and Kazakhstan; at the border between China and Kazakhstan the average time at the Chinese BCP was 353 hours and at the Kazakhstani BCP 54 hours.[20] The exception to the long delays is the Chongqing-Duisburg train which has special wagons to facilitate the gauge change and which is subject to simplified border formalities. This last observation and the changes at the Kazakhstan-Russia border suggest that governments could facilitate trade, but the political will to do so for intra-Central Asian trade has been lacking.[21]

The principal corridor from Central Asia to South Asia is through Afghanistan. Apart from security risks, the two main bottlenecks are the BCPs between Pakistan and Afghanistan, and trucks may face lengthy delays due to convoy requirements on segments of the route in either country (CAREC, 2014, 34).[22] Road upgrading could shorten travel times, the BCPs could be better designed to separate passenger traffic

---

[20] Some of this is associated with the change of gauge, but delays are mostly associated with customs, quarantine, etc. It is difficult to allocate the time to one BCP rather than the other because delays at one BCP lead to back-up of trains at the other, e.g. delays entering Kazakhstan lead to back-up at the Chinese BCP, and there is a suspicion that these 2012 data are influenced by the customs union's hardline towards goods entering from China (CAREC, 2012, 21).

[21] Although there is anecdotal evidence that the level and frequency of corruption has declined, the 2012 CPMM annual report found a 32% chance that "unofficial payments" would be demanded at BCPs.

[22] The route from Karachi to Kabul, via Sukkur-D.I.Khan-Peshawar-Torkham, has better roads than the southern route to Kandahar via Chaman and Spin Boldak. However, trucks are required to form convoys at D.I.Khan, and the BCP at Peshawar is 55 km from the border. Trucks took an average 34 hours to pass though the Peshawar BCP in 2014. This entire segment from D.I.Khan to the border is prone to delays, and truckers report a high level of demand for unofficial payments. The average time at the Afghan BCP, Torkham, was 39.5 hours in 2014. At both BCPs, most of the delay was associated with customs procedures, but the queuing also led to large variance in time. Crossing times were even longer at the Chaman-Spin Boldak BCPs, 36 hours and 60 hours respectively, i.e. four days and nights to cross the frontier. The security on this route is poorer than on the Kabul route.

from goods, and improvement in the security situation would also reduce some concerns. However, the principal source of delays is customs procedures.[23]

An alternative route from Central Asia to Pakistan passes through the ancient crossroad of Kashgar (Kashi) in Xinjiang Autonomous Region of China, and there has been an increase in traffic between Bishkek and Karachi via the Karakoram Highway, which is being upgraded by China in the US$43 billion China-Pakistan Economic Corridor Project (Ritzinger, 2015). According to freight forwarders in Pakistan, a truck carrying 20 tons from Bishkek to Karachi via the Karakorum Highway takes 9 to 11 days and costs US$8,500. There are problems due to high altitude and winter closures, and currently the BCP between China and Pakistan is not designed to handle large volumes and officials at the BCP are often unfamiliar with Kyrgyz documents and seals (CAREC, 2014, 33). Traffic has also increased between Dushanbe and Kashgar (CAREC, 2014, 26). Geographically the Karakoram Highway will always be more challenging than routes through Afghanistan, but it provides a feasible alternative route from Central Asia if the transit situation through Afghanistan fails to improve. Current problems at BCPs could be reduced if the Central Asian countries, China and Pakistan, wanted to foster trade along this corridor.

Connections between Central Asia and Iran have been limited in the past, but appear to be on the cusp of improved connectivity.[24] The current rail link from Mashad through Turkmenistan and Uzbekistan is underused, primarily because transit obstacles make it unattractive. In December 2014 the Presidents of Kazakhstan, Turkmenistan and Iran formally hammered the last spike in a new railway along the Caspian coast (Map 6.1 and 6.2). This project reflects increasing engagement of the latter two

---

[23]The two authorities have difficulty sharing information about freight because Afghanistan use ASYCUDA World, while Pakistam uses the proprietary Web-Based One Customs System.

[24]Sanctions were imposed on Iran after the 1979 occupation of the US Embassy and were subsequently modified at various times in relation to the Iran-Iraq War, alleged money laundering and other illegal acts, and Iran's nuclear program. A July 2015 agreement to lift sanctions was implemented in January 2016, although US banks continued to observe some restrictions on financial transactions. In April 2016 meetings, the Iranian and Turkish presidents and the Iranian Prime Minister and EU High Commissioner for Foreign Affairs agreed to work more closely on facilitating trade.

countries in international trade and Kazakhstan's desire for links to Southwest Asia and the Middle East as an alternative to the Caspian Sea crossing or transiting Russia to Black Sea ports. The new railway's connection to the Kazakhstan rail network is potentially important, improving on current rail connections between Russia or China and Southwest Asia. The first Chinese train to Iran reached Tehran in April 2016.[25]

The significance of these new links to South and Southwest Asia is that what was previously a transport system centered on a few major corridors is becoming a network in which users can shop around for alternative routes to their suppliers or markets. These alternatives may not always be apparent when the new road or railway is being constructed. The China-Pakistan Economic Corridor Project of upgrading the Karakoram Highway opened up new options for Central Asian truckers to reach Pakistan because it coincided with improvements in roads from Tajikistan and the Kyrgyz Republic to China, and there could be a virtuous circle as the new option encourages improvements in hard and soft infrastructure between Central Asia and Kashgar and along the Karakoram Highway. Similarly, the Kazakhstan-Turkmenistan-Iran railway could stimulate increased trade not only among those three countries, but also between Russia or China and Southwest Asia; Indian sources are even foreseeing a new link from Mumbai to Kazakhstan via Chabahar port (Map 6.1).[26]

The conclusion from this section is that physical connectivity of Central Asia to surrounding regions is improving, but the soft infrastructure that results in high trade costs remains poor. The two are, however, interconnected in that, as potential traders face more alternatives, there could be a virtuous race to the bottom in reducing obstacles to trade. The Kyrgyz onions case remains a stark warning of the dangers of a tragedy of the anticommons, but Central Asian policymakers are generally more

---

[25]For more details of Iranian connectivity, see "Iran's New Trains: Joining the Dots: Some treats ahead for railway enthusiasts", *The Economist* (London), April 2, 2016.

[26]Chabahar is Iran's only port directly on the Indian Ocean. A master plan for its development was drawn up in the 1970s but shelved after the 1979 revolution. In the 1990s India contributed to some construction work, and since the early 2000s has been negotiating more substantial involvement, with the goal of accessing Afghanistan, and potentially other long-distance rail trade, without transiting Pakistan.

aware of these dangers and of potential gains from trade in the 2010s than in the 1990s.

Conclusion

The SREB and AIIB are initiatives holding economic promise for Central Asia as a central location between China and Europe. With modern technology, the vision of a Eurasian high-speed rail network that includes either a China-Astana-Volgograd-EU mainline or a China-Tashkent-Istanbul mainline with spurs to the Middle East and North Africa is a feasible prospect. Improved connectivity will bring many benefits, including promotion of agricultural specialization and trade, including some areas of past specialization (such as Uzbek melons) and some that have been unexpected (such as Kyrgyz beans), and integration of Central Asian producers into manufacturing GVCs. The diversity of comparative advantage and geographic conditions across China, the EU and Central Asia, not to mention Russia, Turkey, Iran or the Arab world, suggests that such possibilities for specialization and trade are almost endless. Unreliable, slow and expensive transport impacts especially on agricultural products and most of all on small and medium-sized enterprises; the SREB stimulus can be regionally broad and economically inclusive.

References

ADB (2006). *Central Asia: Increasing Gains from Trade through Regional Cooperation in Trade Policy, Transport and Customs Transit* (Asian Development Bank: Manila).

ADB (2014). *Central Asia Regional Economic Cooperation Corridor Performance Measurement and Monitoring: A Forward-looking Perspective* (Asian Development Bank: Manila).

Birkman, L., Kaloshnika M., Khan M., Shavurov U. & Smallhouse S. (2012). Textile and Apparel Cluster in Kyrgyzstan (Harvard University Kennedy School and Harvard Business School, Cambridge MA) — available at http://www.isc.hbs. edu/pdf/Student_Projects/2012%20MOC%20Papers/Kyrgystan_Textile%20 and%20Apparel1%20Cluster_Final_May%204%202012.pdf.

Boulègue, M. (2013). Xi Jinping's Grand Tour of Central Asia: Asserting China's Growing Economic Clout, *Central Asia Economic Paper No. 9,* Elliott School of International Affairs, The George Washington University, Washington DC.

Burkitbayeva, S., & Kerr W. (2013). The Accession of Kazakhstan, Russia and Ukraine to the WTO: What Will it Mean for the World Trade in Wheat? *CATPRN Paper 2013–06,* Canadian Agricultural Trade Policy and Competitiveness Research Network (http://www.catrade.org).

Buchanan, J. & Yoon, Y. (2010). Symmetric Tragedies: Commons and Anticommons. *Journal of Law and Economics* 43(1):1–13.

Cadot, O., Carrère C. & Grigoriou C. (2006). *Landlockedness, Infrastructure and Trade in Central Asia* — in two-volumes (World Bank: Washington DC).

CAREC (2012). *Corridor Performance Measurement and Monitoring Annual Report 2012* — available at http://cfcfa.net/cpmm-annual-and-quarterly-reports/2012-annual-report/.

CAREC (2014). *Corridor Performance Measurement and Monitoring Annual Report 2014* — available at http://cfcfa.net.

Grigoriou, C. (2007). Landlockedness, Infrastructure and Trade: New estimates for Central Asian countries, *World Bank Policy Research Working Paper 4335* (World Bank: Washington DC).

Heller, M. (1998). The Tragedy of the Anticommons: Property in the Transition from Marx to Markets. *Harvard Law Review.* 111(3): 621–88.

Hegay, S. (2013). Diversity of Beans Grown in Kyrgyzstan and Marker-aided Breeding for Resistance to Bean Common Mosaic Virus and Anthracnose, Doctoral Thesis No. 2013:35, Faculty of Landscape Planning, Horticulture and Agricultural Science, Sveriges lantbruksuniversitet (Swedish University of Agricultural Sciences), Alnarp — available online at http://pub.epsilon.slu.se/10425/1/hegay s 130510.pdf.

Kaminski, B., and Mitra S. (2010). *Skeins of Silk: Borderless bazaars and border trade in Central Asia* (Washington DC, World Bank).

Kaminski, B., and Raballand G. (2009). Entrepôt for Chinese Consumer Goods in Central Asia: Re-exports through Kyrgyzstan — A Statistical Puzzle, *Eurasian Geography and Economics* 50, 581–90.

Kassenova, N. (2009). China as an Emerging Donor in Tajikistan and Kyrgyzstan, *Russie.Nei.Visions No. 36,* Russia/NIS Center, IFRI, Paris.

Knowler, G. (2015). Time Healing Supplier Pain as China's Go West Policy gathers Momentum,*JOC,* 13 January—http://www.joc.com/international-logistics/time-healing-supplier-pain-china's-go-west-policy-gathers-momentum_20150113.html.

Linn, J. (2004). *Economic (Dis)Integration Matters: The Soviet Collapse Revisited* (Brookings Institution: Washington DC).

Nurbek, J. (2014). Export-driven SME Development in Kyrgyzstan: The Garment Manufacturing Sector, *Institute of Public Policy and Administration Working Paper* No. 26, University of Central Asia, Bishkek.

Pomfret, R. (1995). *The Economies of Central Asia* (Princeton University Press, Princeton NJ).

Pomfret, R. (2006). *The Central Asian Economies Since Independence* (Princeton University Press, Princeton NJ).

Pomfret, R. (2014). Trade Costs and Agricultural Trade in Central Asia, Leibniz Institute of *Agricultural Development in Transition Economies (IAMO) Discussion Paper No. 146*, Halle, Germany.

Pomfret, R., and Sourdin P. (2014). Global Value-Chains and Connectivity in Developing Asia — with Application to the Central and West Asian Region, ADB Working Paper Series on Regional Economic Integration No. 142, Asian Development Bank, Manila.

Raballand, G. (2003). Determinants of the Negative Impact of being Landlocked on Trade: An Empirical Investigation through the Central Asian Case, *Comparative Economic Studies 45(4),* 520–36.

Ritzinger, L. (2015). The China-Pakistan Economic Corridor, *National Bureau of Asian Research, NBR Commentary*, 5 August.

Summers, T. (2013). China: Still 'Going West'? *East Asia Forum Quarterly 5(3)*, July-September — available at http://www.eastasiaforum.org/quarterly/.

Tiezzi, S. (2014) China's 'New Silk Road' Vision Revealed, *The Diplomat*, 9 May — http://thediplomat.com/2014/05/chinas-new-silk-road-vision-revealed/.

Tilekeyev, K. (2013). Productivity Implications of Participation in Export Activities: The case of farmers in Talas Oblast of Kyrgyzstan, *University of Central Asia Institute of Public Policy and Administration, Working Paper No.17.*

UNDP (2005). *Central Asia Human Development Report: Bringing Down Barriers: Regional Cooperation for Human Development and Human Security* (United Nations Development Programme: Bratislava).

Uysal, O. (2014). *Rail Turkey* 3 December 2014 — available at http://railturkey.org/2014/12/03/kazakhstan-turkmenistan-iran-railway/.

Wong, C.T. (2015). Xi'an Readies for Key Role in "One Belt, One Road" Initiative, *Global Times* 21 April — available at http://www.globaltimes.cn/content/917943.shtml.

World Bank (2009). *Bazaars and Trade Integration in CAREC Countries*, report prepared by Saumya Mitra, Bartlomiej Kaminski and Matin Kholmatov, available at http://www.carecinstitute.org/uploads/events/2009/10th-TPCC/10thTPPC-Bazaars-Trade-Integration-Paper.pdf.

Case 6.1   Khorgos Gateway: A major logistics hub along the SREB

Khorgos: A Free Economic Zone at the China-Kazakhstan border

Khorgos (Horgos for the Chinese) was a transit point on the ancient Silk Road during the Tang Dynasty (618–907 A.D.). The city is located in China, Xinjiang province at the Kazakhstan border, 670 km from Urumqi (China), and 378 km from Almaty (Kazakhstan). The initiative of the creation of the Khorgos International Center of Boundary Cooperation (ICBC) was taken during the official visit of the president of Kazakhstan Nursultan Nazarbayev to China in 2002. The formal agreement was signed in 2004. The presidential decree creating the Special Economic Zone (SEZ) "Khorgos-East Gate" was signed in 2011: it is an area of 528 hectares (ha) (185 ha on Kazakhstan side, and 343 ha on Chinese side), including a logistic zone, an industrial zone, and a "dry port" for cargo transshipment, the storage of containers, and reduction of transit time. The capacity of the "dry port" — 200,000 containers per year in 2016 — was expected to reach 500,000 by 2020.

Khorgos is a major logistics hub along the "Silk Road Economic Belt", and one of the biggest Sino-Kazakh joint projects. Khorgos-East Gate combines the functions of a customs checkpoint, logistics hub, free trade area and industrial park. Companies investing in the SEZ are exempted from corporate income tax, land tax, property tax and value added tax. The Khorgos Railway started operations in 2012. The majority of the cargo in 2015 was transshipment moving from China to Europe through the territory Kazakhstan, but the hub also serves the needs of regional trade between Kazakhstan and Chinese Xinjiang province: cargo passing through Khorgos accounted for half of Xinjiang's import/export volume.

Kazakhstan national program "Nurly Zhol" and the SREB

China's Jiangsu province plans to invest US$600 million in the development of Khorgos-East Gate SEZ logistic projects with Kazakhstan Railways (KTZ). China and Kazakhstan are jointly building a logistics terminal in the port of Lianyungang in Jiangsu province (East China), offering rail connections to Kazakhstan, Iran, Turkey and Europe, as well as maritime links with major Chinese ports, the port of Busan (South Korea) and Osaka (Japan).

(Continued)

Case 6.1   (*Continued*)

The terminal began operation in 2014, offering new export opportunities to Kazakhstan. In 2015 the container trains from Lianyungang to Kazakhstan through Khorgos were carrying medical supplies, auto parts and electronic products from southern parts of China, Southeast Asia, Japan and South Korea. They carried ferroalloy, potash fertilizer and wheat from Kazakhstan to China.

There is convergence between Kazakhstan national "Nurly Zhol" (bright path to the future) program for infrastructure development (2015 to 2019), aiming at Kazakhstan integration in the network of Eurasia international corridors, and China's SREB initiative. The two countries are planning, for example, the construction of a trans-Kazakhstan railway line from Khorgos to Kazakh Aktau seaport along the Caspian Sea, providing access to Azerbaijan, Georgia and Turkey. Kazakh and Chinese financial institutions both contribute to project financing.

Sources: JSC "National Company 'Kazakhstan Temir Zholy' (KTZ), Kazinform, KTZE-Khorgos Gateway" LLP, Ministry of Foreign Affairs of the People's Republic of China, SEZ Khorgos-East Gate (ICBC) and The Institute of World Economics and Politics (IWEP).

Case 6.2   Silk Road Railways from China to the EU

After some experimental starts in 2010 and 2011 with individual trains connecting Sichuan province and Chongqing Municipality with Germany, regular service by bonded train between Chongqing and Duisburg was established; 233 trips had been completed between 2011 and the end of 2014, carrying cargo worth US$6.8 billion, half from Chongqing and Chengdu, 30% from the Yangtze Delta region around Shanghai and 20% from the Pearl River Delta region around Guangzhou (CAREC, 2014, 41). By the end of 2015, alternative routes from Chengdu, Wuhan, Suzhou, Zhengzhou and other cities to Europe were also being tried (Table 6.2).

In 2015 the Chongqing-Duisburg train ran on a fixed timetable three times a week, with extension to Spain once a week; 347 trains had gone from China to Duisburg between 2011 and the end of 2015. The service operated as a joint venture between Chinese, German, Kazakh and Russian rail companies. The Chengdu-Łódź train also ran on a fixed schedule, once a week. Other routes

(*Continued*)

Case 6.2 (*Continued*)

appear to be served when trains were full, and on an experimental basis, e.g. trains from Changsha have gone to three different destinations.

Table 6.2   Alternative routes from China to Europe

	Route	Start	Length km	Duration days
Yuxinou	Chongqing – Duisburg (DE)	July 2011	11,179	16
Hanxinou	Wuhan – Mělnik (CZ)	Oct 2012	10,863	16
Sumanou	Suzhou – Warsaw (PL)	Nov 2012	11,200	18
Rongou	Chengdu – Łódź (PL)	April 2013	9,826	10.5
Zhengou	Zhengzhou – Hamburg (DE)	July 2013	10,124	19–20
Yixinou	Yiwu – Madrid (ES)	Nov 2014	13,052	21
Hexinou	Hefei – Kazakhstan	June 2014		
	Hefei – Hamburg (DE)		11,000	15
Xiangou	Changsha – Duisburg/Moscow/Tashkent	Oct 2014	11,808	18
Haou	Harbin – Hamburg (DE)	June 2015	9,820	15

Source: Li, Yuan, Kierstin Bolton and Theo Westphal (2016): The Effect of the New Silk Road Railways on Aggregate Trade Volumes between China and Europe, Institute of East Asia Studies Working Paper No. 109, Universität Duisburg Essen, Germany, 8.

To electronics firms in Western China supplying EU markets (e.g. HP, Acer and Foxconn) and to EU firms shipping parts between their operations in Europe and in China (e.g. Volkswagen, Audi and BMW), the Eurasian rail link offered an attractive price/time option, faster than by sea and at lower cost than by air. CAREC (2014, 41) reports that in 2014 a 40-foot container cost US\$9,600 from Chongqing to Duisburg by rail and took 16–18 days, compared to 45 days by sea, while the sea freight from Shanghai to Rotterdam cost US\$3,000, rail from Chongqing to Shanghai US\$1,000, plus an inventory cost for the 45 days of an estimated US\$2,000. Li, *et al.* (2016, 17) report that the Chongqing-Duisburg rail service undercuts ocean shipping time by 20 days and airfreight cost by 80%.

Chapter 7

Financing China's "Belt and Road" Initiative*

Shi Jianxun

Tongji University, Institute of Finance and Economics

Chinese President Xi Jinping proposed the construction of the "Silk Road Economic Belt" and the "21st Century Maritime Silk Road" (referred to as the "Belt and Road" or "B&R") as a strategic concept in September and October 2013. The initiative is an important means for China's all-round opening-up in the new international context. But it also represents a major contribution — with an immediate as well as a long-term impact — to the trend toward regional and global cooperation, to meeting the development needs of the countries and regions along the B&R, and to greater sharing of development opportunities and achievements among countries.

The B&R run through the continents of Asia, Europe and Africa. The vibrant economic zone of East Asia lies at one end, the developed European economic zone at the other, and in between are a great many countries with vast development potential. Whether it is economic development and improving living standards or dealing with crisis and speeding up adjustment, many countries along the B&R share common

---

*The author thanks Dr. Wang Panpan of Tongji University for his assistance and significant contributions in writing this chapter.

interests with China. Most of them are emerging economies and developing countries. Over the next decade they will see a pick up in the pace of economic development, with an acceleration of industrialization and urbanization, all of which imply strong demand for infrastructure investment. Thus there are broad possibilities for mutually beneficial cooperation between China and these countries. For the countries of Europe, interconnections with Eurasia — the world's largest landmass — at present are quite poor. Greater connectivity with Eurasia would facilitate economic ties, investment and trade between Asia and Europe, greatly reducing transaction costs to the benefit of both the Asian and the European countries.

The B&R initiative is particularly timely and rich in implications. As soon as the concept was put forward, it drew expressions of strong interest and endorsement from the related countries and regions and at the world level. Countries along the "Belt and Road" and in Europe have shown broad support for the initiative, actively linking it into their own development strategies. The B&R initiative can be expected to greatly facilitate the interconnection of Eurasia's mainland coastal areas and hinterlands and contribute to the economic growth of underdeveloped hinterland regions. It will change the global economy's spatial layout and resource flows, thus profoundly altering the geo-economic dependence of coastal areas worldwide and contributing to more balanced global development.

1. Building the B&R Requires Strong Financial Support

The financial system of ancient China effectively supported the construction of the original Silk Road, thus boosting trade and prosperity along the route as well as the integration of East and West. Chinese and foreign coins from the period found along the Silk Road trail, like the copper recovered undersea along the ancient Maritime Silk Road (MSR), reflect the symbiosis of Silk Road trade and financial activity. Finance indeed played an important and necessary role for the ancient Silk Road and MSR. The process of building the Silk Road linked countries closely together through the medium of financial relations. Such ties not only accelerated the successful development of trade and transport, but also effectively encouraged cultural exchange and communication among the peoples of the East and the West.

We can learn from this history that financial arrangements will also play a vital role in the 21st century B&R initiative. Financial support is urgently needed. The goal is to develop comprehensive, three-dimensional, multi-level interconnections, with a focus on promoting connectedness and interlinkages embracing the five areas of policy, infrastructure, trade, finance and interpersonal ties among the B&R countries and regions. Effective means of financial support are essential for this ambitious plan. On the one hand, financing is one of the five key forms of interconnectedness within the initiative; on the other, financing will be integral to the implementation and promotion of all the other dimensions.

Firstly, building the B&R requires funds on a vast scale. The 65 countries (regions) along the B&R have a combined population of about US$4.5 billion and US$20 trillion of economic activity — 63% and 29% of world totals, respectively. These countries are all at an important stage of industrialization and urbanization, and thus have huge economic development potential. It is estimated that by 2030 the region's overall share of world GDP will reach 35%, meaning it will become an important engine of global economic growth. The role of relevant financial support will be particularly important in this process. Annual infrastructure investments of up to some US$800 billion are forecast in Asia alone in coming years, and in 2025 the volume of trade between China and other B&R countries will exceed US$2.5 trillion. The related need for financial services is massive.

Secondly, building the B&R requires diversified sources of funding. Forms of cooperation for B&R projects are quite complex, and funding sources are also quite varied. They include the Asian Infrastructure Investment Bank (AIIB), the Silk Road Fund (SRF), the China-Eurasia Economic Cooperation Fund, the China-CEE Investment Cooperation Fund, the China-ASEAN Maritime Cooperation Fund and other government-level funding bodies. The resources of the World Bank (WB), the Asian Development Bank (ADB) and other multilateral financial organizations will be mobilized. And the initiative will also attract a variety of commercial funds and private capital through public-private partnerships (PPPs). Multiple forms of financing will be used, including loans, guarantees, equity investments and so on, in order to meet specific project needs.

Thirdly, the "Belt and Road" initiative requires complex and differentiated financial services. Projects cover such diverse areas as transport infrastructure, energy resources, trade and investment, industrial cooperation, agriculture, environmental protection, and so on. They involve economic entities at multiple levels — governments, enterprises, individuals and others — engaging in investment, consumption and other activities in multiple business fields. The financial requirements of the "Belt and Road" strategy are thus also extremely complex. The countries along the B&R have three major religions and dozens of languages. They differ widely in their stages of economic development and their economic and financial systems. Financing solutions must take all of these factors into account.

Last but not least, the construction of the B&R involves managing complex financial risks. The political, economic and cultural differences among the countries in the B&R region are quite large and the business climate is complex. Some risk factors are difficult to quantify, like those of a geopolitical, political or religious nature, degrees of social governance, and information security and reputation risks. All of this poses enormous challenges for financial institutions' ability to manage and control risk. In addition, the regulatory environment for financial activities is highly differentiated as regards requirements for compliance, money laundering prevention, liquidity controls and capital adequacy. Thus the effective control of financial risk will be an important issue for B&R-related business.

Clearly, then, advancing the construction of the B&R will demand the continual support of enormous amounts of money and a well-suited international investment and financing system. Financing of the B&R will need to be suited to the development needs of the various countries. It must engage with their development strategy, seeking investment opportunities, providing financial support, and actively contributing to their processes of economic restructuring and sustainable development. Finance for the B&R also needs to promote an interweaving of the complex interests of countries both inside and outside the region. Innovation is called for in offering more public financial products which benefit all parties and promote financial systematization in a spirit of inclusion and openness. Such means of financial support needed to come not only from China, but also from the world, and not only from governments, but also from the private sector.

2. Towards an International Financial System to Support the B&R Initiative

2.1. *AIIB*

The Asian Infrastructure Investment Bank (AIIB) came into being as China fleshed out the B&R strategy, and it has been widely welcomed.

From idea to reality in just over two years

Chinese President Xi Jinping proposed the creation of the AIIB in October 2013 during a visit to Southeast Asia, immediately attracting wide attention and positive reactions in Asia and around the world. Thereafter a total of 57 founding members from Asia and beyond signed up to participate in its creation — significantly more than expected. By the end of 2015, 17 prospective founding members had completed domestic legal procedures, were approved to join the AIIB agreement and had submitted the instruments of ratification. At that point capital subscriptions accounted for 50.1% of allocated shares, satisfying conditions for the bank's formal establishment. The AIIB's opening ceremony took place on January 16, 2016, at the Diaoyutai State Guesthouse in Beijing. Speaking at the ceremony, President Xi Jinping stressed that the proposal for the establishment of the AIIB was a constructive effort on the part of China to assume more international responsibility, promote the improvement of the existing international economic system, and offer international public goods of mutual benefit to the parties involved so that everybody wins.

China, as initiator, actively coordinated efforts during the AIIB's preparatory phase, seeking as far as possible to satisfy the interests and request of the parties involved, and working to ensure the organization's openness, transparency and high standards of governance. Thanks to the sincere cooperation and joint efforts of all parties, the AIIB was successfully launched. This was a landmark event in the process of reform of the international economic governance and financial system. With the launch of the AIIB, a ship full of new hope for Asia and the world set sail. Prospects for the future development of the AIIB are far-reaching.

The AIIB will approve its first lending program this year, with an initial lending scale of between US$1.5 billion and US$2 billion. Annual lending of up to US$10 billion to US$15 billion is projected in the coming five to six years. Initial priority investment areas include energy and power, transportation and telecommunications, rural and agricultural infrastructure, water supply and sewage treatment, environmental protection, urban development and logistics, and so on. Locally, the projects supported by those loans will help accelerate interconnection, enhance self-development capacity and spur economic development in a lasting way. The loans will not only help reinforce the infrastructure engine of economic growth, but will also ensure more efficient utilization of Asian capital and contribute to regional and global economic development. At the same time, they are conducive to an expansion of global demand and will inject new vitality into the world economy to promote world economic recovery.

A strong boost for construction of the B&R

The creation of the AIIB will provide strong financial support for implementing the B&R strategy, with the goals of which it is aligned and complementary. An effective interface between the B&R and the AIIB is key both for the progress of the B&R initiative and for the development of the AIIB. The meeting point of the two is the building of Asian infrastructure. In terms of funding supply, as an investment and financing platform of the B&R, the AIIB can resolve the issues of resource mismatches in Asia and achieve an efficient allocation of Asian savings and investment. The AIIB will also engage in financing and investment globally to support infrastructure development in Asia and the rest of the world, which in turn will improve the investment outlook in the B&R countries. In terms of funding demand, there are currently numerous infrastructure projects in the countries and regions along the B&R that require a large amount of external funding. This is a favorable situation for the use of the AIIB's money.

Currently, the demand for Asian infrastructure financing is huge. The AIIB is positioned to provide financial support for these investment projects, which will foster the building of infrastructure in developing countries, particularly Asia's low-income economies. Thus the AIIB will help these countries accelerate their regional economic integration, share in the fruits of regional and global development, and boost their own level of development along with their capacity for developing links with both emerging and developed economies.

Note that the AIIB will play an important role in promoting the development of information infrastructure, connectivity and internet cooperation throughout the B&R region. A new phase of technological and industrial revolution is now creating a historic opportunity and the internet is increasingly becoming an engine of innovation-driven development. New internet-based industries and commercial activities are evolving rapidly, resulting in huge demand for new information infrastructure. Internet infrastructure and related connectivity are becoming key factors to support and accelerate economic transformation as well as strategic adjustment and growth of innovation regionally and globally.

The AIIB has significant advantages in supporting the needed new infrastructure and investments in connectivity. On the one hand, as a new multilateral financial institution established in the 21st century, the AIIB was born in the information age and has an innate grasp of innovation based on internet technology. On the other hand, the AIIB can also draw on existing multilateral development institutions' many years of accumulated experience and so enjoys the late-mover advantage. On this basis, the AIIB is committed to promoting the integral development of financial services and internet technology, and to closely coupling physical infrastructure projects with the new generation of virtual technology. This will help foster the development of internet cooperation among the B&R economies.

Cooperation with other multilateral development banks

The AIIB will form a healthy and complementary relationship with existing multilateral development banks. Worries that the AIIB could become a strong competitor of the World Bank are unfounded. The world is big enough, and the Pacific Ocean wide enough, for the AIIB to develop alongside other multilateral financial institutions. Given its distinct positioning and business focus, the AIIB has a complementary rather than a zero-sum competitive relation with existing multilateral development banks. There is great space for complementarity among these banks. They can promote each other, learn from each other and contribute better

together to infrastructure, interconnectedness and sustainable development in Asia, through joint financing, knowledge sharing, capacity building and other forms of cooperation and benign competition.

Developing countries have long complained that existing multilateral financial organizations have inefficient project-approval processes,
set excessive limits and thresholds, interfere with borrowers' sovereignty, offer insufficient loan amounts, and so on. The creation of the
AIIB will help to remedy shortcomings in the global financial system
and to fill in the gap of multilateral institutions currently involved in
Asian infrastructure investment. The ADB has estimated that between
2010 and 2020 it needs to invest US$8 trillion in the construction of
infrastructure in the Asia-Pacific region, but the ADB's loans for infrastructure projects are only US$10 billion annually. So there is a huge
financing gap. Currently, the WB, the ADB and other multilateral development institutions are focused on global and regional poverty reduction, and the funds they invest in Asian infrastructure are insufficient to
meet countries' development needs. Over time, the AIIB will strive to
become a professional and efficient investment and financing platform
for Asian infrastructure, helping to boost the level of related financing
and promoting economic and social development. The AIIB will also
pursue open regionalism as a way to complement existing multilateral
lenders, and through its unique features will add new vitality to the
existing multilateral system.

Advanced governance principles for the 21ˢᵗ century

Nor is there any need to worry that the AIIB, led by China, might have
difficulty achieving high standards of governance in its operations.
Admittedly, the AIIB was initiated and is actively promoted by China, and
to a certain extent is considered to bear the Chinese colors — that in fact
is the main reason few people are worried. Because shares are allocated in
proportion to GDP, China is the AIIB's largest shareholder. However, in
decision making and managing operations, China will always adhere to
the principle of collegiality, not acting as a superpower. The AIIB will
always operate as a multilateral development bank owned by all members
under the direct leadership of the board and in accordance with the corporate governance framework agreed upon by all the members. As the initial

promoter of the AIIB, China will continue to firmly support its activities and development. In addition to the timely payment of equity capital, China is also contributing US$50 million to establish a special fund to support the AIIB's less developed member countries in preparing projects for financing. By putting others before itself, adhering to the concept of win-win cooperation and not seeking rights of dominance and control, China is making a selfless contribution as a responsible great power.

The AIIB is a bank which belongs to all its member states and which promotes the common development of the region and the world. In the future, too, the AIIB will continue to adhere to the principles of openness and transparency, actively integrate new members and strive to achieve win-win cooperation. The AIIB aims to strengthen cooperation with existing multilateral development institutions to provide co-financing for investment projects. It will also draw on their experience in the design of its own innovative governance structure and mechanisms for operational decision making, in order to ensure professionalism and efficiency. The AIIB will strive to develop a new type of lean, incorruptible, green and sustainable multilateral financial institutions with advanced 21st century governance principles. Over time this will generate abundant benefits for people in Asia and around the world. The first project financed by the AIIB was the Pakistan motorway in 2016, in partnership with the ADB (Case 7.1).

2.2. SRF

The Silk Road Fund (SRF) is an important Chinese effort to support the construction of the B&R. President Xi Jinping announced on November 8, 2014, at an APEC meeting that China would invest US$40 billion to set up the fund. The SRF was registered in Beijing on December 29, 2014, under the Company Law of the People's Republic of China (PRC), and officially started operation. It was the first of the financial institutions established for the B&R initiative to be launched.

Nature and function of the SRF

The SRF is a long-term development investment fund dedicated to promoting economic and social development and multilateral interconnectivity in the countries and regions along the B&R. As a unilateral financial institution, it is entirely financed by China. The fund has an initial design capacity of US$40 billion, which can be increased on the basis of investment performance and demand. Its first phase of funding, at US$10 billion, is sourced from China's foreign exchange reserves (US$6.5 billion), the Export-Import Bank of China (US$1.5 billion), China Investment Corporation (US$1.5 billion) and the China Development Bank (US$500 million).

As a new member of the financial industry, the function of the SRF is to support construction of the B&R, facilitate outbound investments by Chinese equipment manufacturers and promote international cooperation with regard to production capacity. Through a variety of financing forms, primarily long-term equity-based investments, the fund promotes development and common interests within the B&R framework. Specifically, the SRF will focus on working and aligning thinking at three levels:

First, focus on the macro level, thinking about working together in complementarity. The B&R initiative is highly inclusive and interactive, requiring commonality of approach. President Xi Jinping, speaking at the 2015 Boao Forum for Asia, stressed that the B&R initiative must proceed on the basis of joint discussion, common efforts and achieving joint benefits while aligning countries' development strategies for complementarity. Building the B&R is about promoting the allocation and structural optimization of resources and factors of production across a much wider area. Hence the macro strategies and development requirements of the countries involved need to be coordinated, aligning responsibilities and interests. Financial institutions like the SRF can support the "going out" of Chinese enterprises with a variety of finance and investment tools, offering access to Chinese capital and experience, high-end technology and equipment. In the process, China and the other B&R countries can develop mutual cooperation and achieve mutual benefits.

Second, focus on the industry level, with an eye to forming industrial value chains. The B&R initiative is about creating broad spaces for innovation and industrial advances, and that requires thinking about the formation of industrial value chains. China's opening-up has long been driven by export-led processing, which is in the lower portion of the value chain. More recently, Chinese enterprises "going out" have begun engaging in project contracting, but have lacked sufficient operations management expertise and have had mainly debt financing, with little equity investment. Within the B&R framework, financial institutions like the Silk Road Fund will support a transformation of enterprises' overseas investment from project contracting to a "build-operate-transfer" (BOT) model. The incentive for going global will thus shift from seeking project benefits to expanding the industrial value chain. By supporting equipment exports and cooperation in production capacity, the SRF will promote industrial resource integration and technology upgrades, improve enterprise operation and management, boost capacity for innovation and cross-border cooperation, reshape competitive advantages and eventually, movement up the global value chain.

Third, focus on the financial level and thinking about capital. Capital outflows are important for supporting construction of the B&R, so the effective use of capital needs careful consideration. The experience of industrialized countries shows that, along with production capacity cooperation, capital mobility is necessary for obtaining high-quality industry and technology. That means a higher degree of opening-up. China has the world's highest savings rate, so enterprises undertaking outbound investment can take advantage of abundant liquidity with rational financial planning. Thinking about capital means using capital outflows to drive outbound investments by businesses via financing arrangements. The use of varied forms of financing, such as equity, bonds, funds, credit, credit insurance and currency combinations, can provide projects with effective financial support, accelerate capital cycles and improve investment efficiencies. The SRF and a number of other recently announced investment funds will become primary sources of equity investment and will encourage greater capital investment. In addition, internationalization of the renminbi (RMB) is facilitating diversified multi-currency foreign investments.

Operating principles of the SRF

As a long-term development investment fund, the SRF is focused on supporting infrastructure, resource development, industrial and financial cooperation, and other projects under the B&R framework. It does so on the basis of market standards, seeking long-term financial sustainability and a reasonable returns on investments. In providing financial and investment support for economic and trade cooperation as well as for bilateral and multilateral ties between China and relevant countries, the SRF follows the four principles of connectivity, economic benefit, cooperation and openness.

The first principle is connectivity. The investments of the SRF promote coordination and integration of the development strategies of the countries involved, giving priority to investments which advance the "Belt and Road" initiative for the mutual benefit of the parties.

The second principle is economic benefit. The SRF mainly engages in long-term equity investments according to market principles, with appropriate internationalization and specialization. The fund invests in projects which offer reasonable long-term returns, strictly abiding by the laws of the country of investment as well as international standards and regulations.

The third principle is cooperation. The SRF provides a wide range of investment and financing services in cooperation with domestic and foreign enterprises and financial institutions in order to provide more options for projects with a reasonable and sustainable long-term return. With regard to existing international and domestic financial institutions, the SRF seeks not to substitute them, but to complement them and collaborate.

The fourth principle is openness. The SRF will welcome investors with common objectives to join or cooperate at the level of projects or sub-funds.

Activities of the SRF

A bit more than a year after it was founded, the SRF is already helping companies overcome the bottleneck of capital to support expansion and overseas projects through long-term equity investment based on the combined effect of Chinese capital, Chinese experience, high-quality production and superior equipment. Since 2015, the fund has announced three substantive investment projects. One supports an investment by the Three Gorges Group to build hydropower and other clean energy projects in Pakistan and South Asia. Another supports Chinese Chemical Engineering

Co.'s merger with Pirelli of Italy. And the third was an acquisition of shares in Russia's Yamal liquefied natural gas (LNG) project. What the three investments have in common is they all support overseas investments by industry-leading Chinese enterprises in the form of equity plus debt. These projects fully embody the SRF's investment philosophy and represent its forays into the key areas of greenfield projects, international mergers and acquisitions, and energy cooperation, respectively.

Activities to date thus show how the SRF can help supply companies with capital, reduce their overall debt ratio and improve project financing capacity through equity investment. At the same time, the fund provides further financing support through participation in syndicated loans. Such capital support enables Chinese enterprises to participate in other later investment projects and further integrate into the host country's economy to support local employment and industrial development. The projects promote technological upgrades, green development, value chain re-engineering and other long-term sustainable development goals.

While the demand for financing for B&R projects is vast, the size of the SRF is only US$40 billion, with a first funding phase of US$10 billion. In fact, a greater role of the SRF is to promote the B&R initiative. It can help promote coordinated regional development and economic integration. It can also encourage the participation of B&R countries, providing a demonstration effect to attract the wider participation of international capital. In short, the creation of the SRF is a specific way for China to use its financial strength to directly support the building of the B&R. Over time, the SRF will engage in mutually beneficial and pragmatic cooperation with numerous financial institutions and enterprises to contribute to advancing the B&R strategy.

2.3. The BRICS New Development Bank

The New Development Bank (NDB) was established by the BRICS countries to provide financial support for infrastructure and sustainable development projects in developing countries. It is a cooperation platform for the BRICS countries: Brazil, Russia, India, China and South Africa. But as an international financial institution operating in Asia, Europe, Africa and the Americas, its funds can also be used in Asia. For the building of B&R infrastructure, it has a complementary relationship with the AIIB and the SRF.

Leaders of the BRICS countries agreed in Brazil in 2014 to create a BRICS development bank to provide funding, particularly long-term funding, for infrastructure and sustainable development in emerging and developing economies. In early July 2015, BRICS finance ministers meeting in Russia approved the bank's establishment with the official name "New Development Bank". On July 21, 2015, the NDB began operations in Shanghai. The authorized capital of the NDB is US$100 billion, with initial capital of US$50 billion funded in equal parts by the five BRICS countries. The bank's headquarters are in Shanghai and its first president is from India, with deputy presidents from the four other countries.

The mission of the NDB is to provide support for transportation, energy and other infrastructure projects, as well as for sustainable development, in emerging and developing countries. This is highly consistent with the B&R infrastructure strategy. As a new international financial institution established in the 21st century, the NDB will ensure a more diversified investment and financing strategy, giving priority to the use of local financing channels like bond markets in member states. The bank combines the savings of countries with high savings rates, like China, with other countries' potential infrastructure needs, in order to develop profitable investment opportunities with public spillover effects, and eventually to support projects in developing economies including the B&R countries.

Four of the bank's shareholder members — China, Russia, South Africa and India — are the major economies in the B&R region. The NDB intends in the future, when raising funds, to use hard currency in the international capital markets and local currency in member states' domestic markets. In terms of its financing strategy, the bank is studying the feasibility of financing locally in each country and of helping to develop local capital markets. This would gradually reduce current excessive dependence on developed economies' currency and capital markets while also enhancing the asset pricing, trading, intermediary and other functions of the emerging economies' currencies.

Meanwhile, considering the RMB's relatively stable value in relation to the other BRICS currencies and its wider range of use in international trade and investment, the NDB will issue bonds denominated in RMB to support future internationalization of the currency. At the same time, in order to enliven bond trading in BRICS countries and improve the liquidity of currency swap markets, the bank will sign multilateral and bilateral currency swap agreements with the BRICS countries via their central banks. Growth and development of the currency swap markets will help reduce currency swap costs and dependence on intermediate hard currency. This will give emerging and B&R countries more financing options and greater convenience.

The BRICS members China, India and Russia are the largest countries in Eurasia, and in the B&R region. The active participation of these three countries in the construction of the B&R will place huge financing demands on the BRICS bank. The real challenge, though, is how to turn the B&R countries' huge infrastructure funding needs into real investment opportunities for relevant financial and real-economy entities. To address this challenge, the NDB plans to offer flexible loan and investment products, and to establish differentiated terms for sovereign and non-sovereign loans and warranties. In terms of security and procurement, the BRICS bank will adopt a more flexible and effective framework, relying on developing countries' own policies. In setting the refinancing rate and duration, the bank will apply standards at diverse grades for gradual loan implementation in light of specific infrastructure project types and future cash flows. To facilitate joint financing arrangements, it will collaborate on infrastructure projects both with international financial institutions and with local institutions in member states. This approach will ensure greater financial support for infrastructure in underdeveloped areas along the B&R while increasing the multiplier effect of investments, and with the advantage of involving domestic financial institutions familiar with the local situation and risk. At the same time, the BRICS bank will work to mobilize private sector participation in the form of equity investments, contract management, public-private partnership (PPP) and through other innovative approaches.

The NDB will also promote the pursuit of information superiority and multilateral platforms in emerging and developing economies. It will study the potential challenges and risks related to politics and legislation as well as credit and management culture that might arise in the context of production capacity cooperation, in order to support the international development of businesses from member states. And in supporting infrastructure construction, the bank will stress cooperation in technology research and development, thus providing intellectual support to enhance managerial talent and investment impact.

2.4. *European bank for reconstruction and development*

On December 14, 2015, the EBRD approved China's application to become a shareholder of the bank. The EBRD's aims of helping countries of Central and Eastern Europe and Central Asia to transform into private sector-oriented market economies coincides quite well with the goals of the "Belt and Road" initiative.

China's accession to the EBRD provides a new fulcrum and opens up new investment channels for the B&R initiative. According to official data, the EBRD is currently doing business in 36 countries. Borrowing member countries include Poland, Hungary and other Central European countries, Bulgaria, Romania and other South-Eastern European countries, Ukraine, Belarus and other Eastern Europe and Caucasus countries, Kazakhstan, Mongolia and other Asian countries, Egypt, Jordan and other countries in southern and eastern Mediterranean, as well as Greece, Russia and Turkey. As can be seen, there is a high degree of overlap between the EBRD's borrowing countries and the countries covered by China's B&R initiative. Thus China's accession to the EBRD will strongly advance interlinkages between the B&R initiative and the EBRD's investment plan. It creates a vast space for cooperation on project investment in Central and Eastern Europe, the Mediterranean and eastern and southern Central Asia.

The EBRD can play a very important role in the construction of the B&R. Established to support the economic transition of Central and Eastern European countries, the bank will share its investment experience and help China to fill in gaps in its financial cooperation with those regions. In the past, when Chinese banks or companies invested in countries along the B&R, they often lacked experience and in-depth understanding of those areas. The EBRD, meanwhile is present and does business in many countries. The bank's employees in those countries are quite familiar with the local market and can help to orient Chinese enterprises in investments there. In fact, for two decades now, when companies had difficulty determining how best to invest in certain larger projects, the EBRD provided them with free advice — especially for investment decisions. When Chinese banks at times lack sufficient local experience for sound decision-making, the EBRD can offer helpful consultations.

Beyond fortifying the B&R initiative, China's membership in the EBRD will also facilitate cooperation between the EBRD and the AIIB. The European debt crisis led a large number of Western Europe banks to divest from Eastern Europe. This has caused financing difficulties in Eastern European countries at a time when they need to boost investment to revive their real economies and help Europe emerge from crisis. Data from the Institute of International Finance (IIF) shows that foreign investment in emerging markets decreased from US$285 billion in 2014 to just US$66 billion in 2015. Foreign direct investment worldwide has slowed as well. Global FDI was about US$1.3 trillion last year, 8% less than the previous year. Amid the overall contraction of investment in emerging markets, the AIIB and EBRD can work together to resolve the funding gap in those countries. Located at either extreme of Eurasia, the two institutions also simultaneously cover many B&R countries. If they can cooperate on major projects that will not only help in terms of risk-sharing, but will also be conducive to the formation of a more equitable financial order. All in all, there are tremendous prospects for cooperation between the AIIB and the EBRD on jointly advancing the "Belt and Road" initiative.

2.5. Public-private partnership

While the AIIB, SRF, BRICS bank and other regional and international organizations are leading the way in funding construction of the B&R, such public capital is insufficient to meet the scale of financing needed for cross-border infrastructure in the region. In order to resolve the funding gap, a full mobilization of private capital is also needed. In this regard, public-private partnership (PPP) is a promising alternative, and will be one of the main features of innovations in financing mechanisms to advance the B&R initiative.

There is no uniform definition of PPP, but the WB, the ADB, the United Nations Development Program, the United Nations Institute for Training and Research, the European Commission, and the British Treasury all seem to coincide in describing PPP as a form of partnership based on a concession agreement in which the public and private sectors share the responsibility and financial risk for the construction of urban infrastructure or the provision of public goods and services. Experience around the world has made PPP a preferred approach to projects. For the B&R, the PPP model is beneficial not only for helping solve the funding gap, but also for improving the efficiency of public goods management and capital allocation.

In the global development context, according to the World Bank, PPP is mainly used in energy, power, transportation and water treatment, as well as in other industries, generally taking forms such as "build-own-operate"(BOO), "build-operate-transfer" (BOT), "build-rent-own-transfer" (BROT), or the like. The global PPP research journal *Public Works Financing* reports that between 1985 and 2011 the total nominal value of global PPP infrastructure projects was US$775.1 billion. Geographically, the PPP model is more mature in the UK and Australia, where its scale is also larger. The use of PPP is less significant in developing countries, but has been growing rapidly in recent years.

PPP plays a significant role in helping governments ease the pressure of public construction costs. During the process of building the B&R, it is thus imperative to attract various types of private capital as direct investments, which will greatly improve the operational efficiency of cross-border infrastructure assets. In China, PPP is currently highly valued and strongly promoted by relevant decision making and administrative departments of the Chinese government as a new mechanism that should be urgently integrated into the B&R initiative. The State Council has made it clear that in the B&R initiative social capital, forms such as debt and funds, will be used to provide long-term foreign-currency support for enterprises "going out". That is needed in order to attract private capital with innovative forms of financing (like PPP), so that the capital chain better meets the needs of large-scale infrastructure projects.

Still, it is undeniable that infrastructure projects, and especially cross-regional infrastructure projects like those in the B&R initiative, generally fall short of the profitability requirements of private capital due to their large-scale, long-term and high-risk nature and their poor short-term returns. In summary, while return on investment is crucial for attracting flows of private capital, cross-border infrastructure projects have a low Return on Investment (ROI). In addition, the business environment in the B&R region involves great uncertainties, including security and political risk factors, which may scare off profit-minded private capital. Globally, in fact, the share of private capital investment in infrastructure is less than 0.8%, and the financing market for cross-border infrastructure is deficient: the suppliers of funding are mainly governments and international organizations, with little development of investment products and projects suited to the participation of private capital.

There is a need, therefore, for a more diversified investment and financing framework. More innovative approaches and greater security assurances are required to boost the attractiveness of infrastructure projects for private sector investors, mobilize more private sector funding and actively encourage PPP. To begin, it is important to give full play to the leading role of the AIIB, and to design infrastructure projects and products that would be profitable for private capital. Taking into account the real needs of the countries along the B&R and the priority areas for infrastructure development, a project library should be created, including project feasibility reports.

A second step would be the securitization of cross-border infrastructure assets. Specifically, bonds should be issued with the objective of enhancing the returns on such projects. For completed cross-border infrastructure, asset securitization can give investors an exit route. For uncompleted cross-border infrastructure, asset securitization can enable the participation of smaller-scale private capital. Thirdly, B&R cross-border infrastructure stock exchanges can be established to provide a platform for private investment. Finally, at the cross-regional level, B&R countries need to formulate infrastructure investment plans or lists of key projects, with PPP project libraries, to facilitate the development of PPP projects.

Multilateral banks can further promote the issuance of local-currency bonds and/or the development of local debt financing to help attract long-term investors to PPP projects.

The PPP approach took shape in Europe, America, Australia and a number of emerging market economies (such as Turkey) in recent decades, and it has been in the ascendant. China has also initiated a series of PPP practices, but they are still at the start-up and exploration stage. In general, the PPP mechanism offers promise, in the context of building the B&R, for alleviating the financial pressure on governments, boosting the efficiency of construction and operation, and developing markets. It can thus provide mutual benefits for governments, the public and enterprises in a variety of countries in the course of the B&R initiative (See Case 7.2).

2.6. Accelerating RMB internationalization to facilitate the B&R initiative

Internationalization of the RMB and construction of the B&R go together well as complementary processes. The B&R strategy creates investment opportunities, financing support and market conditions for the internationalization of the RMB, while the internationalization of RMB strategically supports smooth trade and money flows throughout the B&R region, helping to achieve the integration of regional investment and cooperation.

The RMB's internationalization will greatly facilitate the development of trade between China and countries along the B&R. From 2009 to 2013, these countries on average accounted for 24.55% of China's overall trade volume. As the B&R initiative strengthens communication and cooperation in the region, bilateral trade can be expected to continue growing and expanding, thus further boosting demand for RMB as a settlement currency.

Consider the Central Asian countries. Since 2006, China has signed agreements on construction of a natural gas pipeline with Turkmenistan, Kazakhstan and other Central Asian countries, and in December 2009, the Central Asia-China Gas Pipeline was inaugurated. Along with increased investments and energy cooperation, China's trade with the Central Asian countries has also increased year by year. Trade with Kazakhstan, for example, grew by 66% in 2007 and 135% in 2008, during construction of the pipeline, and has continued growing stably since then.

Similarly, implementation of the B&R initiative will effectively boost trade between China and other countries as well. China, for its part, is exporting equipment as well as construction and management services to these countries, and they in turn will increase export volumes to China to help repay their debts. According to media reports, some countries are engaging in barter exchanges of goods and services with China. Thailand, for example, plans to provide rice to China in exchange for the construction of a railway. Internationalization of the RMB would enable the invoicing and settlement of such projects in RMB, making trade and settlement more efficient, and thus promoting further growth of trade.

Internationalization of the RMB is also conducive to currency circulation in the B&R region. Deciding which currency to use for monetary and financial activities in the region is a very important issue. Under continued use of the US dollar, the B&R plan would be restrained by US monetary policy. Changes in the value of the dollar would directly affect the efficiency of capital. Global monetary policies are currently differentiated, and the US is about to enter a cycle of rising interest rates. Changes in dollar-based international capital flows are hard to predict. Therefore, using the US$ as a funding vehicle would increase uncertainty in planning for the B&R initiative.

In addition, the RMB's internationalization helps to avoid the exchange rate risk of falling dollar prices for commodities. The countries along the B&R are mostly resource exporters, and commodities comprise a large share of their exports. Data for 2011 to 2013 show Kazakhstan's mineral exports on average accounted for 80% of its total annual exports, with 71% of those mineral exports going to China. In the same period, India's exports of mineral products and metals on average accounted for 44% of its total exports, and 46% of them went to China. The current situation of oversupply in commodity markets is quite difficult to change in the near term, and the impact on commodity prices is being worsened by continued dollar appreciation. Thus bypassing the US dollar, the Japanese yen, the Euro and other international currencies, and using the RMB for transactions, can help avoid the potential risks of US dollar fluctuations and global monetary policy differentiation.

The B&R initiative is dedicated to promoting the interconnection and intercommunication of policy, infrastructure, trade, finance and interpersonal relations. Ultimately, it seeks to strengthen economic cooperation among the countries along the route and gradually give rise to a new type of large-scale regional cooperation across Eurasia. Internationalization of the RMB will help smooth the flow of trade and the circulation of money among the B&R countries. The results of theoretical and empirical research shows that China is the most important trading partner of the countries along the route, and that China leads the region in economic, financial and social development. Increased use of the RMB can effectively guard the region against financial risks, reduce transaction costs, enhance the overall level of economic competitiveness and co-development, provide new risk management mechanisms, anchor financial security and thus make a significant contribution to regional economic and financial stability.

Concluding Remarks

The B&R initiative was proposed by China in the context of the continuing profound impact of the international financial crisis and the various uncertainties related to global economic recovery. The initiative also represents China's new thinking focused on mutually beneficial cooperation after it became the world's second-largest economy and largest trading nation. Implementing this international initiative is like a dragon dance, with China as the leader of the dance. This not only requires China to help reshape the world economy with a global perspective, but also calls for all the countries of the world to cooperate closely for the sake of eventual mutual benefits. Given the financialization of the global economy, it is vital to build an international financial system based on equality, openness, inclusiveness and cooperation. That is an integral part of the Silk Road initiative. Thus the B&R, more than just a strategy for trade and investment, is a strategy for international financial development. It even can be said that it is precisely a finance initiative.

References

Chen, Y. & Qian Y. (2015). *The Belt and Road: A Financial Perspective* [M], Beijing, China: China CITIC press.

Dong, J. (2015). *Grasping the significant opportunities of the B&R initiative: all efforts to enhance the level of financial services* [EB/OL], *Xinhuanet*. Available at http://news.xinhuanet.com/fortune/2015-08/26/c_128168511.htm.

Huang, Y. (2016). Understanding China's Belt & Road Initiative: Motivation, Framework and Assessment, *China Economic Review, 40*: 314–321.

Hongli, Z. (2015). On the Prospect of China's Financial Industry: Go Global with the "One Belt One Road" Initiative, *Frontiers*, 9.

Jin L. (2016). *AIIB: The Propeller of International Economic and Financial Cooperation and Development* [EB/OL]. *Xinhuanet*. Available at http://news.xinhuanet.com/finance/2016-01/05/c_128595084.htm.

Jin, Q. (2015). *How the Silk Road Fund is Supporting the B&R initiative* [EB/OL], available at http://money.163.com/15/1231/02/BC4LC33700253B0H.html.

Liang, H. (2016). The B&R initiative should draw interactive financial communications[EB/OL]. Available at http://www.ftchinese.com/story/001066620full=y..

Li, J. & Zheng, Y. (2015). *The financial opportunities of the B&R initiative* [EB/OL], available at http://finance.ce.cn/rolling/201504/09/t20150409_5059868.shtml.

Liu, Y. (2015). *How to financially support construction of the B&R* [EB/OL], available at http://www.yicai.com/news/4592589.html.

Xinxiang, W. & Xin, X. (2015). The new historical period for the internationalization of the renminbi: the "One Belt One Road" initiative and the future international financial system, *Frontiers, 16*.

Zhang, H. (2015). *The Belt and Road initiative and financial strategy* [EB/OL]. *Caixin* online. Available at http://topics.caixin.com/2015-03-23/100793867.html.

Zhu, L. (2016). The Construction Model of the "One Belt and One Road": Mechanisms and Platforms, in *Annual Report on the Development of the Indian Ocean Region (2015)*, (Singapore: Springer), p. 111–127.

Case 7.1   Pakistan motorway: The first project co-financed by the AIIB

On May 2, 2016, during the Asian Development Bank's Annual Meeting, held in Frankfurt, Germany, AIIB President Jin Liqun and ADB President Takehiko Nakao signed a memorandum of understanding on strengthening cooperation between the two organizations through a series of cooperative financing projects. The memorandum noted that the AIIB is in discussions with the ADB on co-financing projects for roads and water supply. The two sides will hold regular high-level consultations and jointly gather data in order to facilitate the achievement of the sustainable development goals of the United Nations and the Paris climate agreement.

Shortly after signing the memorandum, the two sides agreed to co-finance the construction of 64 kilometers of motorway in Pakistan connecting the cities of Shorkot and Khanewal in Punjab province (See Map 7.1: The China-Pakistan Economic Corridor). The AIIB thus formalized its first project financing and

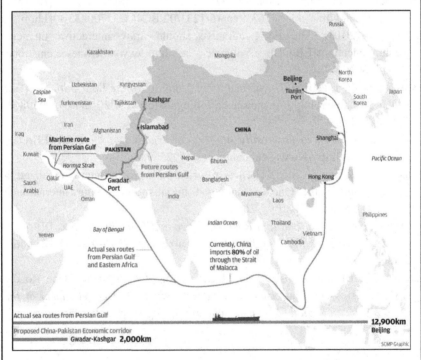

Map 7.1   The China-Pakistan Economic Corridor

Source: South China Morning Post Retrieved from https://www.chinadialogue.net/article/show/single/en/7864-China-s-new-silk-road-What-s-in-it-for-Pakistan.

(*Continued*)

Case 7.1 (*Continued*)

marked its formal start of investing in B&R infrastructure projects. The AIIB's president said on May 2, he was pleased by the further partnership with the ADB. He said the AIIB looks forward to deepening its relationship with the ADB and expanding cooperation to meet the huge demand in Asia for infrastructure financing.

The Pakistan motorway project is the first of the AIIB's widely anticipated initial batch of projects to be announced. The initial projects will be based on co-financing, which is a different approach than that taken by the BRICS New Development Bank. The vice president and chief financial officer of the New Development Bank, Leslie Maasdorp, has said that the New Development Bank would independently finance its first batch of projects on its own, focusing mainly on the field of renewable energy.

The AIIB's first batch of projects is expected to include co-financing with the EBRD and the World Bank. It is known that the AIIB plans to co-finance a project for a ring road in Almaty, Kazakhstan, with the World Bank and the EBRD. It will also work with the EBRD to provide co-financing for a highway in Dushanbe, Tajikistan. Co-financing agreements for both these infrastructure projects in Central Asia were due to be signed in June 2016.

Through initial projects with joint financing, the AIIB can quickly expand its project portfolio and leverage existing institutions' project reserves and capacity for project research and compliance. The ADB, the World Bank and the EBRD can also leverage the AIIB's US$100 billion of capital in order to use their limited funds for more projects.

Sources: Asian Infrastructure Investment Bank, Asian Development Bank.

Case 7.2   The International Common Silk Road Public Facilities Fusion PPP Fund

The United Nations Maritime and Continental Silk Road Cities Alliance (UNMCSR) was established in Beijing on September 11, 2015. Its purpose is to support the cities along the Silk Road in conducting multilateral economic and technological cooperation under the United Nations Framework.

The idea fits well with the B&R initiative. It will further enlarge the common interests of the countries, regions and cities along the Maritime and Continental Silk Road to seek common development and prosperity.

(*Continued*)

Case 7.2   (*Continued*)

In the spirit of the Silk Road, the UNMCSR will promote interaction and exchange between cities of different cultures and play a key role in promoting the joint construction of the "Silk Road Economic Belt" and the "21st Century Maritime Silk Road".

The UNMCSR has a Financial Capital Committee (FCC) whose purpose is to promote cooperation and resource integration for public infrastructure PPP projects among the cities along the Maritime and Continental Silk Road. The FCC initiated an International Common Silk Road Public Facilities Fusion PPP Fund to facilitate international PPP project investments in Silk Road cities. The Fusion Fund will function as an international investment fund, in accordance with the principles of "the government setting the stage", market logic, scientific decision making and risk prevention.

The Fusion Fund's first funding phase will focus on the PPP project "Silk Road internet P&C cross-border public commodity exchanges worldwide networking platform". The project will help develop new growth engines, improve cross-border support for investments in Silk Road cities through a commodity trading platform, and inject new vitality into the Common Silk Road Cities PPP fusion strategy.

The International Common Silk Road Public Facilities Fusion PPP Fund connects Silk Road cities through trading relations and market forces, supports the creation of internet infrastructure, and promotes common development between countries and regions. It aims to facilitate electronic commerce, leveraging international and social capital for the development of infrastructure and trade relationships along an internet Silk Road.

Sources: UNMCSR City Alliance web site http://e.unmcsr.org/ and the United Nations Industrial Development Organization Center for South-South Industrial Cooperation in China (UCSSIC).

Chapter 8

Managing Talents in the Silk Road Cross-cultural Environment[1]

Zhao Yixuan and Zhao Shuming

Nanjing University, Business School

1. Culture and the "One Belt One Road" Initiative

In ancient times, the Silk Road described the trade, political and cultural exchange between China and other countries. There were three "Silk Roads": from Zhang Qian's (张骞) embankment to the West around 138 BCE, there was the "Northwest Silk Road"; the "Prairie Silk Road", which stretched from inner Mongolia to the Tian Mountains; and last, but not least, the "Maritime Silk Road", which stretched from the South China Sea to beyond the Indian Ocean to Africa and Europe (Yuan, 2014). In 2013, Chinese President Xi Jinping stated the "One Belt One Road" as a medium and long-term strategy in China's relationship with foreign countries. The "One Belt One Road" (OBOR) is short for the world's "Silk Road Economic Belt" and the "21st Century Maritime Silk Road". Currently, the "Silk Road Economic Belt" starts from China's Xi'an, through Central Asia,

[1]The authors would like to thank the National Natural Science Foundation of China for supporting this research (Project No.: 71332002).

Russia, before arriving at the Baltic Sea (Yang, 2015). While China has been deeply involved in the process of economic globalization by positively "introducing" in the last 38 years "reform and opening-up", OBOR signifies the arrival of a new stage of China's globalization and the promotion of more collaboration between China and other related countries. While OBOR seeks to connect major Eurasian economies through infrastructure, trade and investment (Hoffman, 2015), the strategy also includes financial integration, regional information and communications technology networks, unimpeded trade, policy coordination across the region, people-to-people connectivity and common security.

Duan and Li (2016) argued that from the beginning of human society to the modern industrial era, there existed a few major cultural circles around the world, for instance, the East Asian Cultural Circle, South Asia Circle, the Middle East Circle, Western Europe Circle, as well as other smaller culture and civilizations. In the past, the East Asian tribute trade network covered China, the Korean Peninsula, Japan, Okinawa and Southeast Asia. Throughout history, all of these cultural circles had their own developmental track, with the East Asian and Southeast Asian cultural circles in its most stable state. From 1700, the Western Europe cultural circle underwent major changes, due to the discovery of new sea routes as well as the industrial revolution. For Western Europe, this meant the gradual disintegration of the prior agricultural civilization and the formation of a new industrial civilization that ultimately impacted the entire world.

The OBOR strategy continues the cultural and friendship exchange passed on by the ancient Silk Road concept, and further strengthens ties with Southeast Asia, South Asia, West Asia and Africa, as the northwestern part of China is full of rich human resources, production, folk culture, as well as an integration of religious beliefs (Mi and Wang, 2016). The Silk Road also promotes economic development among the countries on that route.

From an economic standpoint, Yang Hailin, Deputy Team Leader of the "One Belt One Road" Project in the China Strategy and Management Research Committee, analyzed the reasons for China initiating the "Belt and Road". While 38 years of reform and opening-up to the outside world have built a strong foundation for China's economic rise, Yang (2015) argued that the country is now facing the challenge of economic transformation. Through trade cooperation, logistics cooperation and culture communication, China can achieve common development of the world economy, promote economic cooperation with countries along the OBOR initiative, and realize common integration and truly achieve harmonious coexistence.

The implementation of the strategy of the OBOR initiative will not only strengthen cross-cultural cooperation but also bring more opportunities and motivations for Chinese enterprises to "go global" and promote economic cooperation with many other countries. Xu (2015) pointed out that in the first quarter of 2015, bilateral trade between China and countries along the OBOR initiative route was US$236 billion, accounting for 26% of China's total amount of national imports and exports. In countries along the OBOR initiative route, more than 70 cooperated zone projects are under construction, infrastructure investment by enterprises is more than US$8 billion, annual output value is more than US$20 billion, and it is expected to create 200,000 jobs for the local markets.

With an important role in the implementation of the OBOR strategy, Chinese enterprises have a great development opportunity to "go out". Seizing the opportunity can help the relevant industries and enterprises in China to be able to go abroad and export more to the international market. However, the OBOR initiative strategy involves more than 60 countries in three continents, Asia, Europe and Africa, more than 70 economic and trade cooperation zones and more than 4 billion people. If Chinese enterprises want to "go out" and internationalize, they should become more closely involved with foreign enterprises and foreign employees, such as hiring foreign talents and employees. Thus, Chinese managers will inevitably be faced with problems of managing employees from different cultures and countries. Solving the problem of cross-cultural management will be key to successfully "going out", including how to promote Chinese traditional management philosophy in host countries. Similarly, companies from other countries along the Silk Road can also seize the opportunity to have more economic cooperation with both their Chinese counterparts and members of other Silk Road countries.

2. Cultural Differences between China and Europe and the Cross-cultural Environment

The OBOR initiative emphasizes participation, development and cooperation. Therefore, understanding cultural-political differences between
countries along the Silk Road is vital to the success of the OBOR initiative
and individual Chinese enterprises, as each foreign country has different
understandings of Chinese culture and history, including some regional
countries at the heart of political disputes. Alder (1983) indicated that
cross-cultural management is the study of the behavior of people in
organizations located in different countries across the world. It focuses on
the description of organizational behavior within countries and cultures,
on the comparison of organizational behavior across countries and cultures. Most importantly it focuses on the interaction of peoples from these
different countries working in the same organization or same environment. Moran, *et al.*, (2014) stated that culture is a distinctly human means
of adapting to circumstances and transmitting this coping skill and knowledge to subsequent generations. Culture is often considered the driving
force behind human behavior. Hall and Hall (1995) stated that culture
guides the actions and responses of people in every walk of life. In particular cultures, the elements that combine and produce a given meaning
in a culture, events and context are in different proportions depending on
the culture. Hall and Hall (1995) referred to this kind of difference in
terms of high to low context. For instance, many Asian, Arab and
Mediterranean peoples are more high-context as they have extensive
information networks among family, friends, colleagues and clients, and
are involved in close personal relationships. But many Northern Europeans
are not only low-context but also lack extensive, well-developed information networks.

2.1. *Cultural differences between China and Europe*

Li (2014) summarized the culture differences between China and Europe
in terms of cultural characteristics, ways of thinking, as well as life attitudes. First of all, in terms of cultural characteristics, Li argued that
European values originated from Ancient Greek civilization, advocating

mutual independence, freedom, equality, as well as paying attention to self-consciousness and self-centered individual value concepts. As the ancient Greeks lived near the sea and the farming conditions were bad due to the geographical factors, they made their living through overseas trade, and then gradually formed a social spirit of adventuring and forging ahead. Such a personality of adventurism and individualism slowly became the origin of European culture.

European countries mainly advocate Judeo-Christian culture, which emphasizes the equality of humankind and individual human dignity. Another remarkable feature of this culture is its rationality. Western countries generally pursue science and truth, against fuzzy awareness and speculation. Generally speaking, European culture attaches great importance to scientific freedom, freedom of speech and freedom of thinking. In addition, they emphasize the importance of cooperative contracts, with the contract spirit originating from the Bible, which includes both individual and collective contracts, as well as individual responsibility and responsibility to society (Wang and Li, 1999). This contract spirit emphasizes that individuals must comply with contractual agreements, with emotional factors weak among people, rational cooperative contract compliance is highlighted.

In contrast, Chinese native culture is deeply influenced by Confucianism, and at the same time, Taoist culture. It fully reflects human characteristics. Since China's economic reform and opening-up to the outside world in 1978, China has been fine-tuning domestic economic development, and constantly absorbing elements of foreign culture, but the core content of Chinese traditional culture remains unchanged. The Chinese people have been committed to the consolidated family concept since ancient times; they take the family as the foundation unit. This is similar to many other Asian countries with high context cultures.

Secondly, there are differences in the way of thinking between China and Europe. Europe emphasizes quantitative analysis and identifies the value of the whole while paying equal attention to individual interests. Therefore, Europeans put the value of the whole and the individual on the same level. Since their childhood, Europeans have received training to think in terms of democracy, independence and freedom. They fully maintain their rights and can be excessively self-centered (Zu, 2013).

The most prominent Chinese way of thinking is "commonality and completeness" (*tongyuyuan*, "同与圆") due to influence from Confucianism and Taoism philosophies. Unlike Western people's pursuit of revealing their own personality, Chinese philosophy is to seek common ground while resolving differences. Therefore, Chinese people take themselves and the whole environment as a unified whole and strive for common development goals. Chinese people seek common goals and the pursuit of integrity. They also are pragmatic about family values, such as the annual family reunion dinner during the Spring Festival (Chinese New Year's Eve). All these are manifestations of the strong family atmosphere in Chinese traditional culture and the strong concept of social unity.

Thirdly, there are life attitude differences between Chinese and Europeans. Europeans are more practical in life and in work, and are good at practical reasoning. Also, Europeans emphasize logic and reasoning. When problems arise, Western people use the contractual system and frequently rely on rigid legal rules, trying to avoid interference of human factors, such as moral emotions. When situations arise that cannot be coordinated informally, even between close friends or family members, Europeans may still rely on strict accordance with the laws and regulations to deal with problems.

Unlike Western people who attach great importance to practical application, Chinese people pay more attention to spiritual enjoyment. Western culture emphasizes reasoning and analysis, while Chinese people do things more with their past experience and intuition, focusing on humanist spirit and the overall image, neglecting small abstract parts. When Chinese people are faced with practical problems in daily life, they tend to use perceptual thinking, emphasizing more on the interpersonal relationship and each other's feeling, and putting morality and law on an almost equally important position. Chinese believe that "gossip hurts" (*renyankewei* "人言可畏"), so when solving the problem may hurt personal reputation and respect, they will try to avoid using legal means. Chinese families comply with very strict seniority rules; the social relationships are also closely related to kinship, advocating a strict hierarchy system. Elders and teachers in Chinese traditional culture are put in a very high position, reflected in the "respect for teachers and education" even in contemporary Chinese society. For example,

Chinese students use a respectful appellation towards their teachers. The weakness of Chinese culture lies in the lack of rational thinking, including the failure to take the objective world as the center of research, and demanding identity excessively while ignoring the development of individual personality (Liu, 2012).

Russia and other countries along the Silk Road between China and Europe are not mentioned in great detail in this chapter. But what needs to be noted are the similarities between Chinese and Russian culture. As Michailova and Hutching (2006) mentioned, both China and Russia are multinational states with heterogeneous populations dominated by a single ethnic group. Both countries were historically great powers and both were ruled by the Communist Party (formal Soviet Union, USSR, until 1991) for more than 60 years. According to Michailova and Hutching (2006), China and Russia share the "cultivation of personal relationships and networks (in-groups) highly important for substituting the lack of general reciprocity as well as nurturing dyadic reciprocity."

2.2. *China and European enterprise cultural differences*

Shan (2010) analyzed five cultural differences that may arise after the merger or acquisition between Chinese and Europe enterprises, comprising manifested cultural differences; system cultural differences; value differences, differences in thoughts and ways, differences in operation, and human resource management differences.

Manifested cultural conflict in mergers or acquisitions between Chinese and Europe enterprises can be easily identified, due to different meanings which are given to the same expression. Manifested cultural conflict is mainly reflected through language and behavior. For example, the conflicts caused by different languages may be as basic as ways of greeting. When Chinese meet, they usually say: "Where are you going?" "Have you eaten yet?" This is merely a greeting, rather than an inquiry about your movements or eating habits. As a result, people tend to answer vaguely. The actual meaning is just like "Hello!" "How are you?" Such greetings could be misunderstood by Western people, who might infer that you are interfering with their personal lives and privacy. In addition, conflicts may also arise from communication habit differences. Chinese employees stick with the doctrine of "Golden Mean", generally they do not do anything that may offend other people's businesses or upset people, so they usually do not disagree with people face-to-face, but respond with vague words like "Let me think it over" as a euphemistic refusal. In contrast, European employees are generally outgoing, with a clear point, very straightforward, and worry less about other people's displeasure.

Due to the Western countries' relatively complete legal environment, system culture differences can be understood in terms of Western managers' action based on the law. But for their Chinese counterparts, especially those who work in state-owned enterprises, they emphasize the importance of interpersonal relationship between superior and subordinate. For Chinese managers and employees, the main basis of management action is superior instructions, rules and regulations. In many Chinese companies, the employee listens to manager instructions and the individual's identity and status in the company relies on his or her position in the company, as well as personal power and group member relationships. Instructions and files may change with executives' value judgment. Therefore, policy or systems do not require long-term consistency, certainty and predictability, but are subject to flexible interpretation. Western enterprises are different from Chinese firms, with an emphasis on professional opinions, rules and regulations rather than someone's intentionality. People gain status by professionalism, contribution and the ability to judge. These different operating styles between Chinese and Western enterprises inevitably lead to conflict.

Value systems are at the core of culture. Value differences are the most basic differences that we can observe among people. It refers to the evaluation and understanding of different things and is a tool to measure people's beliefs, mores and attitude system. Influenced by tradition and reality, Western enterprise employees believe in working hard and playing hard. They pursue material satisfaction and pleasure through their own hard work, while their Chinese counterparts, because of the feudal hereditary view and mobility difficulties between different classes, are more conventional, lacking in initiative, and are not keen and confident toward changes. However, the Chinese are very zealous about interpersonal relationships, taking work time as an opportunity to communicate between colleagues. So the differences of working attitude may lead to conflict.

Second, managers in the West and China hold different views toward innovation and adventure. Western managers have enormous enthusiasm about the application of new technology, new market exploitation and new products innovation. On the contrary, Chinese managers have a weaker adventurous spirit and they are conventional and cautious about rapid change and taking responsibilities. Usually, it is difficult for Chinese managers and employees to seize opportunities in highly competitive environments, so there will be strategic conflicts between Chinese and European enterprise employees. Third, in Western companies, there is a certain level of rights for subordinates to advise or question their superiors; subordinates have a high level of autonomy and can voice their opinions without fearing the consequence. In China, everything looks harmonious on the surface, but what is under the surface may be the opposite.

Operational thoughts and ways can also be different given different cultural backgrounds. In the West, operational thought emphasizes mutual benefit and reciprocity, efficiency and market response. In China, on the contrary, in terms of mutual benefit, people do not think too much about others' benefits; the concept of market response "basing sales on production" still exists. Industry and products structure still lack scientific rationality. Western enterprises attach great importance to long-term behavior, which is seen as a valuable investment. However, for many Chinese private enterprises, there is often short-term behavior, mainly due to unpredictable policies, with long-term plans becoming a mere formality. For decision making, Western companies are accustomed to personal decisions, taking ultimate responsibility, and implementing decentralized decision making. While Chinese domestic enterprises implement centralized decision making, and decisions are often made by collective efforts, where responsibility and achievement belong to the whole group.

The last type of cultural difference that Shan (2010) identified was the differences in human resource management. For instance, in terms of growth of employee wages, from a Chinese enterprise standpoint, an increase in employee wages is based on the improvement of the general growth of economic benefits. On the other hand, European companies generally think that if there is an increase in the price index and life index, as well as inflation, enterprises need to increase the wage base. Second, in terms of the structure of employee wages, Chinese companies generally take elements like personnel qualifications; experience and education into account, and these are very important factors to distinguish employee wages. While European enterprise employee wages are mainly related to the nature of work, and only when the enterprise personnel's work content changes, will salary adjustments occur. When selecting talents, Chinese enterprises attach importance to personal history and family background, including ability and political integrity and control quality. European enterprises put employees' ability as the first priority.

Using Hofstede's (2015) cultural dimensions, Gao and Ma (2015) analyzed the cultural dimension scores of countries involved in the OBOR initiative. Gao and Ma's research indicated that the higher the Hofstede score, the more that country or region is inclined to one of Hofstede's dimensions. Table 8.1 shows that Chinese culture has the following Hofstede characteristics: power distance is high; individualism tends to be low; more inclined to masculinity; and the degree of uncertainty avoidance is low. Compared to China, Southeast Asian countries have similar power distance with China, while non-Southeast Asian countries are at relatively lower power distant levels; in the dimension of individualism, Southeast Asian countries are relatively lower than China, while other regions have a higher level of individualism than China. European countries are relatively higher than China and other areas are close to China; for uncertainty avoidance, Southeast Asian countries are similar to China, while other countries are relatively higher than China. Although Russia is not listed in this table or included in Gao and Ma's study, its economic ideology is more collectivistic-oriented while the national culture is more individualistic-oriented (Ralston *et al.*, 1997).

For high power distance countries such as Southeast Asia and Arab countries, managers can employ top-down ways of decision making, for example, managing teams with a paternalistic style. Company employees in these regions are used to listening to their managers, and seldom express their ideas to their managers. In countries with low power distance, employees demand equality even between employees and managers, with differences between their positions mainly influenced by different job content. Low power distance employees appeal for personal freedom, with less influence due to hierarchy levels. Western enterprises tend to attach great importance to the independent decisions of individuals

Table 8.1   Cultural differences between China and other "One Belt One Road" countries

Country	Power distance	Individualism	Masculinity	Uncertainty avoidance	Cultural differences with China
China	89	39	54	44	—
Indonesia	78	14	46	48	28.740
Malaysia	104	26	50	36	38.131
Philippines	94	32	64	44	23.875
Singapore	74	20	48	8	75.750
Thailand	64	20	34	64	42.261
India	77	48	56	40	46.109
Pakistan	55	14	50	70	49.729
Iran	58	41	43	59	47.445
Israel	13	54	47	81	86.134
Turkey	66	37	45	85	55.272
Arab States	80	38	53	68	25.671
Czech Republic	57	58	57	74	55.507
Hungary	46	55	88	82	68.593
Poland	68	60	64	93	62.594

Source: Gao, C. and Ma, C.Z. The cross-cultural management of Chinese enterprises "going out" under "One Belt, One Road" strategy [J]. *Human Resources Development of China*, 2015(19).

and to individual responsibility, with managers good at listening to low-level employees and responsive to bottom-up decision making.

In countries with low individualism, companies can input collective ideas into the management process, cultivating their sense of belonging to the enterprises. When employees encounter difficulties, if enterprises can provide necessary help, the employees will pay back with loyalty to enterprises. Employees with low individualism believe that relationships are more important than work, they value interpersonal relationships, and there are close relations between employees. Such low individualism environments mean that the employees hold very high loyalty to their enterprises, which leads to a relatively low turnover. Therefore, Chinese enterprises maintain relatively stable teams. In countries where individualism is high, employees demand that management respects employees' privacy and personal freedom.

In countries with high level of masculinity dimension, the social competition consciousness is strong; the measure of success is wealth and fame. The society encourages and praises workaholics. People tend to solve conflicts in their organization in a "showdown" way. This kind of culture emphasizes fairness and competition, focuses on job performance, and team members often show overconfidence and arbitrariness. Thus, it is easy to build competitive work environments to enhance the staff's work enthusiasm. However, when this dimension score is low, life quality is more the focus, with people generally more willing to adopt reconciliation and negotiation as ways to solve conflicts in the organization. The culture emphasizes equality and unity. People think that the most important thing in life is not material possessions, but the communication of the mind.

In countries with low levels of uncertainty avoidance, the management methods of enterprises are adopted in a benign environment, which encourages innovation. When the uncertainty avoidance is high, enterprises should pay attention to the specification of management, system management, and management regulations and also display respect for individual freedom at the same time. Organizing team management, companies can employ internal rules and provisions to regulate employees' work behavior, reducing uncertainty and fuzziness of any perceived threats. In East Asian countries and the Middle East, the doctrine of religion can be more influential than the rule of law. Also, the regions may have detailed rules, including personal appearance features, practices, living standards and worship. Islam's external influence is extremely strong, which reinforces working together with heart and teamwork to enhance their influence. So, enterprises should take advantage of the positive role of uncertainty avoidance in the development of the market.

3. The Impact of Cross-cultural Environment on Talent Management

There are more than 60 countries along the OBOR initiative, which includes, but is not limited to, countries that were among the ancient Silk Road trade route. Elisseeff (1998) mentioned that "while the Silk Road is a channel for trade and the transfer of technology, it does not always flow at the same pace and towards the same destination." This can also be said of the dissemination of languages and the influence of ideas. Within Chinese international enterprises, the cross-cultural environment will bring challenges for the process of talent management (Shan, 2010). Shan believes that if companies cannot successfully conduct cross-cultural talent management, they may experience four stages of talent management failure. First, differences in the work environment can lead to unpleasant emotions; forcing employees to tend to constrain their own behavior, become timid and constrain their innovative ideas. In these conditions, when managers conduct enterprise management and operate in accordance with rules and regulations, there may be further social distance between managers and the employees. Second, further social distance between managers and employees will lead to less communication between them, which make talent management more difficult. If managers cannot recognize cultural differences and cultural conflicts, they will act according to the behavior of what they think is right, but not the kind of behavior that employees accept. This may lead to employees' irrational revenge behavior, resulting in more intense conflict, enterprise management chaos, decreased internal cohesion and diminished work enthusiasm. All these will make the enterprise's performance targets harder to realize. Finally, if the first three stages do not have effective control and guidance, employees' psychological pressure will slowly accumulate and influence their work behavior.

In addition, Shan (2010) analyzed the negative effects that a cross-cultural environment can have on enterprises. For instance, cross-cultural issues increase the complexity of management. In a cross-cultural working environment, managers are working with employees from different nations with diverse cultures, reflected in different values, religious beliefs, expectations, work motivation and behavior criterion. In the workplace, these employees have different modes of conduct and performance. Therefore, managers are faced with divergent demands, which in turn increase the difficulty, complexity, and costs of enterprise management and enterprise operation. Second, internal cross-cultural environments impact on the effectiveness of decision making, which is mainly reflected in two aspects. In terms of decision making, managers tend to analyze problems from their own perspectives. Combined with the language barrier, it can take time, labor, material and financial resources to quickly reach an agreement. The other aspect is the implementation of decisions, which is impacted by inconsistencies of information, challenges of decoding and implementation principles, procedures and methods influencing employees. Without managing these issues, enterprises will be unresponsive to market changes; therefore, the company may lose a large number of market opportunities, and end up being in a passive position relative to competitors. Third, cross-cultural working environments may promote the emergence of informal interest groups (Li, 2013). Such interest groups may promote cross-cultural conflict, and the internal convergences of culturally similar employees potentially bargain to benefit the group and not the whole enterprise. Internal convergence naturally repels other groups creating so-called internal informal interest groups.

Of course, there are also positive effects for both employees and the enterprise in terms of a cross-cultural environment. For example, the positive effects on employees, including from culture conflicts, make employees aware of the cultural differences and promote innovation and problem-solving, which provides the enterprise with potential competitive advantages. In cross-cultural environments, employees' minds become more open when analyzing and solving problems, which promotes group learning and cooperation.

In terms of the positive effects on enterprises, first, cross-cultural environments can improve the quality of the management of cross-cultural management. Cultural conflicts make managers realize national cultural differences in different countries, and at the same time allow them to constantly reflect on their means and methods of cross-cultural management. This leads to effective learning about managing cultural conflicts. Managers realize that moderate conflicts can play a positive role in enterprise survival and development. In the process of the operation and management of cultural conflict, managers conscientiously leverage cultural differences to develop international markets, discerning the foreign social, cultural, and economic environment, and improving their own comprehensive cross-cultural management ability. Therefore, Chinese cross-cultural enterprises will be more objective when considering consumer needs and expectations from another culture. Second, cross-cultural environments improve the efficiency of decision making. The performance of cultural conflict in the decision making process is the different views and identity among team members. This can help prevent the mistakes caused by personal bias or cognitive judgment and in the decision of operating risk. Third, cultural conflicts promote the development of culture. In cross-cultural enterprises, employees recognize and accept each other's culture and values through constant communication and learning.

Tian *et al.* (2013) analyzed the cultural communication challenges and solutions faced by employees in "going out" Chinese enterprises and "coming in" foreign enterprises, including cross-cultural sensitivity issues. Recent research results show that "going out" enterprises are at a low internationalized and cross-cultural management stage than "coming in" multinationals. Therefore, Chinese employees in the "going out" Chinese enterprises are responsible for tasks that require more market exploration in culturally complex environments than employees in "coming in" enterprises. At the same time, Chinese employees who are in "going out" Chinese enterprises are likely to have a low level of intercultural sensitivity. Second, employees in "going out" and "coming in" enterprises are facing different cross-cultural communication challenges. The "going out" Chinese enterprises face dual challenges with external and internal issues, so they should not only deal with internal management mechanisms, like strategic and tactical issues and language items but also have to deal with government policy and trade matters. "Coming in" foreign enterprises are faced only with the challenges of the internal management mechanism and a few language issues and strategic and tactical issues. Lastly, "going out" and "coming in" enterprises are employing significantly different methods to cope with the challenge of cross-cultural communication strategy: Chinese enterprises are more inclined to adopt methods with the help of external forces like the employees in the host country and local institutions. The "coming in" foreign enterprises tend to adopt methods through internal training to improve Chinese employees' ability to cope.

4. Effectively Managing Talents via Training and Communication

4.1. *Providing cross-cultural training*

Some cases of joint venture failures between Chinese and foreign enterprises show that foreign employees did not understand many elements of Chinese culture before they were expatriated to China. Faced by

Table 8.2   Content of Cross-cultural training

Cross-cultural training system	Knowledge (K)	1. The basic information of the host country 2. The introduction of company in the host country 3. International business knowledge 4. Intercultural knowledge 5. Language knowledge
	Skills (S)	1. Language skill 2. Cross-cultural communication skills 3. Conflict management skills 4. Negotiation skills 5. Cross-cultural management skills 6. Business operation skills in the cross-cultural environment 7. Cross-cultural interpersonal skills
	Ability (A)	1. Cultural sensitivity 2. Intercultural adaptation ability 3. Global vision 4. Cross-cultural learning 5. Cross-cultural cooperation ability

Source: Zhang, Y. (2007). Research on the model of cross-cultural training [D]. Dalian Maritime University, 23–24.

environmental inadaptability, these expatriates were finally sent back home. But, Chinese enterprise managers and employees are even more unfamiliar with cross-cultural management theory, knowledge and methods. This situation has brought great difficulties to Chinese transnational and international joint venture enterprises. Therefore, providing cross-cultural training for Chinese managers and employees is an urgent and arduous task, but also an effective means for cross-cultural management success (Tang and Lu, 2005). Zhang (2007) summarizes the contents of the cross-cultural training as displayed in Table 8.2 above.

Methods and content of training

There are a lot of different methods to solve the problems caused by cultural differences. Training is generally recognized as a basic means to deal with cultural issues and challenges (Zhao, 1997). Zhao found that many multinational enterprises realized the importance of understanding the host country's culture for expatriated managers, improving their investment in training so as to promote the cross-cultural understanding process. Further, many business schools, in order to meet the needs of multinational companies, are strengthening students' understanding of other countries. For example, every MBA student at the University of Southern California is required to visit and do an internship in an Asia-Pacific region company and undertake related projects. In 1997 to 2002, again in mid-October 2016, groups of 50–70 MBA/EMBA students from University of Southern California conducted study tours and projects with companies in Jiangsu province, China, facilitated by the School of Business, Nanjing University. Similarly, Chinese managers urgently need to understand the methods and business philosophy of multinational business management from different cultural backgrounds, business methods and management philosophies. There are five benefits of cross-cultural training: first, to reduce culture shock of expatriates; second, to help local staff promote their understanding of the company's management idea and practice; third, to maintain good and stable relationships in organizations; fourth, to maintain the information flow and the efficiency of the decision making process; and fifth, to strengthen the team cooperation spirit and cohesion.

There are two basic choices for multinational companies to carry out training: the first one is through the internal training departments to provide training programs and courses; the second is to use external training organizations, such as business schools and consulting companies to provide company tailored programs. The School of Business, Nanjing University, has provided executive development programs (EDP) for many companies in China, with other Chinese top business schools having similar programs. For training about cultural differences, many companies employ external training organizations. There may be limits within Chinese firms to conduct cross-cultural training. Since cross-cultural training has little to do with technical or commercial secrets, it can be outsourced to third parties. Moreover, if the scale of the company is small or the number of participants is limited, third party training can reduce the training costs.

In terms of the content of training, companies should first pay attention to language training as having a common language is the most direct way to communicate. Holding multiple levels and various forms of language training can also invisibly increase the cohesion of the enterprise. The study of language and culture can significantly reduce language barriers, allowing people to better understand foreign cultures and thinking patterns. Such communication ability gained through cross-cultural training is what Chinese enterprises urgently need. Second, cross-cultural training and cultural exchange activities should be combined together. Enterprises should carry out a variety of cultural exchange activities, and consciously carry out cross-cultural training and education, to promote exchange between different cultures and strengthen the understanding of national culture and corporate culture from all over the world. Third, gaining knowledge about cross-cultural sensitivity and adaptability is important in its own right. Cross-cultural awareness is based on the understanding of cultural differences, and the ability to make a response in the face of the cultural differences. Good cross-cultural consciousness is based on "cultural sensitivity", which refers to the understanding of the host country culture system. Managers with high cultural sensitivity are not confined to a narrow range of thinking, and they often reason from a broad perspective. Fourth, training improves the ability of enterprise members to engage in cross-cultural communication and conflict handling. Cross-cultural awareness training can enable trainees to understand the values of other cultures, their habits and moral standards, improve the ability of employees to master other cultural knowledge, encourage staff to understand and respect other cultures, all of which reduce the cultural conflict and improve the ability to solve cultural conflicts. The implementation of cross-cultural training can keep good and stable relationships within the enterprise between the manager and employees. It is a powerful tool to realize the integration of management mode and create harmonious corporate culture.

Things that cannot be neglected in the process of training

Currently many enterprises emphasize pure technical training while ignoring the cross-cultural training for employees, especially managers (Li, 2006). Cross-cultural training content generally includes knowledge and understanding of culture; cultural sensitivity and adaptability training; training in language, customs and way of living, and cross-cultural communication and conflict-handling ability training. Such training of cultural values, ethics, customs and legal system improve staff awareness of each other's culture and cultural sensitivity and guide employees to understand and respect each other's culture, reduce cultural conflict and improve the ability to resolve the cultural conflict. Cross-cultural training includes training and developing staff's observation ability and the ability of face-to-face communication to make the staff understand and learn each other's culture in a real enterprise environment (Li, 2006).

In cross-cultural training, there are two things we need to consider. The first is whether trainees have the opportunity to fully interact with other cultures. As noted earlier, the essence of culture training is to interact with other cultures to explore potential cultural conflict, so individuals really understand and feel these implicit cross-cultural assumptions. In other words, abstract concept teaching is not enough for trainees to understand other cultures. They should strengthen their real understanding of other cultures through personal experience. Second, the quality of training personnel is critical. Cross-culture is not about just pedagogy, psychology and other professional knowledge and skills, but training personnel must first understand the culture of trainees before they may impart other cultural values to them. A trainer who does not understand China's methods of training may upset Chinese employees (Zhao, 1997).

4.2. *Establishing good cross-cultural communication channels*

Ess and Sudweeks (2001) defined cross-cultural communication as consisting of intercultural, multi-domestic and cross-gender communication. In cross-cultural communication, meaning and interpretations are derived collectively and individually through interaction, thus it is implied that culture in which norms are developed will be reflected in all interactions regardless of the communication medium. The need for transparent information sharing has gained widespread recognition at the management level in multinational enterprises because information is an important resource in modern social and economic organizations. To establish a cross-cultural management mode that is conducive to the two-way communication between different cultures is particularly beneficial for the business development of joint ventures. Japanese companies have been successful in foreign countries, displaying a strong adaptability. Their success is attributed to Japanese firms being "learning organizations", with the flow of information across the firm. In the Japanese "learning organization", employees from different cultural backgrounds have the rights (and obligations) of participating in enterprise management. They can equally and freely speak on this platform, communicate with each other and learn. The result is a gradual diminution of the national consciousness, improved global business philosophy and different cultural fusion (Shan, 2010). Japanese firms' successful experience provides a lesson on cross-cultural management to Chinese enterprises that want to grasp the economic and business opportunities provided by the OBOR initiative and "going out".

Cross-cultural management communication mechanism is the fundamental guarantee of cross-cultural management in enterprises. Tang and Lu (2005) posited that cross-cultural communication refers to a process where two people or groups with different cultural backgrounds express ideas, send out information, communicate emotion and form interactions. The essence of intercultural communication is to respect and understand each other. Respect refers to holding positive attitudes toward cultural differences. Establishing multi-level, institutionalized, formal and informal communications is the basis to ensure information flows and effective communication. It is also one of the key elements for the success of cross-cultural enterprise management. Only constant communication and trust can lead to understanding, cultural integration and innovation.

Cross-cultural communication is of great significance for the success of multinational business and the improvement of competitiveness. The cross-cultural communication ability of China's overseas enterprises is weak and also faces enormous challenges. From the standpoint of communicating with different people from different countries on the OBOR initiative, and from the perspective of cross-cultural communication, it is best when China's overseas enterprises learn the local language and culture as the main communication tools. English also plays an important role. Xia and Feng (2009) came up with three measures to improve the effectiveness of cross-cultural communication. First, use the host country's language or a commonly-used language like English to conduct culture media publicity. Second, attract, train and hire local Chinese students to accelerate the localization process of enterprises. Third, attach importance to local talents in order to enhance the effect of cross-cultural communication.

Stuttard (2000) proposed that the ancient Silk Road emerged as a natural outcome of the supply and demand market condition, especially the needs of people who lived along the Silk Road. The current OBOR initiative not only resembles historical prerequisites but also builds more regional cooperation, creates political flexibility and improves economic growth. Many Chinese companies have already gone international and set up overseas subsidiaries in many of the countries along the Silk Road. In the telecom and ICT sector, Huawei has developed a strong presence in all European markets, and adapted its corporate culture and human resource policy to this environment (Case 8.1).

5. Chinese Management and German Culture: The Case of Phoenix Contact

Since the setup of Phoenix Contact China in Nanjing in 1993, it was rated the most trusted local company (Zhang, 2013). As a foreign-owned enterprise, Phoenix Contact (electrical engineering and automation) was 99.7% German, but the management team was 100% Chinese, the technical personnel was 100% Chinese and the employees in the company were 100% Chinese (Zhao and Li, 2009). As a German invested company in China, Phoenix Contact China not only owned the German technology but more importantly, integrated the spirit of the German culture and local management. At the beginning of business, the company set up "inspire the national spirit and serve the society" as the principle of management action. Li Musong, former Chair and President, one of the founders of Phoenix Contact China, once told the media during an interview: "excellent enterprise and outstanding performance are created by excellent teams. In foreign-owned enterprises in China, if Chinese management is just as second-class citizens, the enterprise will never succeed." The company's current president, Gu Jiandang stated, "the European management is very professional, and for Chinese companies, they must manage the change and breakthrough. Phoenix Contact China combined the two perfectly. So in today's Phoenix Contact in China, what we can see is not only efficient German management but also China's human management."

Phoenix Contact China invested in human resources training and development as the company's first investment priority and social obligation. It introduced a dual channel development system and a framework for career planning. Employees can make a choice of their career planning according to their own personality traits, personal expertise and value orientation. The company also provided corresponding resources to support employees' self-development, so as to adapt to the strategic need of the company's rapid development. The company also integrated its business development with personal development needs through a well-organized training system, which combined internal training and training abroad. Training provided employees with more opportunities for learning and education. Employing the strategy of "going out" and "calling in", Phoenix Contact China sends employees abroad to receive training, sends middle-level management to study MBA and EMBA programs at the School of Business, Nanjing University and business schools in Beijing, Shanghai, and other places. The company also invites experts from the headquarters in Germany and the United States to provide training for employees on languages, communication skills and management, and at the same time invites customers and department supervisors to go to Germany to visit headquarters.

In 2005, Phoenix Contact China won the prize for its "special contribution of national enterprise culture construction"; in 2006 the "National Customer Satisfaction Award" and the "2006 National Excellent Enterprise Culture"; and in 2007 the "Excellent Enterprise Culture Construction Unit". President Gu was also awarded the "2016 National Outstanding Entrepreneur" award. The number of enterprise culture construction prizes awarded were a sign of Phoenix's phased achievement in enterprise culture construction and also social recognition for its success in China. Within the company, there was a strong traditional Chinese culture. On the enterprise management in Phoenix, traditional Chinese culture had an important position and played an important role during the process. In its factory in the Jiangning District, Nanjing, we can see slogans like "Behave yourself before commanding others" (*zhengrenxianzhengji, zuoshixianzuoren* "正人先正己，做事先做人"). Here, the traditional Chinese culture and modern Western culture are combined together, forming a unique corporate culture.

President Gu was also the first Chairman of the Phoenix labor union. Gu said: "although we are employed by a German company, we still insist on our independence, insist on running the enterprise according to Chinese law, make decisions according to China's national conditions". In this foreign-owned company, the Chinese are the real owners. Chinese managers and workers won the trust of the German Phoenix partners. In Phoenix's corporate culture, trust is the core. Phoenix trust mechanism is not polite trust; it is real strategic interaction and understanding of the responsibility and mission. Trust and responsibility cover all aspects of the enterprise; they are long-term cooperative relations with the society, customers and the employees. Phoenix's trust mechanism is the dynamic combination of trust and responsibility (Zhang and Zu, 2012).

Conclusion

The "One Belt One Road" national medium and long-term strategy involves politics, economy, society and culture. The OBOR initiative does not just provide new opportunities for the global compliance for the external economy, but also provides new opportunities for regional industrial transformation and development (Gong, 2015). While Chinese enterprises play an important role in this strategy, these enterprises cannot just realize the economic exchanges between countries, but must also promote cultural exchange. For example, hiring foreign employees or sending Chinese employees abroad both require cultural learning and communication. The implementation of the OBOR means that China will play an increased role in shaping the world economic landscape, which brings great opportunities for Chinese enterprises to "go out" into the international markets and for companies in other countries to play important roles in the regional economic development. However, cultural difference is one of the biggest challenges for Chinese enterprises "going out" (and foreign firms coming to China). Cultural differences between each country or between each enterprise mean differences between employees in values, way of thinking, behavior, language and many other aspects that can produce conflicts. To resolve these conflicts effectively, enterprises should first understand the national culture and corporate culture and the differences between enterprises. One way to understand cultural differences is through Hofstede's culture dimension theory and Hall's high-context culture and low-context culture framework. According to the results of such analysis, companies should provide employees and managers with cultural training, comprising three aspects: knowledge (the basic introduction of host country, cross-cultural knowledge, language knowledge, etc.), skills (cross-cultural communication skills and conflict management skills, negotiation skills, etc.) and ability (cultural sensitivity, intercultural adaptability, global vision, etc.). At the same time, an effective cross-cultural communication channel should also be established to ensure the employees are able to communicate in a timely and effective manner.

References

Adler, N. J. (1983). Cross-cultural management research: The ostrich and the Trend. *Academy of Management Review* 8.2: 226–232.

Bai, Y. (2009). *Multinational Corporations' Cultural Predicaments in China and Intercultural Training*. Shanghai Foreign Language University Press.

Chen, J. (2015). Changes that "One Belt, One Road" can bring to our country enterprise management. *Chinese & Foreign Entrepreneurs Journal*, 11.

Chu, Y. and Gao, Y. (2015). Three problems of China's "One Belt, One Road" strategy position. *International Economic Review*, 2.

Di, K. (2015). Strategic thinking of "One Belt, One Road" Construction. *International Review*, 5.

Duan, J. S. and Li, H. K. (2016). Geography, ethic group and culture — The history and reality of the relationship between strategy and southwestern provinces. *Journal of Beifang University of Nationalities*, 2: 43–27.

Elisseeff, V. (1998). *The Silk Roads: Highways of Culture and Commerce*. Berghahn Books.

Ess, C. and Sudweeks, F. (2001). *Culture, Technology, Communication: Towards an Intercultural Global Village*. SUNY Press.

Gao, C. and Ma, C. Z. (2015). The cross-cultural management of Chinese enterprises "going out" under "One Belt, One Road" strategy. *Human Resources Development of China*, 19.

Gong, S. L. (2015). The macro strategy and shortcomings of the "One Belt, One Road". *Vision: The Mirror for Managers*, 7.

Hall, E. T. and Hall, M. R. (1995). Key concepts: Underlying structures of culture. *International Management Behavior*. Blackwell Publishers, Cambridge, Massachusetts. 199–202.

Harris, P. and Moran, R. T. (1987). *Managing Cultural Differences*, Gulf Publishing Company, 6.

Hawes, C. and Chew, E. (2011). The cultural transformation of large Chinese enterprises into internationally competitive corporations: Case studies of Haier and Huawei. *Journal of Chinese economic and business studies*, 9(1), 67–83.

Hoffman, B. (2015). *China's One Belt One Road initiative: What we know thus far.* The World Bank. Retrieved from http://blogs.worldbank.org/eastasiapacific/china-one-belt-one-road-iniative-what-we-know-thus-far.

Hofstede, G. (1980). *Culture's Consequences: International Differences in Work-Related Values*. Beverly Hills, CA: Sage.

Jin, Y. H. (2006). Communication management under intercultural background. *China Water Transport Journal* (Academic Version), 5.

Larçon, J.-P. (2009). *Chinese Multinationals*. Singapore: World Scientific.

Li, D. (2014). *Research on the Cross-cultural Management of China Enterprises in Transnational Mergers and Acquisitions*. Guangxi University Press.

Li, L. and Huang J. (2004). Inspiration of Peugeot Guangzhou's cross-cultural failure [J]. *Enterprise Research*, 10.

Li, W. F. (2013). Cross-cultural conflicts of newly established enterprise in group industry and countermeasures. *Human Resource Management Journal*, 10.

Li, Y. L. (2006). Intercultural conflict and cross-cultural management. *Scientific Socialism Journal*, 2.

Lin, C. Q. (2007). Cross-cultural conflict and management in multinational companies — take Peugeot Guangzhou as an example. *Science-Technical on Middle-Small Business Journal*, 2.

Liu, G. M. (2001). Who's to blame? The reasons that Peugeot Guangzhou collapsed in the "transnational marriage". *China Business Office Journal*, 3.

Liu, Q. (2012). *Research National Culture and Custom of South-East Asian Nations*. Guangxi Social Science Press, 5.

Liu, W. D. (2015). Scientific meaning and problems of "One Belt, One Road" strategy. *Progress in Geography Journal*, 5.

Mi, J. T. and Wang, P. (2016). "One Belt One Road" strategy and the protection of the intangible cultural heritage in the Chinese northwest ethnic region. *Northwest University for Nationalities, Philosophy and Social Science*, 2: 42–45.

Michailova, S. and Hutchings, K. (2006). National cultural influences on knowledge sharing: A comparison of China and Russia. *Journal of Management Studies*, 43(3), 383–405.

Moran, R. T., Abramson, N. R. and Moran, S. V. (2014). *Managing Cultural Differences*. Routledge.

Phatak, A. V. (2006). *International Management*. Machinery Industry Press, 112.

Ralston, D. A., Holt, D. H., Terpstra, R. H. and Kai-Cheng, Y. (1997). The impact of national culture and economic ideology on managerial work values: A study of the United States, Russia, Japan, and China. *Journal of International Business Studies*, 177–207.

Shan, H. Y. (2010). *Cultural Differences in Joint Venture and Research on Cross-cultural Management*. Xibei University Press, 2010.

Stuttard, J. B. (2000). *The New Silk Road: Secrets of Business Success in China Today*. John Wiley & Sons.

Tang, Y. Z. and Lu, W. (2005). Foreign cross-cultural management research and enlightenment. *Modernization of Management Journal*, 5.

Tian, Z. L., Xiong, Q. and Jiang, Q. (2013). Challenges of cross-cultural communication faced by Chinese employees in multinational companies and coping strategies. *Chinese Journal of Management*, 7.

Wang, J. P. (2006). *Hot Issues About Enterprise Culture*. Beijing: China Development Press 22–69.

Wang, X. R. and Li, X. B. (1999). *Introduction to Comparative Culture*. Lanzhou University Press.

Xia, X. L. and Feng, L. (2009). Cross-cultural communication problems in China's overseas enterprises. *China Opening Herald Journal*, 3.

Xu, N. S. (2015). Strategic thinking of Chinese enterprises "going out" under "One Belt, One Road" strategy. *Economic Science Journal*, 3.

Yang, H. L. (2015). "One Belt, One Road" and the inheritance and transmission of Chinese culture. *Journal of News Research*, 20.

Yang, J. H. (2002). *Cultural Differences Analysis in Cross-cultural Communication and Comparative Study of Cross-cultural Training Mode*. Huadong Normal University Press.

Yuan, X. T. (2014). The analysis of the "One Belt, One Road" national strategy. *Theory Monthly Journal*, 11.

Yun, Z. (1993). "Cross-culture training" came into being, World's Knowledge Journal, (8).

Zhang, P. and Zu, Z. X. (2012). Phoenix Contact — A foreign company that adheres to China's characteristics. *Enterprise Management Journal*, 1.

Zhang, Y. (2007). *Research on the Model of Cross-cultural Training*[D]. Dalian Maritime University Press, 23–24.

Zhang, Y. L. (2013). Responsibility lifted the Chinese Phoenix — Phoenix (China) Investment Co. Ltd. became the first foreign company that won "national demonstration base of the enterprise culture". *Modern Enterprise Culture Journal*, 11.

Zhao, S. M. (1997). Challenge for the multinational companies in China: cultural differences and cross-cultural management. *Management World Journal*, 3.

Zhao, S. M. and Li, Q. W. (2009). Innovated mould of Phoenix Contact (China)'s company culture [J]. *Journal of Management Case Studies*, 4.

Zhao, Y. L. (2012). *Research on Chinese Enterprises Internationalization of Cross-cultural Management, Based on Conflict-Adaptation-Cooperation.* Tianjin University Press.

Zu, W. H. (2013). Influence of European and American culture on contemporary college students' humanities cultivated manners. *Forward Position Journal*, 6: 131–132.

Case 8.1 Huawei building on local talents in the Nordic-Baltic region

Huawei is a leading global information and communications technology (ICT) solutions provider. Founded in 1987, Huawei has grown from a US$5,680 small company to a global company with a sales revenue of over 390 billion yuan, or about US$60 billion in 2015, with a business presence in over 170 countries and regions thanks to the tireless efforts of its employees and the company's global mindset.

Larçon (2009) mentioned three internationalization paths for Chinese multinationals. Huawei is among the second category of companies that followed a "normal path". Huawei began the internationalization process step-by-step, despite the growing competition of foreign products. Currently, Huawei has business operations not just in Asia, but the Americas, as well as the Europe, Middle East and Africa (EMEA) region. In Huawei's 2015 annual report, we can see that in the EMEA region, there was a 27.2% increase in revenue over 2014.

Hawes and Chew (2011) categorized Huawei's cultural transformation techniques into five interrelated levels: defining the corporate philosophy and values; creating corporate "myths" that shock employees into a realization of the importance of the firm's values; setting up rituals to celebrate the firm's heroes and to publicly criticize those who fail to embrace the firm's values; fixing the values in place; and leading by example, ensuring that the CEO is subject to the same values as everyone else in the firm. Hawes and Chew further described the negative aspects that Huawei has run into during cultural transformation among its workforce. For example, in the initial period of growth, Huawei relied on "rewards and penalties to mold the behavior of their employees and to inculcate their core values". However, as a greater proportion of highly-skilled and educated employees from many different countries are required, many of these employees are less willing to endure the military-style discipline, constant supervision and grueling working hours.

Huawei's market entry into Europe is an international success story that multinationals can reference. The company set up its first European office in Kista, Sweden, in 2000 and now has 11 offices with some 800 staff in the Nordic and Baltic region in both management and R&D. For Leo Sun, President of Huawei Brussels office in 2014: "Our general vision is to transform the whole company into a truly global enterprise and to acquire the best talents in the

(Continued)

Case 8.1 *(Continued)*

industry no matter where they are". The company, which opened in 2012 a new R&D facility in Helsinki had recruited some 160 employees at the end of 2015.

Although Huawei has not yet developed a standard model for cross-cultural talent management, most of the operational positions at Huawei Europe are taken by Europeans, and Huawei has started recruiting foreigners in key positions at the level of its Shenzhen headquarters.

Sources: Baltic Management Institute, Company data, and Invest in Finland.

Special Contribution

Russian Multinational Enterprises and Chinese "Belt and Road" Initiative

Andrei Panibratov

Saint Petersburg State University, Graduate School of Management

Relationships between China and Russia

Sino-Russian relations are based formally on the Treaty of Good-Neighborliness and Friendly Cooperation between China and Russia of 2001. In recent years, relations between China and Russia continue to develop in a wide range of cooperation areas. The interaction in the political sphere is stable, and there are coincidences in the positions of Moscow and Beijing on major areas of the international agenda. In total, there are more than 300 intergovernmental treaties and agreements between the two countries.

According to the Federal Customs Service (FCS) of Russia, in 2015 the trade turnover between Russia and China reached US$63.6 billion. Russian exports to China amounted US$28.6 billion, with imports from China amounting to US$34.9 billion. More than half of Russia's exports go to the supply of mineral fuel, oil and petroleum products (60.7%), followed by wood and wood products (9.4%), non-ferrous metals (9%), fish and seafood (3.5%), and chemical products (3.3%). The main import categories are: machinery and equipment (35.9%), clothing (13.7%), chemical products (9.1%), furs and fur products (5.6%), footwear (5.3%) and furniture (3%).[1]

Since 2010, China has been the largest trading partner of Russia, its share in foreign trade turnover in 2015 amounted to 12.1% (in 2008, this was 7.6%). Russia occupies 16th place in the ranking of Chinese partners. According to the Bank of Russia as of October 1, 2015 the volume of accumulated foreign direct investment in China in the Russian economy amounted to US$1.5 billion (15th place among countries-investors). Russian investments in China amounted to US$172 million.[2]

"One Belt One Road" and Russian Multinational Enterprises' interests

On May 8, 2015, Russia and China signed an agreement on the conjugation of the Eurasian Economic Union and Silk Road Economic Belt (the "Great Conjugation"). It was the culmination of an unprecedented Russian-Chinese rapprochement. Russia gained a powerful symbol of support from the second world economy during the confrontation with the West, the ability to upgrade their infrastructure and the first international agreement concluded between the Eurasian Economic Union (EEU) and countries outside the former Soviet Union.

The "Great Conjugation" — the strategic partnership with China's "One Belt One Road" (OBOR) initiative — gave Russia a unique opportunity to solve its traditional problem of infrastructure. It benefited from the existing surplus of China's funds for investment, its 30 years of experience in the construction of roads in the most difficult conditions, and of the widespread opinion among the Chinese elite that the country investment must bring the love of its citizens. Next, transport and infrastructure development will lead to the expansion of trade. The developing of mutual trade through the use of national currencies should lead to stability in the monetary policy. Last but not least, the observance of the main conditions — political stability and ensuring social security guarantees should support the country party

---

[1] http://tass.ru/info/1956459.
[2] http://tass.ru/info/1956459.

to the "New Silk Road". Thus, the "New Silk Road" could be the key to regional stability and security.[3]

Russian Multinational Enterprises (MNEs) have the following interests in the OBOR initiative:

(1) For Russia in general, it is essential to integrate into the Trans-Eurasian transport corridor, or the "New Silk Road"*, thereby consolidating its position as a major transit country. Russia should become a full "Eurasian bridge" between the East and the West;

(2) Russian MNEs' participation in the project and increasing the transit through Russian territory will dramatically enhance the MNEs' revenue, the return on investment in transport infrastructure will result in the active development of many regions of the Asian part of Russia, making them more attractive for production and living;

(3) Against the background of difficult relations with the West at the time of writing, Russia is interested in strengthening and widening cooperation with China. Joint major projects between Russian and Chinese MNEs are the most reliable way of building long-term partnership;

(4) Russia needs to expand cross-border relations with China through multiple joint projects between Russian and Chinese MNEs — without such projects, it is hardly possible to complete the economic development of the regions of Siberia and the Far East. Border regions need to be close to markets to export their products and to attract tourists from China;

(5) Russia, as well as China, is highly interested in establishing political stability with the countries of Central Asia and the Middle East, as well as in the active economic development of these countries. For both Russia and China, drug production in Afghanistan and the related drug trafficking pose a real threat, as well as the Islamic fundamentalist militants and uncontrolled migration flows arising in the

---

[3]The strategy of the New Silk Road development in the 21st Century (Стратегии развития нового Шелкового пути в XXI веке), URL: http://moluch.ru/archive/95/21393/.

* In this chapter the "New Silk Road" refers to the coordinated development of the Eurasian Economic Union (EEU) and China's Silk Road Economic Belt.

course of military conflicts. Ultimately, the total elimination of these threats is possible only through the accelerated economic development of all countries in the region — only the improvement of living standards could become the basis for political stability. The "New Silk Road" project could play a crucial role in this regard, becoming an incentive and a tool for peace and economic prosperity in Eurasia.[4]

Undoubtedly, the OBOR initiative opens various strategic opportunities for Russian MNEs because it will create a flow of investments from China and an increase in the flow of Chinese tourists. This will help Russian MNEs to integrate deeper into the Eurasian economic community, create new economic links with Chinese MNEs and strengthen existing ones.

China-Russia MNEs' Cooperation

Once the potential benefit of a strategic partnership between Russian and Chinese MNEs became obvious, signed agreements followed, examples of which are listed below.

On September 22, 2016, Sergey Mukhin, executive director of Russian MNE FESCO Transportation Group, stated at the IX International Forum on "Transport and Transit Potential" in Saint Petersburg that today the "New Silk Road" is our reality. He stressed the ultimate importance of the project, and that therefore, FESCO Transportation Group will take advantage of the strategic partnership with Chinese MNEs.[5]

At a meeting in Ürümqi, China on August 31, 2016, Kazakhstan's Air Astana and China discussed the joint construction of a regional air transport market, cooperation in aviation safety and security at airports and aviation infrastructure. Air Astana intensified the air communication between Astana and Ürümqi within the OBOR initiative.[6] This indicated one more potential area for strategic partnership for Russian MNEs.

On June 17, 2016, the Moscow government signed the agreement to build a high-speed train Hyperloop that will operate in Moscow and will

---

[4]The New Silk Road, URL: http://ruxpert.ru/Новый_шёлковый_путь.
[5]https://regnum.ru/news/economy/2183829.html.
[6]http://russian.cctv.com/2016/09/01/ARTIrsS91qlj0TpplqxIfHpz160901.shtml.

allow traveling across Moscow at maximum pace. However, the main aim of cooperation with Russia Hyperloop is the construction of a "New Silk Road", according to Sherwin Pishavar.[7]

On June 20, 2016, JSC "Speed line" — a subsidiary of JSC "Russian Railways" — and a consortium of companies and designers, with the participation of JSC "Mosgiprotrans", JSC "Nizhegorodmetroproekt" and China Railway Eryuan Engineering Group Co. Ltd. signed an agreement for the development of the project documentation for the construction of the "Moscow-Kazan" high-speed railway (HSR) "Moscow-Kazan-Yekaterinburg". The signing took place in Saint Petersburg in the framework of the 2nd meeting of the Intergovernmental Russian-Chinese Commission on Investment Cooperation, chaired by the First Deputy Prime Minister Igor Shuvalov and Deputy Chairman of the State Council of China Zhang Gaoli. The Russian participants of the consortium are to undertake the engineering surveys around the site "Moscow-Kazan". The Chinese participants of the consortium will contribute as consultants supporting the engineering survey work: optimization of the developed trails in order to meet the requirements for the safety and comfort of passengers, and participation in the design of the most critical infrastructure subsystems and their elements.[8] This agreement created a new economic link between Russian Railways and a Chinese partner (Case 9.1).

---

[7]http://www.rbc.ru/business/22/06/2016/576a22c69a79477cd9c44eb8.
[8]http://www.vestifinance.ru/articles/58998.

Case 9.1 The "Moscow-Kazan" high-speed railway

The project

The "Moscow-Kazan" high-speed rail project was first proposed by Russian Railways in 2009, with the objective to spur innovation and increase population mobility. Russian President Vladimir Putin announced the decision to go ahead with the project in 2013, and China expressed initial interest in 2014.

The "Moscow-Kazan" rail track, with a length of 770 kilometers, will run through seven territorial entities and regions of the Russian Federation: Moscow, the Moscow region, Vladimir, the Nizhny Novgorod region, Tatarstan, and Udmurtia. It will have fifteen stops, including Vladimir, Nizhny Novgorod, Cheboksary and Kazan. The travel time between Moscow and Kazan will be reduced to three and a half hours from the current fourteen hours.

The line will be extended later to Yekaterinburg and will become part of the planned Beijing-Moscow high-speed corridor.

Managing the project

Russian Railways (RZD) defined in 2015 the principles guiding the development of the project: a cooperation between a Russian and Chinese company to jointly develop and manufacture a high-speed train. In 2016, Sinara Group and CRRC Changchun Railway Vehicles signed an agreement to jointly build trains for the "Moscow-Kazan" high-speed rail.

Sinara Group, founded in 2001, is a diversified private Russian company active in property development, transportation and the financial services sectors. Sinara is already cooperating with Siemens in the field of transport engineering through a joint venture Ural Locomotives. China Railway Construction Corporation Limited (CRRC) is one of China's biggest state construction companies, specialized in infrastructure construction, including railways, underground, port and airport infrastructure. Changchun Railway Vehicles Co., the CRRC subsidiary, is based in the capital city of Jilin province. It has extensive experience in manufacturing electromagnetic unit vehicles for alpine high-speed rail lines. This will be a competitive advantage because Kazan, the capital of Tatarstan Republic, is located in a high altitude area.

The production will be localized in Russia, with the objective of reaching 80% of local production.

(Continued)

Case 9.1 (*Continued*)

Financing the project

The overall cost of the project is expected to exceed US$15 billion, and diverse sources of funding are to be structured. According to RZD, China is ready to provide a US$6 billion loan for the "Moscow-Kazan" high-speed rail.

German companies, including Siemens and Deutsche Bahn, are also interested in participating in the project and its financing. The manufacturing of the wagons and locomotives will start in 2020. The opening of the railway is expected in 2021.

Sources: China Daily, Lenta, Russia Beyond The Headlines, Russian Railways, Sputnik International, Tass, Think Railways and Vedomosti.

Special Contribution

Alliances and Joint Ventures along the "New Silk Road"

Pierre Dussauge

HEC Paris

The "New Silk Road" initiative to better link China to the rest of the world, and notably to Western Europe, has spawned a significant number of alliances and joint ventures along the way. Indeed, for many Chinese firms, collaborating and entering into joint ventures have become one of the preferred modes through which to expand internationally. Along the New Silk Road ("Road"), joint ventures have been formed to finance and create the infrastructures of the Road itself, to exploit these infrastructures, and to develop new business opportunities made possible by the Road. In this contribution, we will examine some of the joint ventures formed in these three areas.

Joint ventures and alliances to create the infrastructure for the Road

A lot of the new infrastructure projects that are being developed to enable the Road are built in the context of joint ventures or other forms of collaboration between Chinese firms or government entities and local partners. At

221

the very root of the initiative, one of the major financial institutions set up to finance such projects is the Asian Infrastructure Investment Bank (AIIB), itself a joint initiative of several countries affected by the Road and in which, in addition to China, the leading partner, India and Russia are also major shareholders. Numerous infrastructure projects have also been developed as joint ventures between Chinese partners and foreign investors. For example, the Lianyungang Port Authority formed a 49%/51% joint venture with Kazakhstan Temir Zholy (KTZ) to build a logistics terminal in that port city, at one of the ends of the Road. At the other end of the Road, China Merchants Group (CMG) is building an outer sea port in Klaipėda (Lithuania) and is planning for it to become one of the largest seaports in the Baltic region. On an even broader scale, China Merchants Holdings International acquired a 49% stake in Terminal Link, the company set up by CMA CGM, one of the largest shipping companies in the world, to build and then manage container terminals in large ports around the world (see Case 10.1). Other similar agreements have been signed to establish the infrastructure needed to create and improve the rail connections linking China to Northern and Western Europe. Notably, Russian Railways has decided to cooperate with Chinese partners to develop the new "Moscow-Kazan" high speed railway. The fact that this project has received significant funding from the New Silk Road Fund (SRF) has led some observers to speculate this line could later be extended all the way to Beijing, making it another component of the Road initiative.

Overall, the infrastructure associated with the Road needs to be created in a number of countries located between China and the Atlantic Ocean. Such projects raise issues of national sovereignty and strategic interests for the countries involved, making the formation of joint ventures involving Chinese entities and local partner institutions a preferred choice for financing and building the necessary infrastructure.

Joint ventures and alliances to manage operations associated with the Road

As the infrastructure associated with the Road is created, joint ventures and alliances are formed to manage many of the facilities and services associated with operating the infrastructure itself.

For example, in the area of railway logistics services, the Yuxinou Logistics Company is a joint venture associating the railway logistics services arms of a number of large national railway companies from China, Russia, Kazakhstan and Germany, set up to provide services such as freight forwarding and customs clearance along the China-Asia-Europe rail route that will link Chongqing and the coastal regions of China to Europe in less than 14 days. Towards the western end of the Road, the China Shipping Group and the Shanghai International Port Group (SIPG) agreed to collaborate with A.P. Moller-Maersk (APM), one of the largest maritime terminal operators in the world, and to acquire a 24% stake and a 25% stake respectively in the APM terminal in Zeebrugge (Belgium). This agreement was signed in the presence of Xi Jinping, the president of China, and Elio di Rupo, the prime minister of Belgium, signaling its importance for both countries.

Many service oriented joint ventures, mainly in the area of logistics and handling, have been created as joint ventures between Chinese partners and local service providers, enjoying the necessary connections with local administrative and customs authorities. For example, CMG and Lithuanian Railways are setting up a joint venture that will take care of freight handling and forwarding services between Lithuania, Belarus and China. S.F. Express, China's largest private courier company, has formed a joint venture called Post 11 with Omniva, the parent company of the Estonian Postal Service, to speed up the delivery of goods between China and Europe and thus support the development of internet sales by Chinese online merchants abroad.

Joint ventures and alliances to exploit opportunities along the Road

Finally, numerous investments have been made along the Road to exploit the economic opportunities it is creating. Again, many of these investments are made in joint ventures and alliances set up by Chinese firms in collaboration with local partners.

One of the most publicized collaborative projects is the plant set up by Midea, a Chinese leader in household appliances, as a joint venture with Horizont, a Belarussian electronics and appliances company. The joint venture plant, owned 55% by Midea and 45% by Horizont, is located in a free economic zone near Minsk and will produce water heaters, water coolers, microwave ovens and other household appliances, essentially for export to Russia, Kazakhstan and other CIS countries. It is expected that parts and components will be shipped from China for assembly in Belarus, taking advantage of the enhanced logistics made possible by the Road. Another similar project is a joint plant established by automobile manufacturer Zhejiang Geely in partnership with Belarus Autoworks (BelAZ). The plant will assemble Geely cars from semi knocked down kits shipped in containers from China to Belarus.

Many other projects of this type are expected to develop over the next few years, as the Road initiative develops. Many of these projects will undoubtedly be undertaken as joint ventures between Chinese firms and local partners along the way.

Case 10.1   Terminal Link, a joint venture between CMA CGM and China Merchants Holdings International

Port container terminals play a strategic role in shipping, especially with the development of giant container ships. CMA CGM, founded in Marseille, France in 1978 is among the top three shipping companies worldwide. The company operates in 150 countries and employs more than 18,000 people. Terminal Link is a subsidiary of CMA CGM, established in 2001, which operates a network of container terminals located in Northern Europe, around the Mediterranean Sea, in West Africa, North America and Asia.

In 2013, CMA CGM entered a strategic partnership with China Merchants Holdings International (CMHI) to cooperate for terminal development and management. CMHI acquired from CMA CGM a 49% equity interest in Terminal Link valued at 400 million Euros. It was the first agreement of this kind along the "Maritime Silk Road" (MSR). Terminal Link owned 15 container terminals in eight countries:

- in the North Sea and Atlantic Coast: Zeebrugge and Antwerp (Belgium), Dunkirk, Le Havre, and Montoir (France)
- around the Mediterranean Sea: Fos (France) and Malta
- in North and West Africa: Tangiers (Morocco) and Abidjan (Ivory Coast)
- in North America: Miami (USA)
- in Asia: Busan (South Korea) and Xiamen (China)

The two companies also signed a 12-year deal through which CMA CGM's container ships will increase their calls at China Merchants' ports.

China Merchants Holdings International is the port unit of CMG, a large central state-owned enterprise (SOE). CMHI is China's largest operator, with a presence in the largest ports of China: Dalian, Guangzhou, Hong Kong, Ningbo, Shanghai, Shenzhen, Tianjin, Xiamen and Yingkou. CMHI's "go global" strategy began in 2008 through acquisitions and partnerships in many areas including Southeast Asia, East and West Africa, the Baltic Sea Region and Russia.

The partnership with CMA CGM helped CMHI become one of the world's largest port operators with 320 terminals in 29 ports around the world. In 2016, China Merchants Group was said to be planning the construction of key infrastructure projects, such as specialized marine terminals, in countries

(Continued)

Case 10.1   (*Continued*)

along the MSR, notably in Djibouti, Sri Lanka and Belarus during China's 13th five-year plan (2016 to 2020). CMHI also changed its name to China Merchants Port Holdings Company Limited in 2016.

Sources: CMA CGM (http:://cma-cgm), CMHI (http://www.cmhi.com.hk).

Conclusion

Striving for Achievement

Jean-Paul Larçon

HEC Paris

In October 2013, Chinese President Xi Jinping, delivering a speech at the foreign affairs conference of the Chinese Communist Party (CCP), said that China "would strive for a sound neighboring environment for its own development and seek common development with neighboring countries", signaling the opportunity to take new initiatives on the international scene.[1]

China's "Belt and Road" (B&R) initiative is a clear example of this new policy, characterized by ambitious long-term goals and priorities as well as clear guidelines and detailed operational action plans. It is a grand strategy endowed with significant financial resources. The "New Silk Road" strategy is pragmatic and opens various possibilities that serve a common objective: the development of Chinese international trade and international investment, as well as China's innovation-driven economic development. Chinese multinational enterprises are simultaneously the instruments and the pilots of this venture.

China's initiative can also serve the mutual economic interests of China and Europe and the first years of development of the EU-China

---

[1]Xi Jinping: China to further friendly relations with neighboring countries (October 26, 2013). *Xinhua*, english.news.cn.

cooperation along the Silk Road are already providing inspiring lessons for entrepreneurs and decision makers. The benefits of such cooperation depend not only on geopolitical factors but also on the operational success of projects jointly developed along the way.

The economic impact of the B&R initiative

Long-term investments in infrastructure are key for the governments, regions and cities involved in the Sino-foreign project and the fact that China is bringing new long-term financing solutions to these projects is a powerful incentive to seize the opportunity and create a competitive advantage over rivals. In this sense, China's initiative is advancing the process of concentration of trade roads on specific routes with logistics hubs able to manage very large volumes and to efficiently connect with key end markets.

The European Union (EU) has a strong influence on the elaboration of long-term priorities in terms of transport infrastructure in Europe, but there is no integrated and coherent EU response to Chinese initiatives, which are dealt with at the bilateral level such as Chinese investments in Piraeus and the Budapest-Belgrade railway connection. China's B&R initiative is a growth opportunity for countries and regions that are either landlocked or at the periphery of major trade routes and markets. It is the case of China's western provinces, Central Asia, Belarus, the seaports and industrial clusters of the Baltic Sea and Central Europe countries.

China's initiative is also an opportunity for Nordic countries, which are oriented towards international trade and innovation, and have not yet fully exploited the opportunities linked to the cooperation with Chinese firms in the region or in third countries.

China's initiative is a source of added revenue for the largest European logistics hubs such as Rotterdam, Antwerp, Hamburg and Duisburg. These cities and their hinterland already have a key role in China-Europe trade and they have the technical and financial means to further invest in infrastructure and advanced logistic solutions. Germany is the leading force of China-Europe cooperation and will benefit further from the increase of China-Europe trade: it will consolidate German presence in the Chinese market and attract more Chinese investment in Germany; it will provide new incentives to the technological cooperation between China and Germany such as the Industry 4.0.

In some cases, projects linked to the "New Silk Road" are perceived as a major opportunity at the local or at the company level, but with more skepticism at a national level. In Poland, cities like Gdańsk, participating in the maritime road, and Łódź, active along the railroad connection, are strong supporters of China's initiative which has a direct impact on their regional economy. But, at the national level, the Polish government's priority is more focused on the development of Polish exports to China than on the development of Chinese investments in the country.

Finally, the trade imbalance between China and Europe is a major concern which leads to various forms of protectionism at the EU or at the national level. China could overcome this challenge in opening more of its domestic market to foreign firms, helping European small and medium-sized enterprises (SMEs) to enter the Chinese market, and promoting economic cooperation between specific provinces of China and European regions.

The entrepreneurial dimension of China's B&R

Many sectors are impacted by the B&R; the energy sector, transport and logistics, port management, maritime industry, shipping, high-speed train, construction companies, engineering, e-commerce and tourism. But the opportunities are not limited to companies or institutions operating directly in these sectors or located physically along the B&R. China's Belt and Road is an opportunity for their suppliers such as engineering companies and the ITC sector. It is the case of Alstom, manufacturing passenger and freight electric locomotives in Astana in partnership with the national railway company KTZ or the case of Wärtsilä manufacturing marine engines in China with China State Shipbuilding Corporation. It is also an opportunity for companies such as Geely-Volvo, to reorganize their activities along the road, with new localizations for their R&D, manufacturing sites, assembly plants and distribution units.

Many companies, on the Chinese side, are state-owned enterprises which benefit from the political and financial support of Chinese government. Some of these companies have a very successful record in terms of international operations such as China Merchants or Cosco. However, in

Europe, these companies will either have to adopt a more European stance in regards to leadership and organization or to work jointly with European partners. This would lead to major changes in the management of human resources.

On the European side, state-owned organizations, such as port authorities and national railway companies are China's natural partners along the B&R. These companies, following the example of DB Schenker, will have to further develop their international orientation, services to international clients and collaboration with foreign counterparts.

Chinese, European and global companies are already key actors along the Silk Road: leading firms of the shipping industry, port management and marine engineering for the "Maritime Silk Road", leaders of the construction industry and railways technology for the "Silk Road Economic Belt"; leaders of the ICT and e-business companies for both. But these firms will not work alone; they will build on the capabilities of smaller regional enterprises, potentially those which are more specialized, operating in their ecosystem.

Chinese or European, state-owned or private, all companies operating in the framework of the B&R will have to quickly develop new capabilities:

- The art of managing international large projects in terms of quality of planning, speed of implementation and quality control.
- The art of managing multi-cultural talents to develop an international culture inside the firm.
- The art of balancing economic performance and responsiveness to society and environment.

We are at the very first stage of China's grand strategy for the "One Belt One Road" initiative, and the initiative is facing challenges at the political and economic level. However, China has a long-term vision, a strong political will, a strong interest to develop its economic cooperation with Europe, and the financial resources to support its ambitions.

The Chinese way focuses on trade and economic cooperation but the project also contributes to building bridges between distant cultures and nations. Distance still matters, but barriers are reduced step-by-step.

China's "New Silk Road" initiative is a unique venture. There is no doubt that the challenges it faces will lead to concerted international action, technological innovation and new management practices.

The "New Silk Road", like the Hanseatic League, should be a fertile breeding ground for entrepreneurship and innovation.

Postface

The "Belt and Road" Initiative as the Bridge between China and Europe

Liu Zuokui

Chinese Academy of Social Sciences, Institute of European Studies,
Department of Central and Eastern European Studies

The "Belt and Road" is a brand new initiative introduced by China in the new era. It mainly aims to promote the connectivity and the economic cooperation between China and the countries involved. Moreover, it actively pushes forward the policy coordination, currency circulation as well as the people-to-people bond. Europe or the EU plays quite a significant role under the "Belt and Road" (B&R) initiative. For China, the EU is the biggest trading partner, the leading source of foreign investment, a key supporter of the Chinese economy and the very focus of the B&R initiative. The B&R initiative will undoubtedly become the crucial link between the two major civilizations and two huge markets and further contribute to the comprehensive cooperation between China and Europe.

In terms of construction, both the "Silk Road Economic Belt" and the "21st Century Maritime Silk Road" are closely linked to Europe, especially Central and Eastern Europe.

At present, there are basically two routes in the layout of building the B&R in Europe, namely, the north route and the south route. The north route refers to the Eurasian Land Bridge which starts from the inland provinces and the west of China and reaches Europe via Xinjiang, Central Asia, Russia and Central and Eastern Europe. Many freight trains have come into operation on this route including the Chongqing-Xinjiang-Europe International Freight Train (from Chongqing, China to Duisburg, Germany), the Wuhan-Xinjiang-Europe International Freight Train (from Wuhan, China to Prague, Czech), the Chengdu-Europe Express Rail (from Chengdu, China to Łódź, Poland), the Zhengzhou-Xinjiang-Europe Freight Train (from Zhengzhou, China to Hamburg, Germany), the Yiwu-Xinjiang-Europe Freight Train (from Yiwu, China to Madrid, Spain), the Suzhou-Warszawa Block Train (from Suzhou, China to Warszawa, Poland) and the Hunan-Europe Express Rail (from Changsha, China to Duisburg, Germany).

The south route is a sea route which starts from the coastal cities in the south of China and ends at the Piraeus Port in Greece via the Mediterranean Sea. The Piraeus Port, the largest port of Greece, is known as the "South Gate of Europe". In the past, Chinese goods had to be delivered to Europe through a circuitous route as passing through the Indian Ocean, rounding the Cape of Good Hope in the south of Africa, crossing the Atlantic and traveling through the West African coast. Now, through the Piraeus Port, Chinese freighters are able to directly cross the Red Sea and the Suez Canal and unload the cargo at the Piraeus Port which will be directly transported to European hinterlands via the Greece-Macedonia-Serbia-Hungary Railways. The new route has become the shortest sea route between China and Europe, cutting 7 to 11 days of delivery by sea. So far it has become a project under the B&R initiative pushed by the Chinese decision makers in the past two years. When the Chinese Premier Li Keqiang visited Serbia in December 2014, he had an in-depth exchange of views with the related parties and confirmed the plan of building the China-Europe Land-Sea Express Passage on the basis of above-mentioned routes.

China's B&R initiative has caused diverse repercussions in European countries, especially in Central and Eastern European countries (CEEC) (16 CEEC were listed as the countries along the "Belt and Road"). The EU has been following the B&R initiative and expecting the synergy between the initiative and the existing projects and plans of the EU.

The EU's response to the B&R initiative suggests that the initiative enjoys popularity in Europe and Europe expects to get a lift from the rise of the Chinese economy and develop economic and trade relations with China by making full use of the various initiatives and mechanisms launched by China. However, to understand the real attitude of Europe towards the initiative, the official declarations of the European countries are far from enough. Therefore, it is necessary to further analyze the motives behind European responses and the potential of the bilateral cooperation between the two sides. In this book, the editors and the authors have made concrete analysis on the European responses and contributed greatly to the construction of the B&R between China and CEEC.

The publication of this book is a huge promotion of mutual understanding between China and CEEC on the B&R and a very successful event in academia which will surely pose a successive and long-lasting influence on the research on both sides.

Bibliography

Aalto, P., Blakkisrud, H., & Smith, H. (eds.) (2008). *The New Northern Dimension of the European Neighbourhood*. Brussels, Belgium: The Centre for European Policy Studies (CEPS).

Aglietta, M., & Guo Bei, G. (2016). *13th Five-Year Plan. In pursuit of a "Moderately Prosperous Society"*. CEPII Policy Brief 2016–12. Paris, France: CEPII.

Antola, E. (2009). *EU Baltic Sea Strategy. Political Challenges for the Baltic Sea Region*. London, UK: Konrad-Adenauer-Stiftung.

Arvis, J.-F., Saslavsky, D., Ojala, L., Shepherd, B., Busch, C. & Raj, A. (2014). *Connecting to Compete. Trade Logistics in the Global Economy. The Logistics Performance Index and its Indicators*. Washington, DC: The International Bank for Reconstruction and Development/The World Bank.

Austermann, F., Vangeli, A., & Xiaoguang, W. (eds.) (2013). *China and Europe in 21st Century Global Politics*. Newcastle upon Tyne, UK: Cambridge Scholars Publishing.

Barauskaite, L. (2009). *Chinese FDI and Economic Relations with the BSR Countries*. Turku School of Economics, Pan-European Institute Electronic Publications, 6.

Barré, G. (2016). *Les Entreprises Chinoises et la Mondialisation*. Paris, France: CNRS Editions.

Bellora, C., & Jean, S. (2016). *Granting Market Economy Status to China in the EU: An Economic Impact Assessment*. CEPII Policy Brief 2016–11. Paris, France: CEPII.

Bondaz, A., Cohen, D., Godement, F., Kratz, A., & Pantucci, R. (2015). *"One Belt, One Road". China's Great Leap Outward*. The European Council on Foreign Relations. Paris, France: Asia Centre.

Bordachev, T. (ed.) (2016). *Towards the Great Ocean 4: Turn to the East*. Valdai Report. Moscow, Russia: Valdai Discussion Club.

Callaghan, M., & Hubbard, P. (2016). The Asian Infrastructure Investment Bank: Multilateralism on the Silk Road. *China Economic Journal*, 9(2), 116–139.

Callahan, W. A. (2016). China's "Asia Dream": The Belt Road initiative and the new regional order. *Asian Journal of Comparative Politics*, 1(3), 226–43.

Carlsson, M., Oxenstierna, S., & Weissmann, M. (2015, June). *China and Russia — A Study on Cooperation, Competition and Distrust*. Report FOI R 4087. Stockhom, Sweden: FOI.

Casaburi, I. (2016). *Chinese Investment in Europe 2015–16*. Barcelona, Spain: ESADE Center for Global Economy and Geopolitics.

Chen, L., & Zhang, W., (2015). China OBOR in perspective of high-speed railway (HSR)—Research on OBOR economic expansion strategy of China. *Advances in Economics and Business*, 3(8), 303–321. Doi: 10.13189/aeb.2015.030803.

Clerc-Renaud, P. *La Mondialisation Chinoise Surles Rails* (July 25, 2016). LaTribune.

Council of the Baltic Sea States (2014). *Declaration of the Council of the Baltic Sea States on the Implementation of the Vilnius Declaration on A Vision for the Baltic Sea Region by 2020*. Stockholm, Sweden: Council of the Baltic Sea States.

Dabrowski, M. (2016, January). *Belarus at the Crossroads*. Bruegel Policy Contribution, 2. Brussels, Belgium: Bruegel.

Di Minin, A., & Zhang, J. (2010). R&D strategies of Chinese companies in Europe. *Review of Policy Research*, 27(4), 433–455.

Di Minin, A., Zhang, J., & Gammeltoft, P. (2012). Chinese FDI in R&D in Europe: A new model of R&D internationalization? *European Management Journal*, 30, 189–203.

Dong, Li., & Glaister, K. W. (2007). The management of culture in Chinese international strategic alliances. *Asia Pacific Journal of Management*, 24, 191–205. Doi:10.1007/s10490-006-9010-7.

Dragneva, R., & Wolczuk, K. (2012). *Russia, the Eurasian Customs Union and the EU Cooperation, Stagnation or Rivalry*. Chatham House Briefing Paper 2012/01. London, UK: Chatham House.

Drelich-Skulska, B., Bobowski, S., Jankowiak, A.H., & Skulski, P. (2014). China's trade policy towards Central and Eastern Europe in the 21st century, example of Poland. *Folia Oeconomica Stetinensia*, 14(1), 149–174.

Ekman, A. (2015, July). *China in Asia: What is Behind the New Silk Roads? Ifri Policy Paper*. Paris, France: Ifri.

Elms, D. K., & Low, P. (eds.) (2013). *Global Value Chains in a Changing World.* Fung Global Institute (FGI), Nanyang Technological University (NTU), and World Trade Organization. Geneva, Switzerland: WTO Publications.

Éltető, A., & Szunomár, Á. (2016). Chinese investment and trade — Strengthening ties with Central and Eastern Europe. *International Journal of Business and Management*, 4(1), 24–48, Doi: 10.20472/BM.2016.4.1.002.

EU Commission *Elements for a New EU strategy on China* (22 June 2016). Joint Communication to the European Parliament and the Council. Brussels, Belgium: EU Commission.

EU Commission Staff Working Document. (2015, June). *European Union Strategy for the Baltic Sea Region. Action Plan.* Brussels, Belgium: EUSBSR.

European Bank for Reconstruction and Development (2013). *Transition Report (2013). Stuck in Transition.* London, UK: European Bank for Reconstruction and Development.

Fallon, T. (2015). The New Silk Road: Xi Jinping's grand strategy for Eurasia. *American Foreign Policy Interests*, 37, 140–147.

Ferdinand, P. (2016). Westward Ho — the China dream and "One Belt, One Road": Chinese foreign policy under Xi Jinping. *International Affairs*, 92(4), 941–957.

Fey, C. E., Pavlovskaya, A., & Tang, N. (2004). A Comparison of HRM in Russia, China, and Finland. *Organizational Dynamics*, 33(1), 79–97.

Garcia-Herrero, A. (2015, October*). Internationalising the Currency while Leveraging Massively: The case of China.* Bruegel Working Paper 2015/12. Brussels, Belgium: Bruegel.

Garcia Herrero, A., & Xu Jianwei, (2016). *China's Belt and Road Initiative: Can Europe Expect Trade Gains?* Working Paper 5. Brussels, Belgium: Bruegel.

Garlick, J. (2015). China's trade with CEE EU members, 2004–2014. *Acta Oeconomica Pragensia*, 23(4), 3–22.

Ghauri, P., & Fang, T. (2001). Negotiating with the Chinese: A socio-cultural analysis. *Journal of World Business*, 36(3), 303–325.

Griffith-Jones, S. (2014, March). *A BRICS Development Bank: A Dream Coming True?* UNCTAD Discussion Paper 215. Geneva, Switzerland: UNCTAD.

Grigas, A., Kasekamp, A., Maslauskaite, K., & Zorgenfreija, L. (2013). *The Baltic States in the EU Yesterday, Today, and Tomorrow.* Paris, France and Berlin, Germany: Jacques Delors Institute.

Grunfelder, J., Rispling, L., & Norlén, G. (eds.) (2016). State of the Nordic Region. *Nordregio Report 2016.* Stockolm, Sweden: Nordregio.

Grushevska, K., & Moskvichenko, I. (2013). Competition among ports on the Eastern Coast of the Baltic Sea for the Russian and European market. *WspółczesnaGospodarka — Contemporary Economy*, 4(3), 25–44.

Gu, J. (2015). *China's New Silk Road to Development Cooperation Opportunities and Challenges*. Tokyo, Japan: United Nations University Centre for Policy Research.

Hanemann, T., & Huotari, M. (2016, February). *A New Record Year for Chinese Outbound Investment in Europe*. Berlin, Germany: MERICS.

Henningsen, B. (2011). BSR Identity. *On Identity — No Identity. An Essay on the Constructions, Possibilities and Necessities for Understanding a European Macro Region: The Baltic Sea*. Copenhagen, Denmark: Baltic Development Forum.

House of Lords European Union Committee (2014). *EU and Russia Before and Beyond the Crisis in Ukraine*. 6th Report of session 2014–15. London, UK: House of Lords.

Hu Jintao (2012). Report to the 18th National Congress of the Communist Party of China on November 8, 2012. *Xinhua*. Available at http://www.china.org.cn/china/18th_cpc_congress/2012-11/16/content_27137540.htm.

Humpert, M. (2014, October). *Arctic Shipping: An Analysis of the 2013 Northern Sea Route Season*. Washington, DC: The Arctic Institute.

Islam, S. (ed.) (2016). EU-China relations — New directions, new priorities. Discussion Paper Summer 2016. Brussels, Belgium: Friends of Europe.

Ivanov, L.S. (ed.) (2015). *Development of Russian — Chinese Trade, Economic, Financial and Cross-Border Relations*. RIAC Working Paper 20. Russian International Affairs Council. Moscow, Russia: Spetskniga.

Jing, M. (ed.) (2014). EU-China relations and diplomacy. *European Foreign Affairs Review*, 19 Special Issue.

Kaarlejärvi, J., & Hämäläinen, M. (2012). *New Opportunities for China-Finland R&D&I Cooperation*. Tekes Review 295/2012. Helsinki, Finland: Tekes.

Kaartemo, V. (2007). *The Motives of Chinese Foreign Investments in the Baltic Sea Region*. Turku School of Economics. Electronic Publications of Pan-European Institute 7/2007.

Kaczmarski, M., & Jakóbowski, J. (2015). *China on Central-Eastern Europe: '16+1' as seen from Beijing*. OSW Commentary 166. Warsaw, Poland: Centre for Eastern Studies.

Kalotay, K., & Sulstarova, A. (2013). Long-term prospects of inward foreign direct investment in the Baltic Sea Region. *Journal of East-West Business*, 19, 79–90.

Karin, E. (ed.), Auelbaev, B.A., Kushkumbayev, S.K., Syroezhkin, K.L., & Dodonov, V. Y. (2015). *Central Asia — 2020 Four Strategic Concepts*. Astana, Kazakhstan: Kazakhstan Institute for Strategic Studies.

Ketels, C., & Pedersen, H. J. (2016). *2016 State of the Region Report*. Copenhagen, Denmark: Baltic Management Forum.

Klein, M. (2014, September). *Russia: A Euro-Pacific Power? Goals, Strategies and Perspectives of Moscow's East Asia Policy*. SWP Research Paper 8. Berlin, Germany: German Institute for International and Security Affairs.

Klimenko, E. (2014, September). *Russia's Evolving Arctic Strategy: Drivers, Challenges and New Opportunities*. SIPRI. Policy Paper 42. Solna, Sweden: Stockholm International Peace Research Institute.

Kowalczyk, U. (2012). *Hub and Hinterland Development in the Baltic Sea Region*. Gdańsk, Poland: Maritime Institute in Gdańsk.

Laaksonen, E., & Mäkinen, H. (2013). The Competitiveness of the Maritime Clusters in the Baltic Sea Region: Key challenges from the Finnish perspective. *Journal of East-West Business*, 19(1–2), 91–104, Doi: 10.1080/10669868.2013.780502.

Lain, S., & Pantucci, R. (2015). *The Economics of the Silk Road Economic Belt*. RUSI Occasional Paper, November 2015. ISSN 2397-0278 (Print). London, UK: Royal United Services Institute for Defence and Security Studies.

Lamy, P. (2014). The World Trade Organization: New issues, new challenges. Policy Paper 117. Paris, France: Notre Europe — Jacques Delors Institute.

Larçon, J.-P. (ed.) (2008). *Chinese Multinationals*. Singapore: World Scientific Publishing.

Le Corre, P., & Sepulchre, A. (2016). *China's Offensive in Europe*. Washington, DC: Brookings Institution Press.

Lee, S., Shenkar, O., & Li, J. (2008). Cultural distance, investment flow, and control in cross-border cooperation. *Strategic Management Journal*, 29(10), 1117–1125.

Liu Zhun, China Ocean Strategic Industry Investment Fund to Promote "Belt and Road" Initiative (October 23, 2016). *Global Times*. Available at http:// www. globaltimes.cn/content/1013140.shtml.

Liu Zuokui, *The Role of Central and Eastern Europe in the Building of Silk Road Economic Belt* (September 18, 2014). Beijing, China: China Institute for International Studies.

Lo, B. (2016, March). *The Illusion of Convergence-Russia, China, and the BRICS*. Russie. Nei. Visions 92. Paris, France: Ifri.

Lukin, A. *Russia, China and the Emerging Greater Eurasia* (August 18, 2015). The Asan Forum. Seoul, Korea.

Lv, P., & Spigarelli, F. (2015). The integration of Chinese and European renewable energy markets: The role of Chinese foreign direct investments. *Energy Policy*, 81, 14–26.

Lynton, N., & Beechler, S. (2012, October). Using Chinese managerial values to win the war for talent. *Asia Pacific Business Review*, 18(4), 567–585.

Melchior, A., Thori Lind, J., & Mee Lie, C. (2013). *Norway, Asia and the Global Value Chains — Asia's Growth and Norway's Economic Links to Asia*. NUPI Report. Oslo, Norway: Norwegian Institute of International Affairs.

Merk, O. (ed.) (2014). *Competitiveness of Global Port Cities: Synthesis Report*. Paris, France: OECD.

Ministry of Foreign Affairs, the People's Republic of China. *The Suzhou Guidelines for Cooperation between China and Central and Eastern European Countries* (November 24, 2015). Beijing, China.

Montesano, S. M., & Okano-Heijmans, M. (2016, June*). Economic Diplomacy in EU–China Relations: Why Europe Needs its Own 'OBOR'*. Clingendael Policy Brief. The Hague, Netherlands: Clingendael.

Morrison, W. M. (2015). *China's economic rise: History, trends, challenges, and implications for the United States*. CRS Report. Washington, DC: Congressional Research Service.

Moser, R., Migge, T., Lockstroem, M., & Neumann, J. (2011). Exploring Chinese cultural standards through the lens of german managers: A case study approach. *IIMB Management Review*, 23, 102–109.

NDRC (2015). *Vision and Actions on Jointly Building Silk Road Economic Belt and 21st-Century Maritime Silk Road*. Beijing, People's Republic of China: the National Development and Reform Commission, Ministry of Foreign Affairs, and Ministry of Commerce of the People's Republic of China, with State Council authorization in March 2015.

Nicolas, F. (2014). China's FDI in the EU. *China Economic Journal*, 7(1), 103–125.

Nicolas, F. (2016). China and the global economic order. *China Perspectives [Online]*, 2016/2, 7–14. Available at: http://chinaperspectives.revues.org/6960.

OECD (2013). *Interconnected Economies: Benefiting from Global Value Chains*. Paris, France: OECD Publishing.

Ojala, A. (2015). Geographic, cultural, and psychic distance to foreign markets in the context of small and new ventures. *International Business Review*, 24(5), 825–835.

Ojala, L., Kersten, W., & Lorentz, H. (2013). Transport and logistics developments in the Baltic Sea Region until 2025. *Journal of East-West Business*, 19(1–2), 16–32.

Okano-Heijmans, M., & Lanting, D. (2015, October). Europe's response to China's activism. Clingendael Report. The Hague, Netherlands: Clingendael.

Ordabayev, A. (2015, June). *The Geopolitics of Transport Corridors in Central Asia*. Working Paper. Almaty, Kazakhstan: The Institute of World Economics and Politics.

Peyrouse, S. (ed.) (2014). *How does Central Asia View the EU*. EUCAM Working Paper 18. Brussels, Belgium: EU Strategy for Central Asia, EUCAM.

Poncet, S. (2015). China's emergence and its implications for Europe's economies. *Global Economic Review*, 44(4), 387–419.

Rodrigue, J.-P., Comtois, C., & Slack, B. (2016). *The geography of transport systems*. London and New York: Routledge.

Schäfer, M., Wei Shen, & Loesekrug-Pietri, A. It's in our interest to join Belt and Road Strategy (July 31, 2015). *China Daily European Weekly*, 12.

Schulte Beerbühl, M. (2012). *Networks of the Hanseatic League*, in Leibniz IEG, Mainz, Germany: Institute of European History Online (EGO).

Sheng Bin (2015, April). *China's Trade Development Strategy and Trade Policy Reforms: Overview and Prospect*. Winnipeg: Canada: The International Institute for Sustainable Development.

Simola, H. (2016). *Economic Relations between Russia and China — Increasing Inter-dependency?* BOFIT Policy Brief 6. Helsinki, Finland: Suomen Pankki — Finlands Bank.

Simurina, J. (2014). *China's Approach to the CEE-16*. Ecran Short Term Policy Brief 85. Brussels, Belgium: Europe China Research and Advice Network (ECRAN).

Skylar Mastro, O. (2015). *Why Chinese Assertiveness is Here to Stay*. The Washington Quarterly. Winter 2015.

Sørensen, C. T. N. (2015). The significance of Xi Jinping's "Chinese Dream" for Chinese foreign policy: From "Tao Guang Yang Hui" to "Fen Fa You Wei". *Journal of China and International Relations*, 3(1), May.

Stiglitz, J. E. (2015). Leaders and followers: Perspectives on the Nordic Model and the economics of innovation. *Journal of Public Economics*, 127, 3–16.

Stiller, S., & Wedemeier, J. (2011). *The Future of the Baltic Sea Region: Potentials and Challenges*. HWWI Policy Report (6). Hamburg, Germany: Hamburg Institute of International Economics.

Stopniece, S. (2015). China-Finland cooperation, trade, and investment: In search of common ground. *Journal of China and International Relations*, 3(1), 130–150. Retrieved from http://journals.aau.dk/index.php/jcir/article/view/1149/970.

Su, P., & Lantaigne, M. (2015). China's developing arctic policies myths and misconceptions. *Journal of China and International Relations*, 3(1), 1–25.

Sun, L. (2010). Chinese maritime concepts. *Asia Europe Journal*, 8(3), 327–338.

Szunomár, Á, Völgyi, K., & Matura, T. (2014). *Chinese Investment and Financial Engagement in Hungary*. Centre for Economic and Regional Studies HAS Institute of World Economics Working Paper 208, 34–54.

Timofeev, I., & Alekeseekova, E. (2015, December). *Eurasia in Russian Foreign Policy Interests, Opportunities and Constraints*. Ifri Policy Paper 89. Paris, France: Ifri.

Tri Vi Dang, D., & Qing H. (2016). *Bureaucrats as Successors CEOs*. BOFIT Discussion Papers, 13. Helsinki, Finland: Suomen Pankki — Finlands Bank.

Tung, R. L., Worm, V., & Fang, T. (2008). Sino-Western business negotiations revisited — 30 years after China's open door policy. *Organizational Dynamics*, 37(1), 60–74.

Vadcar, C. (2016). Value creation and global chains: New business models. *Paris Tech Review*, June 29.

Van der Putten, F.-P., & Meijnders, M. (2015, March). *China, Europe and the Maritime Silk Road*. Clingendael Report. The Hague, Netherlands: Clingendael.

Vandenberg, P., & Kikawa, K. (2015). *Global Value Chains along the New Silk Road*. ADBI Policy Brief (2) (May). Tokyo, Japan: Asian Development Bank Institute.

World Bank (2016). *The Impact of China on Europe and Central Asia*. ECA Economic Update Spring 2016 (April), Washington, DC: World Bank.

Yan, X. (2014). From keeping a low profile to striving for achievement. *Chinese Journal of International Politics*, 7(2), 153–184. Doi: 10.1093/cjip/pou027.

Zhang, Y., Marquis, C., Filippov, S., & Steen, M. van der (2015, February). The challenges and enhancing opportunities of global project management: Evidence from Chinese and Dutch cross-cultural project management. Harvard Business School Organizational Behavior Unit Working Paper No. 15–063. Available at SSRN: http://ssrn.com/abstract=2562376.

Zhang, H. (2015). Building the Silk Road Economic Belt: Challenges in Central Asia. *Cambridge Journal of China Studies*, 10(3), 17–35.

Index

245

Printed in the United States
By Bookmasters